3 KILLERS
AT DALLAS

3 KILLERS
AT DALLAS

TRACEY — MY INVESTIGATION
REPORT IS THE CLOSEST YOU WILL
EVER COME TO SEEING THE TRUTH
ON WHAT REALLY HAPPENED IN DALLAS
THE DAY JFK WAS KILLED. WOULD
BE GOOD FOR YOUR NEXT STORY
            Phil

Chief Phil Doherty

Chief Phil Doherty

To order additional copies of this book, contact:
Xlibris LLC
1-888-795-4274
www.Xlibris.com
Orders@Xlibris.com
633826

CONTENTS

Dallas Police Case # F-85950

Murder of John F. Kennedy

November 22, 1963

Chief Phil Doherty

ACKNOWLEDGEMENTS

The author wishes to thank Lorraine Heffner for preparing the outside cover for the book. A word of thanks to Mike Davis for assisting in the clarifying the ballastic information. JFK expert, Arthur Brown, provided interesting questions regarding the Officer Tippit murder, prompting an additional review of that section. A website has also been established to provide a venue for feedback from readers. Lynn Appleget of Appleget Associates, quickly made that possible.

The author is extremely grateful for the many hours that Lyriss Underwood toiled in assisting me to organize and to clarify the work in many of the chapters. Ms. Underwood was able to point out contradictions and areas that required revisions, as well as eliminating some of the grammar errors and typos.

The author did the research, wrote the manuscript, typed the product, assembled the index, bibliography and citations, so any errors still present are strictly those of the author.

Phil Doherty

CHIEF DOHERTY'S
OTHER BOOK

"The Miami Police Worksheet, self-published by Xlibris Press, 2012

Note: All net proceeds from this book were donated to the Miami Police Veterans Association's Scholarship Fund. Funds provided for seven grants being awarded to first year college students. Thank you for your patronage.

Portions of this book are on-line at www.mpdvets.org/history

DEDICATION PAGE

NOTE: For those dedicated authors and researchers who have labored diligently, regardless of being pro sole assassin or pro-conspiracy, my thanks. Numerous serious researchers have spent years delving into this infamous crime and I salute them. Perhaps someday the entire story will surface.

INTRODUCTION

John F. Kennedy, the 35th President of the United States, was nearing the end of his third year in office when he and his wife traveled to Texas on a political trip. JFK arrived at Love Field in Dallas, Texas, aboard Air Force One on Friday, November 22, 1963, at 11:40 A.M. The presidential party that day included JFK and Mrs. Kennedy, Texas Governor John Connally and Mrs. Connally, Vice President and Mrs. Johnson and several congressional VIP's.

The motorcade left the airport in an open 1961 Lincoln limo with the top down. President Kennedy and Governor Connally were in one car with their wives and two Secret Service agents. Vice President Johnson was in a following car, with the other VIP's following behind in cars and busses. The motorcade through Dallas was heading for the Trade Mart where JFK was scheduled to make a speech.

As the motorcade turned left off Houston Street onto Elm Street, adjacent to the Texas School Book Depository building, 411 Elm Street, Dallas, (formerly the Sexton building.) on the north side of Elm Street, heading into Dealey Square, several shots rang out, resulting in injuries to both President Kennedy and Governor Connally. The motorcade sped on to Parkland Hospital, four miles away, with the wounded men. President Kennedy was soon pronounced dead but Governor Connally survived. Vice President Johnson left Parkland Hospital and was taken back to the airport where he was sworn in as President aboard Air force One. The Dallas police department began a homicide investigation led by Captain John Will Fritz.

An hour or so later, a Dallas P.D. officer, J.D. Tippit, was shot and killed on East Tenth Street, in the Oak Cliff section of Dallas, several miles from the scene of the Kennedy assassination. The officer was shot by a white male whom the officer was attempting to converse with. Minutes later, several blocks away, a man was seen by a citizen, ducking into a store alcove just as a uniform police car was passing. The citizen followed the man who was then observed entering the Texas Theater, a few blocks from the officer-shooting. The theater employee, alerted by the observant citizen, called the police. Approximately fifteen officers promptly arrived and the man was arrested in the theater after striking an officer and pulling out a revolver. The suspect was identified later as Lee Harvey Oswald, 24, who turned out to be an employee of the School Book Depository building, the location from which it was thought that the shots were fired at the presidential motorcade.

A second homicide investigation commenced, led again by Captain Fritz of the Dallas P.D., under Chief of Police Jesse Curry. Oswald was held and interrogated at Dallas headquarters until Sunday morning when he was to be transferred to the Dallas County Jail. During the chaotic transfer from the basement of the police department, with numerous police officers and media present, Oswald was shot and killed by a Dallas night club operator, Jack Ruby. The tragic event, shown live on national television, opened up a third murder investigation.

Now as President, Lyndon Johnson federalized the presidential killing in the following days and organized a special commission on November 29th (the Warren Commission), headed up by Supreme Court Chief Justice Earl Warren. Johnson expressed a fear that Kennedy's murder might result in the starting of a nuclear war with the Soviet Union, as Oswald had now been publicly identified as a communist who had lived in Russia for several years.

The Warren Commission presented an 888 page report the following September, followed by twenty-six volumes of the hearings and exhibits. The commission concluded that Oswald had been the sole shooter and that there was no conspiracy involved. The Tippet and Oswald murder cases had already been closed by the Dallas police immediately after Oswald's slaying. Jack Ruby was subsequently tried and convicted and sentenced to death. His conviction was overturned and Ruby died of natural causes prior to a second trial. The commission harshly criticized the carelessness of the FBI, the Secret Service and the Dallas police department and recognized the need to improve measures for protecting American Presidents. At the time of the Kennedy murder, the murder of a president was not covered in the federal crime statutes, although it is now.

From the time of the Warren Commission Report and continuing to the present, the public opinion in America concerning the JFK case has consistently opined that there was indeed a conspiracy to kill the young president. Further, there strongly exists in the minds of many that Oswald may not have actually fired the fatal shot, or if he did so, it was in conjunction with other assassins.

During the 50 plus years since this sensational case occurred in November of 1963, there have been thousands of books, magazines, articles and websites dissecting the assassination. As recently as 2013, Bill O'Reilly's book, "Killing Kennedy", topped the best seller book lists for months. The answers to the conspiracy question still tantalize the public, not only in America, but around the world as well.

This author has maintained an interest in this case since day-one, often speculating that if one of the victims was other than the U.S. president - someone of a lesser profile - the investigation of the murder case might have been more concise and organized, without the enormous

Political ramifications, nationally and globally, being present, and with a more definitive result.

The frame of reference in this book is primarily from the viewpoint of a trained police officer who desires closure while still on the green side. This version may be a bit sophomoric to the 'real' scholars and researchers of the Kennedy investigation, but I have hope that the general public can better understand my 'Joe Friday' version rather than studying numerous complicated published texts, good and bad, seeking answers.

Few mortals in 1963 would have entertained the notion that a cabal of organized crime, anti-Castro terrorists, and a branch of the U.S. government's Central Intelligence Agency would commit the premeditated murder of a popularly elected President of the United States. Fifty years of investigation by government committees and aggressive civilian investigators, most who are amateur investigators, have turned that notion on its head. Most now believe that there was a planned conspiracy and that 'our" government was up to its neck in involvement. Lets look at the totality of the facts, some solid and some nebulous.

Much of the public today receive their news in 140-character bursts. I do think (and hope), however, that a certain portion of this public will go beyond that level in seeking the same closure as I have.

Chief Phil Doherty

PART I

OVERVIEW

THREE MURDERS IN DALLAS

A half century has slipped by since a young, energetic U.S President, John Kennedy, was assassinated in Dallas, Texas in November of 1963. Thousands of books and periodicals have since been written and millions of Americans, some of whom were not yet born when the tragedy occurred, exhibit an intense interest in the assassination. A majority of our citizens still do not believe that Lee Harvey Oswald acted alone that fateful day, despite the continued authoritative claim by the Dallas police, the Federal Bureau of Investigation, and the Warren Commission, that there was no conspiracy.

The author, a long retired Miami police officer, has maintained an interest in this case since November 22, 1963, and has studied the various chronicles that delved into every aspect of the event and the players. The recent 50th anniversary of JFK's killing has renewed the author's interest. No longer hampered by the need to work and having ample time to give these cases another long look, the author has re-read most of the heralded literature, plus having the luxury of the utilizing the Internet, which provides long forgotten material as well as new revelations by the many scholars who still labor to seek the truth regarding this case that created a drastic change in the psychic of the American people.

Not claiming to be an academician, the author has decided to approach the case as a police investigator. I do hope that his type process produces some new avenues for others to complete the solving of this fascinating puzzle.

My starting point will be a fairly basic overlook at the initial event. I then examine the attempted murder of a retired Army General, Edwin Walker, in Dallas, several months earlier, as the event is crucial to the subsequent murder cases. We will then examine the murder of President Kennedy and the immediate law enforcement response, followed by the murder of Officer Tippit, and then of Lee Oswald himself.

I will also focus on the initial police response as I would if I was the on-scene commander. These officers are supposedly well trained observers. We will then follow the examination of the responses and statements of the civilian bystanders, especially prior to them having the opportunity to elaborate on a "more rational" response to their initial observations.

THE KENNEDY I RECALL

The author first met John Kennedy during his campaigning for election to the U.S. House of Representatives, 11th Massachusetts district, in the late 1940's. That district's incumbent congressman, James Michael Curley, a famous Bay State politician, was leaving the congressional seat in 1946, in order to campaign for the post of Mayor of Boston, (in which he was successful). John Kennedy appeared at my youth baseball awards banquets in Woburn; one year at a civic hall adjacent to the rail station and two years later in the basement meeting room of Woburn's police station. Kennedy, was elected to that U.S. House seat three times, serving from 1946 to 1952, at which time he was elected to the U.S. Senate. My age at these initial events was approximately nine and eleven years old. I remember little of his brief speech to us kids, but he appeared to be a nice man. (1)

By the time Kennedy campaigned for President in 1960, I was a young rookie police officer on the Miami police department, having been recently discharged from the U.S. Air Force. I did cast my first presidential ballot for JFK, as he was a fellow Boston Irishman whom I admired and who had represented our family in Congress. My next personal sight of Kennedy was at Miami's Orange Bowl on January 1, 1961, shortly after his election to the

Presidency, but prior to his taking office. I was assigned to stadium security detail that day when a Navy football team (9-1) battled the University of Missouri. Halfback Joe Bellino, Navy's Heinsman Trophy winner that year, hailing from Winchester, MA. (My high school's rival,) scored a TD that day, although it was not enough to carry the day. Both Kennedy, a Navy veteran, and I were disappointed. Noteworthy that day was the very loose security that surrounded Kennedy during his Orange Bowl visit, the films of which are still available on Google for viewing.

On December 29, 1962, John Kennedy and his wife, Jackie Kennedy, addressed a large crowd at Miami's Orange Bowl to greet and honor the Cuban Bay of Pigs veterans who had recently been released from Cuban prisons in a deal with Fidel Castro. Again, I was assigned to the security detail, which had been significantly beefed up during this visit. Kennedy was presented with the Cubans' #2506 Brigade flag, which the president promised to return to them some day in a free Havana. Three days later, JFK returned to the Orange Bowl on January 1st, to attend the Alabama -Oklahoma Orange Bowl game, which was won with quarterback Joe Namath leading the University of Alabama. My partner Officer Tommy Payne and I tail-ended the presidential motorcade at game's end back to the police station where Kennedy boarded the Air Force helicopter for his return to his Palm Beach vacation home. That was the last time I seen John Kennedy in person.

Kennedy did visit Miami on November 18, 1963, a few days prior to his murder. Security for this visit was very tight due to warnings that the Miami police had received stating Kennedy would be gunned down from a high office building while his motorcade headed from the airport to Miami Beach for a speech. The plan was changed and the motorcade scrapped, as JFK was instead flown by helicopter from Miami International Airport directly to Miami Beach for the political meeting. While working as an aide to Assistant Chief Glen Baron and Patrol Commander, Major William Harries, I was aware of a staff meeting that week with the Secret Service and our police Intelligence Squad, as well as several other police staff members, where it was recommended that there be no motorcade on the 18th. (Details in a later chapter) Five days later JFK was gunned down in Dallas.

Several years later, in 1969, while assigned as Commander of the Strategic Information Unit (Intelligence) of the Miami police department, I listened to the audio recordings that Sergeant Everett Kaye had made with informant Willie Somersett just prior to Kennedy's murder and had long discussions with Sergeants Kaye and McCracken on the subject, who were then assigned to my unit.

On the day of JFK's murder, November 22, 1963, I joined millions around the globe in shock upon hearing the assassination news from the department's communications center, while on duty as an assistant to the Patrol Commander. For the next several days, all of us were glued to the television, watching each interview and event, including the gunning down of Lee Oswald by Jack Ruby in the basement of the Dallas police department. It was incomprehensible to me.

The American public initially seemed to accept the Warren commission findings that Oswald had indeed been the lone assassin and ruled out any conspiracy, and I shared that opinion. My American roots and values go back on my maternal side to the 1600's in New England, with ancestors fighting in wars from Revolutionary war, Civil war, as well as the 20th century battles. At age 17, I joined the Air Force and was well bred in the love of country AND government (at that time0. I purchased a copy of the Warren Report and came away with a few questions. During the following years, I avidly devoured each government commission report (there were several) and any and all newspaper and magazine stories about the assassination. I even have a vague recollection of asking myself, "Why is this author Mark Lane guy so harshly criticizing my government?".

I recall flying into Miami while on leave from the Air Force to attend the Orange Bowl game the same day as Castro took over Cuba and began his march to Havana. The crowds in the downtown Miami area were large and noisy, with columns of horn tooting autos parading in the streets. Exactly one year later on January 1, 1960, I was discharged from the Air Force and landed at 3:00 A.M. in warm Miami, leaving a Times Square freezing celebration in New York's Times Square. In Miami, the Cubans were still celebrating their new government which had taken over governing Cuba from the corrupt Batistia regime.

The late 1960's were a busy time for our country and myself, with work, studying for exams in my vocation, marrying, buying a home, and beginning to raise a family. I continued attending college and was an active Air Force reservist in Miami. Civil unrest and the burgeoning of the drug culture in our cities kept me busy at work. The big story in Miami, however, was the invasion of Cuban citizens fleeing from communist Cuba.

CUBANS ARRIVE IN MIAMI

Jump forward a couple of years and one observed a different atmosphere in Miami where I now was a young police officer. Anti-Castro organizations of all shapes and sizes and philosophies had sprung up and the émigrés were signing up at open recruiting stations to volunteer for some sort of invasion to uproot the now openly communist government of Cuba. To the field patrol officer of our police department, it seemed that every other Cuban we encountered in the Miami streets or when handling calls, claimed to be employed by the CIA. It was not unusual that a suspect we had arrested and booked into jail, would soon be seen leaving our police station - not handcuffed, accompanied by crew-cut suit-clad Americans, obviously in the employ of the Central Intelligence Agency (CIA).

The author was a field patrolman in the Little Havana area during the run-up to the Bay of Pigs. All of us field officers knew the invasion was imminent. During the last few nights prior to the jump-off, the field officers were instructed to not stop or search cars in the areas close to the Miami River unless a 'normal crime' like burglary or robbery had occurred. The carrying of a gun by the Cubans in that area was about as common as a pocket knife. This did not pose any great danger to us patrol guys as the Cubans knew we were 'on the same side'.

Beginning in late 1963 into 1964, I was assigned to Miami police's Task Force, a group of fifty or so officers who patrolled in pairs in plain un-marked cars and did not receive any radio calls. We were the offense. Castro had emptied the prisons and nut houses and was forcing Miami Cubans who had sailed to Cuban ports to pick up their remaining relatives, to also take the 'thieves and nuts', back to Miami with them. I had the fortune of being paired with a Cuban born police officer, bi-lingual Bill Zamora, a Marine veteran and a Georgia Tech grad, who taught me some Spanish as we worked Little Havana streets. We became personally acquainted with many of the Anti-Castro people whose names are mentioned in the press when the CIA plots of the 1960's and the assassination are discussed.

About the time (spring of 1963) President Kennedy put the brakes on the anti-Castro raids to Cuba, a number of my police friends (and myself) became well acquainted and friendly with an auto mechanic, Eddy XXXX, who had a repair shop in the rear of the infamous Trojan bar on SW 8th

Street in Little Havana. Eddie was a fierce anti-communist who would periodically disappear for a few days, leaving our personal junk cars awaiting repair to sit and wait for his return. Usually, when he did come back, he would tow in a large cabin cruiser for repairs as we speculated on what target he and his crew had struck on his latest raid in Cuba. This type of scenario was replicated all over the Miami area, especially in shops near the Miami River.

By 1969, the Miami police department had a new Police Chief, Bernard Garmire, a true professional law enforcement manager from Arizona who transformed our department into a modern police agency despite some foot dragging from a cadre of old timers. I was transferred from being a uniformed patrol Lieutenant to command the intelligence unit (Strategic Information Unit). One of the Sergeants who worked for me was Everett Kaye, a smart old detective, who had in late 1963, recorded the conversation between right wing radical Joseph Milteer and an informer, Willie Somersett, where it was stated that JFK would be assassinated by a rifle shot from a high building while in a presidential motorcade. This warning was relayed to the Secret Service and Federal Bureau of Investigation at that time by Lieutenant Charlie Sapp, head of Miami P.D.'s Intelligence Squad.

THE INVESTIGATING COMMITTEES

The Warren Commission Report in 1964 claimed that Oswald acted alone in the killing of the President. Their conclusions merely confirmed what FBI Director J. Edgar Hoover claimed the day after the killing that Oswald acted alone and that there was no conspiracy. () A later reading of the witness interrogations were replete with examples of leading the witnesses toward the theory that all the shots came from the 6th floor window of the school book depository building (TSBD) and that Lee Oswald was the shooter. Other important witness was not interviewed and a possible conspiracy was not even considered. Many witnesses who testified have come forward and stated that their interviews by the Federal Bureau of Investigation (FBI) were not accurate in describing what the witnesses actually said. (2) The convoluted autopsy, the amazing 'magic bullet' theory and the suppression of previous contacts that the FBI had with Oswald were downright disingenuous. The CIA purposely suppressed evidence and displayed obvious criminal intent with the repeated disinformation they provided to the Warren Commission. Even some of the commission members, particularly Representative Hale Boggs, claimed that the Warren Commission investigation was a "farce".

The Warren Commission was composed of Chief Justice Earl Warren, Sen. Richard Russell, Sen. John Cooper, US Representatives John Coyners, Hale Boggs and Rep Gerald Ford. Allen Dulles, former head of the C.I.A. (Previously fired by Kennedy) and statesman John McCloy rounded out the committee. The General Counsel was J. Lee Rankin, a former solicitor general of the US.

There were fourteen Associate Counsels and twelve staff members. The Commission's report was submitted in September of 1964, followed by the release of the twenty-six back-up volumes. In November of 1964. The Commission was disbanded upon the release of the report. An excellent index of the Warren Report was later prepared by author Sylvia Meagher, a task that the Commission neglected.

The Warren Commission excluded the use of the adversary procedure. Neither the American Bar Association nor any private attorneys took part in the exam of the 395 witnesses that testified before the commission.

One author, Edward Jay Epstein, who wrote three JFK assassination books including "Inquest", characterized the Warren Commission's efforts at reaching for the truth as: "by far, the most serious error of the Warren Commission was altering the data to fit a preconceived model." (3)

The Rockefeller Commission was ordered formed in 1975 by President Gerald Ford and headed up by Vice President Nelson Rockefeller. The Executive Director was David Belin. This Commission conducted a limited review of the Kennedy assassination. They also inquired into the possibility that former CIA Agent Howard Hunt and anti-Castro hawk Frank Sturgis, were present in Dallas, on November of 1963, perhaps being two of the 3 "tramps" collared in the rail yards behind the Depository building shortly after the assassination. Howard Hunt, a CIA employee in 1963, who retired in 1971, was a propaganda specialist known as "Edwardo" to the anti-Castro Cubans. Allegedly, Sturgis was not a paid CIA asset directly.

Both denied that they were in Dallas on November 22, 1963. Frank Sturgis' alibi was his wife and her nephew. Hunt said he didn't know Sturgis until 1972, a fact disputed by many.

In 1978, the Select Committee in Assassinations, conducted by the U.S. House of Representatives, know as the HSCA, was a much more independent effort to seek the truth despite problems initially in the administration of the commission. The Committee, headed by Chairman Louis Stokes, presented a final report in January of 1979 (Sixteen years after the assassination). The representatives on the sub-committee that handled the JFK killing were Rep. Richardson Preyer, chairman, and House members Yvonne Burke, Christopher Dodd, Charles Thone, Harold Sawyer, with Louis Stokes and Samuel Devine, as ex officio members. The Chief Counsel and Director was Robert Blakey.

The Committee's final report stated "the committee, therefore, concluded that the testimony of witnesses in Dealey Plaza on November 22, 1963 supported the finding of the acoustical analysis that there was a high probability that a shot was fired at the President from the Grassy Knoll... There were also reports of suspicious activity in the vicinity of the knoll. The committee also stated, "The committee found that the scientific acoustical evidence established a high probability that two gunmen fired at President John F. Kennedy". (4)

The committee found that Oswald fired three shots at Kennedy, the first one missing and the second and third shots hitting the President. They claimed that the shots were fired by Lee Oswald from the 6th floor of the Texas School Book Depository building on Elm Street. They pointed the finger at Oswald mainly because Oswald owned the rifle and that he had access to and was present on the 6th floor. A fact unsaid was that 74 other employees in this building also had access to the 6th floor and no one seen Oswald in possession of, fire the rifle, or was even seen on the 6th floor after 11:50 A.M. that day. The Committee also went on to say that the US Secret Service did not provide adequate protection that day (obvious) and that the FBI and CIA failed to share information, before and after the assassination and that the Warren Commission failed to investigate the possibility of a conspiracy.

The Secret Service also failed to advise the agents planning the Dallas trip of the threats preceding Kennedy's visits to other cities in the weeks before his Texas trip. It was also noted that President Kennedy himself was said to not allow escort police motorcycles to ride alongside his limo during motorcades and prohibited Secret Service agents from riding on the rear of his car, although this version has not been precisely verified for the Dallas trip. Also, it supposedly was the President himself that did not want the bubble top to be placed on his limo during the Dallas motorcade despite the fact that thirty four threats against the life of Kennedy were received from Texas during the period of 1961 and 1962.

The Dallas motorcade's first published notice was on September 13th, although the political trip has been planned for months.

GOVERNMENT ASSASSINATION REPORTS

The FBI Investigation Report - December 1964

Warren Commission Report - 26 volumes, 1964

Alleged Assassination plot - Foreign leaders - 1975

Sub-Committee report on Committee to Study governmental Operation with Respect to Intelligence Activities. Church Committee" - Jan 1975

"Select Committee to Study Government Operations with Respect to Intelligence Activities. Headed by Senator Schweiker and Senator Gary Hart.

Investigation of JFK Assassination - Book V, Select Senate Committee-1976

Report of the Select Committee on Assassinations - US House, 1979

Report to the President by Commission on CIA - 1976

Texas Supplemental Report on JFK case - 1976 by Texas Attorney General Waggoner Carr

Assassination Records Review Board, 1998

Senator Richard Schweiker of the Church Committee was appointed to chair the Select Committee to Study Governmental Operations with Respect to Intelligence Activities. Regarding Oswald, Schweiker was quoted saying, "We do know Oswald had intelligence connections. Everywhere you look with him, there are fingerprints of Intelligence".

City of Dallas, Tx., Archives/JFK, Opened to the public by ordinance, 1964

DEALING WITH FEDERAL AGENCIES

In an effort to acquaint the reader with the dynamics of the relationship between federal and local law enforcement agencies during that period, I will provide examples of my experience when I was the intelligence unit commander in 1969-70.

This intelligence unit was the formal contact point for the department between the various federal agencies that we toiled with, such as the FBI, the Secret Service, the CIA, Customs, etc. A couple of situations occurred that ties in with some later chapters. Soon after taking command of the unit, I noticed an FBI agent, Lenny Peterson, visiting our office almost each morning. Lenny would be given the unit's 'read file' by our secretary Rose Gold, takes notes, and often have Rose make him a copy of a particular report. The 'read file' was a copy of each confidential report made by unit investigators as well as our supervisory reports to the Chief. A few days later, I needed some additional information on a particular organized crime subject and asked Peterson for a copy of the FBI's profile or report on same. His reply, "Sorry, I cannot give you the FBI report but I will try to answer any question you might have concerning the matter". The following morning Lenny was quite surprised and shocked when he was informed that he would no longer have access to our 'read file' nor could he have copies of same. I did offer, upon his written request, that we would provide answers to his specific questions on specific cases.

Another amusing incident soon occurred when my boss, Captain Tom Mullin (also an attorney), and the author was invited to a get-acquainted lunch with the head of Miami's CIA office. (We had no idea what his real name was) At lunch at the Northwest 14th Street Holiday Inn, the CIA guy advised that he had a few 'surplus' rifles in his supply room that he wanted to gift us as a 'personal present'. This caused both Tom and I to break out laughing as it was so obvious what the intent was. The CIA guy seemed a little shaken but we went on to have a nice lunch on Uncle Sam. We learned some weeks later, that the guy did in fact 'lend' our department some rifles, which were then merged into the regular SWAT team's equipment locker. That same guy also 'lent' our intelligence unit a fancy and expensive long-range camera to 'field test'. Another of my Sergeants, Gene McCracken and I, did in fact try out the camera up in Miami's northeast section, where most of our Mafia guys lived. One morning, we spotted notorious national jewel thief, John Cook, walking in the neighborhood. Cook walked two blocks north to the home of another hood and we photographed both crooks together. We could not make out who the other guy was due to the distance, but when the photos were developed, the other guy was identified as a big time national hoodlum and a convicted felon. One of the provisions of Cook's probation was that he was not to associate with felons. Detective McCracken took the photos to the US Attorney and Cook was jailed. FBI Director J. Edgar Hoover sent us a nice letter of commendation.

One last story before getting back to the JFK case. In early 1970, Miami Police Chief Garmire and my section commander, a Major, visited our intelligence office. As they were departing, the Chief (with whom I had a good relationship) remarked, "Phil, I hope you have sense enough to insure that no markings are on our wire tap equipment that would identify the items as belonging to the Miami police". I advised him that it did not make any difference as I had ordered Sgt Kaye, our technical equipment guy, to never take the equipment out of our office unless I gave him a copy of a federal search warrant which would later result in notifying the target at some point, the identify of the agency that had run the tap. I further explained that Bobby Kennedy was probably looking for some one to bang for violating the new wiretapping federal law and it damm sure was not going to be me. The bosses left the office with red faces. The following Monday, I was called to the Chief's office and informed that I had been selected to attend the prestigious Southern Police Institute (SPI) and would be leaving for the University of Louisville the following week. Attendance at SPI was a real plum for any municipal or state law enforcement officer and I had hoped to attend some day. I did not, however, even apply this time, but off I went for four months. My boss, Tom Mullins, a probationary Captain, was called in that day and advised that he was being busted back to Lieutenant. Also, that same week our section commander, the Major mentioned earlier, hosted an office visit from an IRS Intelligence supervisor. A few days later, Captain Tom Mullins was notified that he was being audited by the IRS and had to dig-up all his records for the past three years. Coincidence?

Shortly after, my old SIU (intelligence) crew set up and ran a four month wiretap surveillance on Frank Martin's gas station. Martin was Miami's notorious court 'fixer'. That tap provided sufficient evidence to apply for the federal warrant. The real legal tap then provided enough admissible evidence to snare several local Criminal Court and City Court judges and charge them with corruption. I later remarked to one of my old troopers who worked the case that I was delighted with the results but had been worried that the federal authorities might catch them with the illegal tap. My guy replied that it was not a problem as the feds worked with them from 'day one', before and after the wiretap warrant was issued.

Upon my return to the department from the Southern Police Institute in Louisville, I was assigned as an aide to Chief Garmire in his office for the next year or so writing grants and supervising the Budget and Computer Operations Units. Captain Mullin beat the demotion but was assigned (with two other old Captains) to sit at the front information desk, performing no duties, where they stayed until their retirement.

PART II

ATTEMPT ON WALKER

ATTEMPT MURDER OF
GENERAL WALKER

Skipping the basic known facts for now on these three November, 1963 murder cases, let's look at an event that occurred several months earlier at which a well known retired U.S. Army General was the victim of an attempted murder at his home in Dallas. We now (2014) know with almost certainty that Lee Harvey Oswald attempted to kill General Edwin Walker by firing a rifle slug thru a window of Walker's home, narrowly missing his head while the General was sitting at a desk in his study. The attempt on Walker is a key event, as if Oswald had indeed shot at Walker; it becomes easier for many to believe he did shoot President Kennedy seven months later.

Some brief facts of the attempt on Walker follows: On Wednesday, April 10, 1963, at approximately 9:00 P.M., one rifle bullet was fired from outside the Walker home at 4011 Turtle Creek Blvd., Dallas, Texas. The bullet passed near General Walker's head as he was seated preparing some income tax forms.

The Warren Commission, in considering whether Oswald fired the shot, (1) A note Oswald left for his wife, (2) photographs of the Walker home were found among his possessions after the JFK killing, (3) ballistics of the spent bullet recovered in Walker's home, and (4) alleged statements made by Oswald to his wife by Oswald.

OSWALD'S NOTE

The handwritten note in Russian, confirmed as written by Lee Oswald by FBI expert James Cadigan, is telling. (5)

1- This is the key to the mailbox which is located in the main post office in the city on Ervay Street. This is the same street where the drugstore, in which you always waited, is located. You will find the mailbox in the post office which is located 4 blocks from the drugstore on that street. I paid for the box last month, so don't worry about it.

2- Send the information as to what happened to me to the Embassy and include newspaper clippings (should there be anything about me in the newspaper). I believe that the Embassy will come quickly to your assistance on learning everything.

3- I paid the house rent on the 2d so don't worry about it.

4- Recently, I also paid for water and gas.

5- The money from work will possibly be coming. The money will be sent to our post office box. Go to the bank and cash the check.

6- You can either throw out or give me clothing, etc. away. Do not keep these. However, I prefer that you hold on to my personal papers (military, civil.)

7- Certain of my documents are in the small blue valise.

8- The address book can be found on my table in the study should need same.

9- We have friends here. The Red Cross also will help you (Red Cross in English)

10- I left you as much money as I could, $60 on the second of the month. You and the baby (apparently) can live for another 2 months using $10 a week.

11- If I am alive and taken prisoner, the city jail is located at the end of the bridge through which we always passed on going to the city (right in the beginning of the city after crossing the bridge.

This note was found after the Kennedy murder in a book in Mrs. Ruth Paine's garage and turned over to the police by Mrs. Paine (a close friend whom the Oswald family was living with) on December 2, 1963, An analysis of the note firmly indicated it was written by Oswald in the spring of 1963, around the time of the attempt on Walker.

On the Wednesday evening of the Walker shooting, Marian Oswald testified that Oswald left their apartment after dinner. When he failed to return by 10:00 P.M., Maria discovered the note. When Oswald did return he was very pale according to Mrs. Oswald. "He only told me that he shot at Walker but did not know if he hit him". The following morning Oswald stated to his wife that "he was very sorry that he had not hit him".

The references in the note made clear that the note was written while the Oswald's were living on Neely Street (in Dallas) after 3/3/1963 and prior to 5/14/1963. In Maria's testimony to the Commission in February, 1964, she stated that Oswald advised he had been planning the attempt on Walker for two months. He later showed her a notebook containing photos of Walker's home and a map of the area. The notebook had been destroyed but three of the photos were certified as being taken at Walker's home. The photos were found by Dallas detectives during a second search of Mrs. Paine's garage. (Oswald claimed after his arrest, that the photo was a fake, his face pasted onto the photos after the fact). An exam of the window at the rear of General Walker's house, the wall the bullet passed through, and the fence behind the home indicated that the bullet was fired from a position near the point where one of the photos were taken. Another of the photos depicted the entrance to Walker's driveway from a back alley. Also seen in one photo is the fence on which the assailant rested the rifle in Walker's back yard.

Oswald purchased a money order for the rifle on March 12th, 1963. The weapon was shipped on March 20th and the shooting occurred on April 10th. FBI experts were able to determine that this photo was taken by the Imperial Reflex camera owned by Oswald. (6) Mrs. Oswald advised that her husband told her that after the attempt, he had hidden the rifle in bushes near a railroad track, consistent with the photos mentioned above. Maria testified that several days after the shooting, Oswald recovered the rifle and brought it back to their apartment.

The Dallas police recovered a badly mutilated bullet from Walker's study. The Dallas county lab was unable to determine the type weapon because of the condition of the bullet. Later the bullet was forwarded to the FBI and examined by expert Robert Frazier, who was unable to reach a conclusion that the bullet was fired from the same rifle found at the Dallas School Depository Building after the Kennedy killing. Frazier advised that the general rifling characteristics of the rifle are of the same type as the Walker bullet and it "could have been from the rifle". (7) Frazier also testified that he found no evidence that would indicate that the bullet was not fired from the Mannlicher-Carcano rifle owned by Oswald. The 6.5 mm bullet, according to Frazier, is one of a 'relatively few" types of rifles that could provide the characteristics found on the bullet. Another expert, Joe Nicol, generally agreed with Frazier, linking Oswald to the Walker shooting.

It is significant that Oswald went to great lengths writing the note to his wife that contained instructions on what to do if something went wrong with the Walker attempt, but no such Oswald note was discovered after the JFK killing. The Warren Commission concluded after considering all the facts mentioned, that Lee Oswald did attempt to kill General Walker on April 10, 1963.

MOTIVE TO KILL WALKER

What would be Oswald's motive to kill Walker, especially in view of the reported history of Oswald, that he had not displayed any violent tendencies up to this point in his life? General Walker, a renowned Army leader who had served ably and courageously (Silver Star holder) during WW II (Europe) and Korea was now heavily involved in right wing political activities around the country. Walker's last active Army assignment was commanding thousands of troops. When JFK was elected, Walker and other military leaders were advised to "calm down" their public rhetoric regarding the need to educate their troops on the dangers of Communism. (The author recalls attending mandatory lectures of this type during his active military service (Air Force) in the late 1950's)

Before leaving the Army, Walker was sent by President Eisenhower to command the federal troops that were sent to Little Rock, AK, to quell the disturbances that arose during the integration of the high schools in that city. Records show Walker accomplished his mission ably. Walker later resigned his Army commission and was one of the most vocal leaders against the integration of the U. of Mississippi. Walker was arrested by order of Attorney General Robert Kennedy and Defense Secretary Robert McNamara and an attempt was made to commit Walker to a mental institution for a 90-day evaluation. The General's lawyers obtained his release after five days and the charges of leading the riots were later dropped.

Walker, during the period of the early 1960's, became one of the most vocal leaders of the rightwing in America, touring the country to give anti-communist speeches to rather large crowds. The author recalls attending one of his rallies in 1962 at the Dade County Auditorium in Miami and another (date unknown) at the Miami Beach Convention Center. My purpose however, was not political, but as a young single guy, was much more interested in renewing a relationship with a cute hostess that was working for the firm that produced the rallies.

General Walker's exploits were widely reported in southern cities such as Miami, New Orleans, and Dallas. Many 'progressives' deemed his message 'fascists'. Walker was particularly vocal regarding Fidel Castro and his communist takeover of a country 90 miles from the United States. Oswald, in fact, wrote Arnold Johnson of the US Communist Party in 1963 that he (Oswald) had attended an ultra right meeting headed by Walker in Dallas (possibly on October 23rd). Oswald was heard to express great anger at Walker as he was constantly railing at Fidel Castro, whom Oswald was said to admire.

General Walker, at the time of the shooting, had believed that a former employee of his was the suspect in the attempt to kill him and did hire two private detectives to investigate. The detectives found no evidence concerning this suspicion.

———

21

A remarkable fact on this attempt on Walker that occurred to me was that Oswald, from 100 feet distance, in a quiet setting with the gun barrel resting on a fence, fired at a sitting Walker in a well lighted room, and MISSED. Yet seven months later, allegedly hit three head shots at a person riding in a moving auto, from the sixth floor of a building. Also keep in mind is that the Walker bullet was heavily mangled, (which is not unusual) but this fact was not consistent with the 'magic' bullet allegedly found on a gurney at Parkland Hospital after the Kennedy/Connolly shootings.

The act of Oswald attempting to kill General Walker certainly shows that he had the propensity for committing murder.

PART III

THE ASSASSINATON

THE HOMICIDES

Three murders occurred in Dallas, Texas in late November of 1963, all apparently related. At about 12:30 P.M. CST, on November 22, 1963, John F. Kennedy's presidential motorcade turned off Houston Street onto Elm Street in Dallas, Texas, en route to the Dallas Trade Mart. Just as JFK's limo passed by the Texas School Depository Building in the Dealey Square area, three or more rifle shots rang out, two of which struck President Kennedy and another striking Texas Governor John Connally, who was riding in the same car. Secret Service agents rushed the two victims to Parkland Hospital where President John Kennedy was pronounced dead, but the Governor survived. This act of murder began a Dallas police department homicide case.

The second murder occurred about an hour later on East Tenth Street in Dallas, a couple of miles from the first scene, when Dallas police officer, J.D. Tippit, was killed by several shots from a revolver fired by a man whom the officer was confronting. The alleged killer in both these homicides was Lee Harvey Oswald, a 24 y year old white male. Oswald was arrested at a theatre shortly after the Tippit murder.

The third case occurred on the following Sunday morning in the basement garage of the Dallas police department, where the suspect Oswald was being transferred to the county jail. The killer, Jack Ruby, a Dallas night club owner, was seen by millions on national television, firing one fatal revolver shot at Oswald, as Dallas detectives were walking Oswald to a waiting transport vehicle.

The killings were initially investigated by the Dallas Police Department, headed up by Chief of Police Jesse Curry. The lead investigator was Captain Will Fritz, commander of the Robbery-Homicide bureau of the department. The Kennedy case was federalized by President Johnson the following day, despite the fact ---- at that time --- the killing of a U.S president was not a federal crime. (It now is)

Several days later, on November 29th, President Johnson appointed a special commission to investigate JFK's death. The commission would be headed by the Chief Justice of the U.S. Supreme Court, Earl Warren, and would include two U.S. senators and two U.S. House members, as well as Allen Dulles the former head of the Central Intelligence Agency, and a veteran statesman, John McCloy. The general counsel selected was J. Lee Rankin, assisted by 14 assistant counsels and 12 staff members. The Federal Bureau of Investigation, headed by J. Edgar Hoover, was to provide investigators for the commission. The commission would be forever known as the Warren Commission.

THE MOTORCADE

The make up of the motorcade was as follows:

1- Dallas PD motorcycle officers - to clear back bystanders

2- PILOT CAR - A Dallas PD car with officers to clear back bystanders, driving about ¼ mile ahead of main motorcade. Occupied by Deputy Chief Lumkin and Deputy Chief Turner of D.P.D., Lt. Col Whitmeyer and Detective Senkel.

3- Four Dallas PD motorcycle officers - to keep crowd back

4- LEAD CAR - Dallas Police Chief Curry driving, with Dallas Secret Service Chief Forest Sorrels, Dallas County Sheriff Decker and Secret Service agent Winston Lawson.

5- PRESIDENTIAL LIMO - JFK and wife in rear seat, Governor Connally and his wife in jump seats. The driver was Secret Service Agent William Greer, with Agent Kellerman as the radio man. The limo was an open top 1961 Lincoln, without the bubble top in place.

6- Dallas PD motors, two on each side of JFK limo, riding slightly to the rear

7- FOLLOW-UP CAR - An 8-passenger 1955 Caddy with eight Secret Service agents (four in and four outside car) and presidential aides Powers and O'Donnell.

8- VICE PRES. LIMO - Vice Pres. Johnson and wife, Senator Yarborough, with Texas state patrol officer, Hurschel Jacks, driving.

9- VP FOLLOW-UP CAR - with 3 Secret Service agents and Johnson aide, Cliff Garter.

10- 5 cars with dignitaries, press and presidential staff

11- Two busses with press

12- A Dallas PD uniform car and several Dallas motor men.

The motorcade route was determined by the presidential staff and Secret Service, with consultation with the Dallas P.D. The route, published in the November 19th Dallas Times-Herald, "the motorcade will pass through downtown Dallas on Harwood, then west on Main, turning back to Elm Street at Houston and flowing out Dealey Square to the Stemmons Freeway to the Dallas Trade Mart, four miles away.

The motorcade schedule had it in front of TSBD at 12:25 P.M., although it was five minutes late, as the shots rang out at exactly 12:30 P.M.

The Secret Service basically performed what they were trained to do, before, during and after the assassination (with exceptions as noted later). And, of course, they failed to notice a gunman in the 6th floor window of the TSBD building as the motorcade passed the 'kill' zone on Elm Street. Noteworthy was the swift actions of Secret Service Agent Clint Hill, who leaped onto JFK's car just as the shots were fired and Agent Rufus Youngblood, smothering Vice President Johnson to protect him. There were no Secret Service agents assigned to Dealey Square at all, nor did any embark there after the shots.

After the shootings, the motorcade sped to Parkland Hospital, four miles away. At the time the shots were fired, the speed of the motorcade was calculated at 11 miles an hour. None of the Secret Service agents observed the TSBD shooter(s) or Grassy Knoll suspects, if any existed, as the shots were fired.

The trip to Dallas was originally planned on June 5th, 1963, during a meeting with President Kennedy, Vice President Johnson, and Governor Connolly. The trip was announced to the public in September. The advance route was planned by Secret Service Agent Lawson in the days preceding the November 22nd motorcade.

The preplanning and execution of the motorcade appeared to follow the basic normal protocols of a typical presidential motorcade, from the original planning, test runs, and meeting with local officials. However, deviations were made, some minor and others significant, and some huge mistakes were made, which will be discussed in detail later. The author has participated in numerous presidential motorcade experiences, including that of lesser officials, Vice President, visiting VIP's, candidates such as George Wallace, etc. These motorcades usually follow long established Secret Service guidelines. The Secret Service is in full charge of the motorcades with the local police providing the back-up manpower.

The author was totally surprised while researching this book, that the Secret Service's Dallas trip planners did not take into account the threats that were made concerning Kennedy's Miami trip, as well as the threats during the Chicago and Tampa trips, all just prior to his Texas visit.

UNPLANNED DEVIATIONS

The only deviation of motorcade security that I experienced during my career was an unplanned side trip that President Ford made during a Miami visit. Gerald Ford, in the mid-1970's, was attending a function (rally) at the downtown Howard Johnson hotel in downtown Miami. The Secret Service notified the author, the commander of Miami Police security detail that Ford wanted to make an unscheduled trip over to Miami Beach to visit comedian Bob Hope, who was performing at a hotel on the north end of Miami Beach. The Secret Service requested that Miami police provide an escort to the Beach hotel. I quickly assigned one uniformed car manned by Sergeant Bob Sullivan and two of his SWAT members, who led the way onto the expressway ramp and headed north on I-95, followed by the presidential limo with Ford and a second Secret Service car with three agents and myself. We ran with emergency lights and siren up to the north causeway and turned over to the Beach, an area that was not in Miami's jurisdiction. I quickly contacted the Beach and Metro (Sheriff's department) to man a few of the major intersections to facilitate our run. I doubt that they were very thrilled by this unplanned assignment. We arrived at the hotel and entered through the rear door. We walked right onto the stage where Hope was entertaining a large crowd. Hope appeared surprised, although I seriously doubt that he was. President Ford and Bob Hope swapped a few quick comments, with the President adding a few comments to the audience.

The three-car caravan then reversed our route back to Miami. I questioned the Secret Service prior to the unplanned trip concerning this side venture which had such little security. The agents advised, that due to the trips non-publicized nature, there was minimal risk.

Another quick story about an un-planned presidential situation. President Ford, on a separate trip to Miami, was to address a federal judicial group at the downtown Colonial Hotel, along Biscayne Boulevard. A group of émigrés had gathered across the street in Bayfront Park and were quite vocal. I had only a small group of officers assigned, mainly in the front of the hotel where President Ford was to enter. At the last moment, I was notified that President Ford would make his entrance at the side door of the hotel on N.E. 2nd Street. It was initially planned that local political leaders were to greet the president on his arrival, but for some reason, none of the local political (Democrats) leaders wanted to be seen with President Ford.

The presidential limo arrived at the side entrance and out stepped President Ford. I instantly recognized that there was no one to greet the president, so I stepped out and declared, "Welcome to Miami". We exchanged greetings and were joined by the manager of the hotel. Ford's staff had anticipated that the chats with the local politicians would take about twenty minutes. Instead Ford went upstairs to a room to change and freshen up. He soon emerged back into the lobby although he had to wait 20-25 minutes until the time for his address. I had the pleasure of chatting with Ford, mainly about the subject matter of the address he was about to make to the judges and prosecutors, as well as some current law enforcement issues. I was delighted to have that opportunity and to help him avoid the embarrassment of being shunned by the local politicians. The following day, Ford was escorted to the airport for his departure to Washington and asked me to be photographed with him. He expressed his appreciation for the courtesy extended to him by the Miami police. I still have that photo on my wall.

The point of these last two stories is that the protectors must be flexible when performing this vital task when protecting our national chief executive during this era when there are so many forces determined to violently upset the applecart of our democracy, but the risks rise.

SHOTS FIRED IN DEALY SQUARE

The crowd was large and friendly to observe the young president as he rode in the rear seat of the open Limo alongside his wife. Seated in front of Kennedy were Texas Governor John Connolly and Mrs. Connolly. Two Secret Service agents were in the front sear, with Agent William Greer driving and Agent Roy Kellerman handling the car radio. Dallas police motorcycle officers were on each side of the limo, slightly to the rear. As the presidential limo passed the Texas School Book Depository on Elm Street, at least three shots rang out, two of which struck Kennedy and one hit Governor Connally. The limo was traveling at eleven miles an hour as it turned onto Elm Street from Houston Street and was observed coming to almost a complete stop after the first shot. The Warren Commission concluded that all shots were fired from the sixth floor of the TSBD. These brief moments in Dealey Square were recorded by many bystanders with cameras, especially by the Zapruder, Nix, Muchmore and Bronson films, the Altgens photo, the Dillard photo, etc. One researcher has pointed out that there were 510 photographs produced by 75 different photographers in Dealey Square that day, before, during and after the assassination.

The author visited Dealey Square in the mid 1970's. He also viewed the Zapruder film several times, as well as some of the other films mentioned, while attending a Dignitary Protection Seminar in Washington, D.C., during the first two weeks of March, 1976, with the first week at the FBI Academy and the second week at the Washington Secret Service headquarters.

The Warren Commission examined the Zapruder film in detail, frame by frame. They stated in their report that there is "very persuasive evidence for the experts" that the same bullet which pierced Kennedy's head, also caused the Connally wounds. However, the reaction of bystanders, moving abruptly, indicates that the first shot was fired before frame #204 of the Zapruder film. At that precise time, the president was concealed from the Book Depository window by tree foliage (Frame 3166-204), a point where a sniper in that window could not have seen or aimed at Kennedy. The Warren Commission stated that the Zapruder film did not see JFK at the moment he was first shot because of the intervention of the Stemmons Expressway street sign. Mr. Zapruder however testified, "I heard the first shot and I saw Kennedy lean over and grab himself in the left chest area.

The Governor at that time showed no evidence of being shot. The earliest time frame which Connally was shot was frame #228, or maybe #233., as his hand was not injured until that time, according to the account in Sylvia Meagher's book, "Accessories After The Fact", page 27-35., which examines the shots. The head shot to President Kennedy came at frame #313 and caused the president to be violently thrust back against the rear seat, the opposite direction that a sniper shot from the Depository would travel. A simpler layman's explanation of the Commission conclusion was that shot #1 hit JFK in the shoulder, exiting through his neck, Shot #2 hitting Governor Connally and shot #3 hit JFK in the head. Commission counsel Arlen Specter (later a United States Senator) came up with the magic bullet theory that shot #1 went through Kennedy and continued on into Governor Connally, wounding him in several places, finally exiting Connally at his wrist. Shot #3's bullet fragmented after blowing off the President's skull.

It is the author's opinion (not a forensic expert) that Specter would have been laughed out of court if he had presented that theory in a trial. Spector described the bullet traveling in a zig-zag fashion, which defies the laws of physics. The idea that a speeding bullet could travel sideways is incredible and the fact that learned men would believe such a conclusion is absurd.

We now look at the Commission's evidence that a sniper accurately fired three rounds from an old junk Italian rifle at a person in a moving vehicle (11 miles an hour) away from the sixth floor window, in less than six seconds. The author, an 11 year military veteran and a big city police officer for over two decades, including SWAT training (and C/O of that unit), and a witness to many, many displays of firearm proficiency at military and police ranges, has very serious doubts as to whether one could achieve that feat, even with a top graded rifle and without tree foliage and signs that would hamper the aim. That a former Marine radar technician, four years removed from his military service and not to have been known as a particularly good shot and without evidence of any recent practice, could hit the target in a moving auto three times at that distance, is preposterous. We will visit this subject again later but must remind readers that the military (and police) categorizes shooters in four different skill levels, from the lowest - Marksman, to Sharpshooter, to Expert, and to Master, the highest level. Suspect Oswald recorded military score was 191, just over the bare minimum for a Marksman.

The author's past performance at the range was slightly better than Oswald, but I always seemed to be one of the least proficient of the members during rifle practices over the years. There is no way possible that suspect Oswald accomplished what the Commission claimed he had done - three accurate shots in six or seven seconds. No way.

NUMBER OF SHOTS FIRED

The presidential motorcade was traveling about 11 miles per hour as it approached the turn onto Elm Street from Houston Street. After the first shot was fired, the presidential limo, driven by Secret Service Agent William Greer, slowed to almost a stop, according to the Zapruder film and witnesses. The first shot rang out after the limo had completed the turn from Houston Street.

An unanswered question remains; if all the shots originated from the sixth floor of the TSBD, by a 'lone assassin', why did the shots begin after the turn onto Elm Street instead of beginning as the motorcade was approaching and facing the TSBD, a much easier target than a vehicle moving down and away from the sniper nest?

The original Warren Commission Report concluded that only three rifle shots were fired. Other questions as to the number of shots still remain to this day. A bystander, James Tague, was struck in the face and a fresh bullet mark was found on the curb near where Tague was standing. His position was not lined up with the other shots. Tague immediately reported the hit to a deputy sheriff, to Officer Haygood, a Dallas officer, and to authorities at city hall a short time later. (8-) The police report on the Assassination (9) does not include any affidavits from or any references to Tague.

The following day, two Dallas newsmen, Tom Dillard and James Underwood, took film and photographs of the mark on the curb. (10) In July of 1964, the Warren Commission finally took testimony from Tague and Sheriff's deputy Walthers (11), regarding this shot. The mark on the curb was measured to be 260 feet from the limo's position (placed by the Zapruder film) to the mark on the curb.

The case of the mark on the curb and Tague's injury, is evidence that a bullet or bullet fragment that almost certainly did not come from any of the three bullets which were fired from the 6th floor of the TSBD. The commission reasoning that only three shells were found - and downgrading objective evidence of more than that number of bullets fired - concludes that this mark were unresolved.

Harold Weisburg, in his book, "Whitewash II", (12) discusses evidence of a second apparent bullet mark on the sidewalk on the north side of Elm Street. This mark, considered by two witnesses to be a bullet mark, was called to the attention of the FBI two days after the Warren Report was issued, without any mention of such a mark.

On Elm Street, between Houston Street and the triple underpass the FBI located a 'wide dug out scar' about four and a half inches wide, and reported to the Warren Commission that the scar lies in such a direction that if it had been made by a bullet, it could not have come from the direction of the 'window' of the TSBD.

Harold Feldman, in his article "Fifty-One Witnesses: The Grassy Knoll", has provided an impressive analysis of eyewitnesses testimony and has demonstrated that fifty one witnesses represented in the Hearings and Exhibits section of the Warren Report "thought that the shots had come from the 25 foot high Grassy Knoll". (13)

In 1978, the original 'Dictabelt' recording of the Dallas police radio traffic which was made the day of the assassination was recovered from the home of a retired police intelligence supervisor. Scientific analysis of this recording indicated that four rifle shots were fired. This fact assisted the US House Committee to conclude "a 'fourth' shot was fired from the Grassy Knoll". (14) A few years later the Ramsey report, conducted by government contractors, refuted this theory, saying "the study was flawed". (15) The US House committee stuck by their original conclusion saying Ramsey's analysis was itself flawed. (16)

House Committee Chief Counsel Robert Blakey insisted "on balance', I say there were two shooters in the Plaza -apart from the acoustics. Indeed, its existence of all the other evidence and testimony that makes me thinks the acoustics is right" (17)

Secret Service agent Roy Kellerman, a passenger in Kennedy's limo, said that the last sound he recalled was "like a double bang-bang-bang… like a plane going through the sound barrier". (18) Secret Service agent William Greer, the limo driver, said "the last shot cracked out, just right behind its predecessor". (19) Both comments suggest two shots very close together - far closer together than one man could achieve with a bolt-action rifle. Governor John Connally, himself a hunter, remembered that because of the "rapidity" of the shots, the thought immediately passed through my mind that there were two or three people involved, or more, in this, or that someone was shooting with an automatic rifle". (20)

HSCA Chief Counsel Blakey, in his summary report, stated, "According to the acoustical analysis conducted by the (US House) Committee, four shots, over a total period of 7.9 seconds, were fired at the presidential limo. The first, second and fourth shots came from the TSBD and the third shot from the Grassy Knoll". (21) The House acoustical experts concluded "that the third shot was "fired from a point along the east-west line of the wooden stockade fence on the grassy knoll, about eight feet west of the corner of the fence". (22)

Forrest Sorrels, the Secret Service boss of the Dallas office, was riding in the lead car ahead of the presidential limo. He reported "I looked toward the top of the terrace to my right as the sound of the shots seemed to come from that direction". (23) Secret Service agent Paul Landis, riding in the car behind the presidential limo, states his reaction as the second shot rang out, "my reaction at this time was that the shot came from somewhere toward the front....and looked along the right hand side of the road". (24) Dallas County Sheriff Bill Decker, also riding in the lead car, immediately got on the police radio and said, "Notify Station Five to move all available men out of my department back into the railroad yards".(25) The rail yards are located beyond the wooden fence on the grassy knoll.

The observations of a Dallas police officer J. W. Foster is interesting as it sheds light on yet another bullet being shot. Foster, a nine year veteran officer usually assigned to accident investigations, was assigned that day to the triple overpass to prevent people from standing on the bridge at the time of the motorcade. Officer Foster was stationed on the east side and Officer J.C. White on the west side. Foster heard the shots, which "he thought came from the Elm Street & Houston Street intersection area". His reaction was to run to the rear of the TSBD building then searched the railroad (26) until relieved by Sgt. Harkness. Foster then went to the front of the building and contacted Inspector Sawyer, who advised him to stay in the front area of the Plaza. "I then moved down the roadway (Elm Street). I found where one shot had hit the turf there, adjacent to a manhole. The shot had hit the edge of the manhole and then plowed into the turf. I called the crime scene unit who photographed the scene". (27)

In the book, "Crossfire", by author Jim Marrs, he states "of twenty sheriff deputies watching the motorcade, sixteen placed the shots near the triple overpass. Three gave no opinion and one said the TSBD. Four Dallas police officers said the Grassy Knoll was the origin, four said the TSBD and four others had no opinion. (28)

Setting aside the 'Grassy Knoll' shot for now, lets look again at the three shots from the Texas Book Depository Building. Although there are disputes about most details of the President Kennedy assassination, there seems to be almost universal acceptance that three rifle shots were fired from the 6th floor 'sniper's nest at the TSBD'. Three spent cartridges were found on the 6TH floor scene by detectives and the two workman watching the parade from the window on the floor below, Bonnie Ray Williams and James (Junior) Jarmen, They heard spent cartridges hitting the floor above them and advised that 'debris' was falling on them from the ceiling as the shots were fired. Many other witnesses still in the building testified that they clearly heard the three shots ring out inside the building. (29)

Now we shall look at whether or not that rifle, the 6.5 Mannlicher-Carcerno, serial number C-2766, was capable of firing three shots in the time frame by either Oswald or by some other person according to an analysis of the Zapruder film.

The Warren Commission had the cartridge cases examined by firearms experts who concluded that two bullet fragments found in the JFK limo and the one whole bullet found on a stretcher at Parkland Hospital were in fact fired from the Mannlicher-Carcano rifle found on the 6th floor of the TSBD to the exclusion of of all other weapons. One of the experts was a long time FBI agent, Robert Frazier, who has worked in the field of firearms identification for twenty-three years. Another of the experts was Joseph Nicol, head of the bureau of criminal identification and investigation for the State of Illinois. Other bullet fragments found that were only similar in metallic composition to each other. After an exam, these two experts concluded that the three cartridge cases found on the 6th floor of the Depository had been fired from the Mannlicher-Carcano rifle to the exclusion of all other weapons.

The US House of Representatives committee on the JFK assassination(HSCA) appointed a panel of firearm experts in 1977 to examine all the ballistic issues in the JFK case, the Tippit shooting and the killing of Oswald in the jailhouse. Their report is included in Volume Seven of the House (HSCA) report. The report is very detailed and the conclusions reached were similar to that of the Warren Commission experts.

In 2013, author Conner Trafton wrote an article for the American University investigation website, "The JFK Investigation". The article, "The Three Shot Theory", concludes that the three shots could hve been fired in the 7.1 to 7.9 seconds time frame (derived from the Zapruder's film) but this did not mean that Oswald did fire the 3 shots. The story indicates that there are a myriad of other theories with evidence implicating a second shoot. The article concluded that the official lone gunman theory does have basis in fact, and it is completely plausible. (30)

British author Tim Shipman, in an article he wrote for the London Sunday Telegraph newspaper on February 2, 2007, claims that Lee Harvey Oswald "could not have acted alone in assassinating President John F. Kennedy, according to a new study by Italian weapons experts of the type rifle Oswald used in the shootings". Shipman states that Italian army personnel supervised a test of the Mannlicher-Carcano rifle and found that it was impossible to fire the shots quickly enough, even for marksman. The Italian team test-fired a Carcano M91/38 bolt-action rifle and they were unable to load and fire three shots in less than 19 seconds. (31)

The tests were conducted at the former Carcano factory in Terni, Italy, according to Shipman. The tests concluded that the third shot, the kill shot that exploded Kennedy's skull, was, if it was fired from the 6th floor of the TSBD, would have emerged intact rather than disintegrate like the Dallas shot. Each firing of this type weapon, the testers advised, would take several motions for each shot.

Mr. Shipman also pointed out that in May of 2007; researchers at Texas A&M University "argued that the ballistics evidence used to rule out a second gunman had been interpreted". This conclusion is at odds with claims by author Vincent Bugliosi, who published a book in 2007 that claimed that the FBI, and the US Marines, was able to fire the same weapon much faster that the Italian experts claimed. Confusing?

Let us now look at the question of if Oswald could have been as accurate with that old rifle as the Dallas murder result turned out to be. We can break it down to several questions. How good of a shot was Oswald? How much skill was needed to accomplish these accurate shots? Did Oswald practice with this weapon, and if so, to what extent? How recent was this practice? What was Oswald's wife information on her husband's practice or lack of, with this rifle?

The Warren Commission, in Hearings, (32) documented the results of the FBI's test of the rifle used in the assassination. Their experts had to adjust the weapon before they could test it did not achieve the accuracy and speed necessary for a lone gunman to be accurate with at least two of the three shots.

Oswald's military record (33), indicated that Oswald was tested twice while serving in the US Marines. In December of 1956, after three weeks of intensive training (34), he scored a 212, two marks above the sharpshooter category. In 1959, he only scored a 191, one mark above a marksman. An expert, according to the military standard, would have to shoot between 220 and 250.

The Warren Commission attempted to ascertain from Oswald's wife Marina, if her husband went to the range or otherwise practiced with the rifle. She advised that she never seen him practice since he had returned from Russia. He only mentioned practicing once to her, after he shot at General Walker. He did some hunting with a rifle in 1959 with his brother Robert Oswald, but the only firearm he practiced with in Russia was a shotgun, at a hunting club he belonged to. We will in a later chapter relate the alleged sighting of Oswald at a range by a fourteen year old youth and his father. (35)

Using common sense, it does not seem possible that Oswald had either the skill or practice to be that good of a shot on November 22, 1963, if he even fired any shots that day, and that is very doubtful according to the author's conclusion.

BULLET HOLE IN LIMO WINDSHIELD

Before the JFK limo was whisked away from Parkland Hospital and flown to Washington on November 22, 1963, four witnesses observed a bullet hole through and through, in the front windshield. Two of the witnesses were Dallas motorcycle officers, Sergeant Starvis Ellis and Officer H...R. Freeman, both on escort duty that day. The two officers can still be seen on video examining the bullet hole while the limo was sitting in the Parkland Hospital Emergency Room parking area.

Sergeant Ellis told interviewer Gil Toff in 1971: "There was a hole in the left front windshield. You could put a pencil through it....I was right beside it. I could have touched it.....it was a bullet hole. You could tell what it was. (36)

Officer Freeman stated: "I was right beside it. I could have touched it. It was a bullet hole"

St. Louis Post-Dispatch reporter, Richard Dudman, wrote in an article published in the New Republic on December 21, 1963, "A few of us noted the hole in the Windshield when the limo was standing at the emergency entrance…." (To Parkland Hospital). (37)

A medical student at Southwestern Medical University next to Parkland Hospital, Evalea Glanges, told attorney Doug Weldon in 1999: "It was a clean hole…it was very clear, it was a through and through bullet hole through the windshield of the car, from its front to the back….." (38) At the time of the interview in 1999, Glanges had risen to the position of Chairperson of the Department of Surgery at John Peter Smith Hospital in Fort Worth. She had been a firearm expert all of her adult life. One can watch her very credible story on a Google video, stating the above.

A fifth witness was George Whitaker, a senior manager at the Ford Motor Co. Rouge Plant in Detroit. In August of 1993, he told attorney Doug Weldon that on November 25th, he discovered the JFK limo in Rouge Plant B building with the interior stripped out and the windshield removed. He was told by a company Vice President to report to the glass plant immediately. When he entered a locked office he saw the windshield. He was told to make an identical replacement. "And the windshield had a bullet hole in it, coming from the outside through…it was a good, clean bullet hole, right straight through, from the front…this had a clean hole in the front and fragmentation coming out the back. The windshield with the bullet hole was broken up and scrapped ---as ordered -- after the new windshield had been made". Whitaker described the hole as about 4 or 6 inches to the right of the rear-view mirror. The impact had come from the front of the windshield.

Whitaker asked Weldon not to release his name. After his death in 2001, with permission of his family, it was publicized in episode #7 of "The Men Who Killed Kennedy" - "The Smoking Gun", by Nigel Turner. Whitaker was a high ranking Ford employee, supervising five different plants, who had been in the glass business for over forty years. (39)

A sixth witness was Secret Service Agent Charles Taylor, who wrote a report on November 27, 1963, (40) detailing his inspection of the Kennedy limo at the White House garage the evening of the assassination. Taylor met the limo when it landed at Andrews Air Force Base in Washington and rode in it from the base to the White House garage. A portion of his report is as follows: "In addition, of particular note was the small hole just left of the center in the windshield from which what appeared to be bullet fragments were removed".

The windshield in evidence today at the National Archives is NOT the windshield that was in the JFK limo on Dallas's Elm Street on November 22, 1963. After the new windshield was installed by Whitaker's crew at the Ford plant and the old original windshield destroyed, the replacement windshield was inspected in Washington by Secret Service Agent Kellerman, who noted that the outside surface was NOT damaged but the underside was. Later on 11/27/63, Bill Ashby, the crew leader of the Arlington Glass Co. told Researcher Robert Smith (as reported by David Lifton in "Best Evidence") that he (Ashby) removed the limo windshield in Washington after agent Kellerman had felt the interior surface earlier that day and determined it to be damaged on the inside and smooth on the outside. (41)

But, the windshield at the National Archive today exhibits long cracks - not a through and through bullet hole -- and is damaged on the outside, which is opposite of what Kellerman noted by a physical exam on November 27, 1963.

Willard Hess of the auto firm Hess and Eisenhardt, in Cincinnati, Ohio, told Doug Weldon that his company also replaced the windshield in the JFK limo, and that the glass removed was standard safety glass--- consistent with what George Whitaker said his team reinstalled in the limo in Detroit, immediately after the assassination. Hess and Eisenhardt replaced the standard safety glass with special bullet resistant glass made by Pittsburg Plate Glass Co (Presumable, the windshield removed by Hess & Eisenhardt was the second new windshield installed -- by the Arlington Glass Co --on November 27th, and is the one in the National Archive today). Mr. Hess told Weldon that the windshield his company removed was not damaged at the time of its removal.

The clear implication here is that the windshield in the Archive today, which exhibits cracks but not a hole, was intentionally damaged by someone involved in a cover-up after its removal by Hess and Eisenhardt. It is obvious that this alteration and gross substitution of evidence was to suppress evidence of shots from the front (i.e., proof of conspiracy) so the government could more easily promote its lone assassin cover story.

Note: Secret Service Agent Taylor, who wrote the report days after the assassination about the bullet hole, recanted his original story in 1976, after examining the National Archive windshield in preparation of his testimony to the House HSCA Committee. Taylor said, "I did not ever get a good look at the windshield in well lighted surroundings". This statement is hardly credible as Taylor was the only passenger in the JFK limo as it was driven from Andrews Air Force Base to the White Hose garage on November 22, 1963, and examined the car in a well lighted White House garage. (42)

DEPOSITORY WITNESSES

We will examine the movements of the some of the key employees of the school depository building (TSBD) before, during and after the assassination.

The Texas School Book Depository is a seven story building on Elm Street. The 5th, 6th and 7th floors are book storage areas and no employee is assigned to these floors although they may access this area to fill book orders. On the day of the assassination, there were several workers putting down new flooring on the 6th floor, the alleged shooter's point. The depository building has two lunch areas, the main lunch room on the second floor which had the soda machines, and the 'domino' room on the 1st floor where the black workers generally ate. The building had two self operated elevators and one full staircase in the rear of the building from 1st to 7th floor, and another staircase in front, from the 1st to the 2nd levels only.

Four of the floor installers left the 6th floor at 11:45 A.M. for lunch using both elevators, racing each other to see which elevator would reach the bottom first. They were Bonnie Ray Williams, Billy Lovelady, Danny Acre, and Charles Givens. As the elevators passed the fifth floor, they observed Oswald in front of the elevator doors. (Open gates on elevator doors) and Oswald shouted to them, "How about an elevator" and "Close the gate on the elevator/" (otherwise, the elevator would't operate). They did not see Oswald again on the upper floors. (43) We will get back to the floor guys later.

At the time of the JFK murder, there were 75 employees working at the Texas School Book Depository building on Elm Street, the source of where it was alleged that the fatal shots had originated from. A key fact is that approximately ninety seconds after the fatal shots were allegedly fired from the sixth story window of this building, Oswald was confronted by Dallas motor officer Baker and Roy Truly, a supervisor at the depository (TSDB). The officer had run into the front entrance of the building, heading up the stairs toward the upper floors. (44)

At the 2nd story landing, the officer observed Oswald at the entrance vestibule of the lunchroom; the officer approached Oswald with gun drawn. Oswald showed no reaction at all, appearing calm and collected and making no utterances. Immediately behind the officer came Mr. Truly, who advised the officer that Oswald was an employee. The officer later testified that Oswald was not out of breath and showed no suspicious reaction or other angst in being confronted with an armed police officer. Mr. Truly and the officer then broke off contact with Oswald and continued climbing the stairs to the upper levels. Oswald was then observed by other employees, finishing his soft drink and walking calmly and slowly out the front door of the building. He was not seen again that day at the TSBD. Another witness, Roger Craig of the sheriff's department, later testified that he was quite sure that Oswald entered a Nash station wagon occupied by other men. (More on that in a later chapter)

Remember now that Oswald - if he was the offender - had only 90 seconds to discard the rifle emerge from the 'sniper's nest' and descend from the 6th floor to the 2nd floor, where he was observed by the motor officer, displaying a demeanor of calmness.

A paraffin test taken later the day of Oswald's arrest at the Dallas P.D. by Crime Scene Technician W.E. (Pete) Barnes and Analyst Louie Anderson, indicated that Oswald did not fire a rifle in the past 24 hours as no residue was found on his cheek. The Warren Commission said that test is unreliable, a much debatable statement among forensic experts. (45)

The rifle that was found on the floor of the 6th floor sniper's nest, the alleged murder weapon, was a 6.5 Manlicher-Carcano Italian made firearm, manufactured in Italy prior to the mid 1940's. The rifle was initially described by Deputy Sheriff Boone and Special Constable Seymour Weitzman, who found the weapon at 1:22 P.M. as a Mauser 7.65 rifle. The rifle, shells and clip were taken to the Dallas PD by Lieutenant Day and examined. Lt. Day's initial report stated that there were no fingerprints on the rifle and there was no indication of the rifle being cleaned of prints.

Oswald's prints were found on the boxes that were used to shield the southeast corner 6th floor window's 'sniper's nest'. Of course, this was not evidence of involvement in the crime as Oswald's' job at the Depository was to obtain books from these boxes to fill orders which would require him to handle these boxes. There was no indication that Oswald or any other employee, used gloves in this routine duty.

At the time of shooting, the sixth floor of the TSBD building was in the process of having flooring replaced. The day of the shooting the workers were replacing the flooring on the sixth floor. The workers had moved stacks of books in boxes to the front of the sixth floor in order to work. These boxes later were the boxes described as having been arranged to provide the 'sniper's nest'. Three of the contractors performing this duty on the west side of the 6th floor were black males; James (Junior) Jarman, 34, Bonnie Ray Williams, 20, and Harold Norman, 26.

The fifth, sixth and seventh floors of this depository building was utilized as storage floors and did not have any employees regularly on duty on these levels during the day. There are seven sets of windows on the south façade of the building facing Elm Street, with this sixth floor having six rows of columns across the floor with five columns in each row. There were two open view, gate controlled, elevators in this building, which were self operated, allowing access to all floors.

At just before noon or within five to ten minutes prior, the three black floor installers jumped into both elevators to ride down to the second floor lunch area. The men testified that Oswald yelled to them as the elevator passed the fifth floor, "Hey guys, send me an elevator back up". The three black laborers went to the first floor lunch room where, The Warren Commission report (46), indicated, that Bonnie Williams had returned to the 6th floor almost immediately and ate a chicken sandwich before returning to the lunch room about 12:20PM. He reported that he did not observe Oswald on this return trip. Dallas officers testified that they observed remnants of a chicken sandwich and accompanying debris just west of the 6th floor window, estimated to be about 40-60 feet from the southeast window, after the shooting. Williams then proceeded to the 5th floor where he joined his two co-workers to watch the motorcade from a south window. None of the three observed Oswald again that day at the depository building.

Several witnesses outside the TSDB testified that they had seen one -or two - men at the southeast 6th floor window as well as the third window west, prior to the shooting. Another citizen observed a rifle barrel sticking out of the same window but assumed it was a Secret Service man's weapon. None of these witnesses initially described either man as similar to Oswald. No witnesses observed Oswald at any of the south windows of the TSBD. A capsule of these observations follows.

Jeraldean Reid: (Mrs. Robert Reid) Mrs. Reid, a clerical supervisor at TSBD building, testified to Commission on 3/25/64, that she saw Oswald when she returned to her desk at about 12:32 P.M., after the shooting, she said to him, "Oh, the President has been shot, but maybe they didn't hit him". Oswald mumbled something she did not understand and Oswald walked east and south to the stairway, descending to the first floor. He then departed from the main entrance at about 1233 PM, before the building was sealed. "He (Oswald) got a Coke, walked across second floor....at a slow pace" and left the building by way of the front door. (47)

Bill Shelly- a foreman at TSBD said he saw Oswald near the telephone on the 1st floor as early as 10-15 minutes before noon.

Charles Givens, employee, "observed Lee at 11:50 AM reading a newspaper in the domino room where the black employees eat lunch. "In April of 1964, he added in his testimony that he had observed Oswald on the 6th floor at about 1150- A.M. when he (Givens had returned to retrieve his cigarettes.) This fact was never mentioned in several previous statements he made to Secret Service agents between the assassination and the April information.

Givens originally said he left the building and went to the corner of Elm Street and Record Street to watch the motorcade with friends James and Edward Shields.

Givens also pointed out that it was the members of the flooring crew that had moved the book boxes to the front of the 6th floor windows to allow room to replace the flooring. These boxes later were used as a blind for the assassination shooter. Givens had narcotics past and his story about the second encounter with Oswald is questionable.(48)

Inspector J. Herbert Sawyer of the Dallas P.D., who was manning a command post in front of the TSBD, issued a bulletin over the police radio instructing officers to locate Givens, a person with a narcotics past. When located, he was questioned by detectives, prior to Oswald being identified as the alleged shooter. The TSBD not effectively sealed until 12:51 P.M. although my reading is that this was accomplished at 12:37 P.M. by Inspector Sawyer and Sgt. Harkness. At 12:45 P.M. and a BOLO was issued by Inspector Sawyer of Dallas P.D., (Dallas Police Radio call #9.)

Bonnie Ray Williams, black male laborer returned to the 6th floor to eat his lunch. Later, his lunch bag, chicken bones, and pop bottle found. At 1215 or 1220 he left the 6th floor to join his co-workers at a fifth floor window to observe the motorcade.

James (Junior) Jarman, another of the black male floor installers, ate his lunch with fellow laborer Harold Norman. Jarman said he ate lunch in the 1st floor domino room between 12:00 and 12:15. They both then went outside for a few minutes and returned at 12:20 - 12:25 P.M. to go upstairs to the fifth floor window to watch the motorcade. The 'Dillard' photo clearly indicated two black males looking out the 5th floor window. The black male laborers all heard three shots, and indicated that they thought the shots were coming from the floor just above them. Some debris actually came down on them as the shots were ringing out and they could hear the empty shells hitting the floor above them. After pausing a few moments, they ran downstairs where they observed witness Howard Brennan talking to a police officer. They then related their observations to the same officer.

Eddie Piper, 56 years old: Piper was the janitor at TSBD. He said he spoke to Oswald at about 12:00 PM, "down on the 1st floor".

Arnold Rowland, a bystander, said that at 12:15 P.M. he seen two men in the 6th floor window, one holding a rifle in front of his chest. Rowland's wife confirmed that her husband drew her attention to the man. They assumed at the time that the man to be a Secret Service agent. The time of 12:15 P.M. is precise as a passing police radio broadcast was heard that the motorcade was at Cedar Spring Road, at that time. The police logs show that the motorcade was at that location at 1215 or1216 P.M. (49)

Carolyn Arnold, the secretary to the Vice President of the TSBD gave a statement to the FBI on November 26, 1963. She was standing inside of the TSBD waiting for motorcade and "thought she seen Oswald in the hallway". About ¼ an hour (12:15) before the assassination. "I went into the lunchroom on the 2nd floor, and observed Oswald sitting on the right side of the room having lunch. I did not speak to him but I recognized him." Carolyn, who was pregnant, said she had to get a glass of water from the lunchroom. "It was about 12:15PM, "but may have been slightly later".

Jim Marrs, who authored a detailed book on the JFK assassination stated, "A killer who had planned the assassination would hardly have been sitting around downstairs after 12:15 P.M., as the evidence about Oswald suggests, if he expected to open fire as early as 12:25 P.M.", (50)

Carolyn Walther, 4118 Shelley, Dallas, Texas, provided a statement to the FBI on December 4, 1963. She stated she is employed in the cutting room for Miller and Randazzo, a dress factory, on the third floor of the Dal-Tex Mart Building, 501 Elm Street, Dallas.

On November 22, 1963 she and another employee, Pearl Springer, ate lunch at 12:00 noon and left the lunch room at about 12:20 PM to go down on the street to see President Kennedy ride by. They walked out of the front door of the building, crossed the street, and stopped at a point on the east side of Houston Street, about fifty or sixty feet south of the south curb of Elm Street. They stopped next to the curb to await the passing of the President. While standing there, she started looking around, and looked over toward the Texas School Book Depository (TSBD) Building. She noticed a man wearing a brown suit and a very dark shirt leaning out a window of the third floor, somewhere about the middle window of the third floor.

Shortly after this, a man in the crowd across the street to the west of where she was standing apparently had an epileptic seizure, and an ambulance came by and took the man away. Shortly after the ambulance left, she looked back towards the TSBD Building and saw a man standing on either the fourth or fifth floors, of the window on the south side of the building, which faces toward Elm Street. This man had the window open and was standing up leaning out the window with both his hands extended outside the window ledge. In his hands, this man was holding a rifle with the barrel pointed downward, and the man was looking south on Houston Street. The man was wearing a white shirt and had blond or light brown hair. She recalled at the time that she had not noticed the man there a few moments previously when she looked toward the building and thought that apparently there were guards everywhere. The rifle had a short barrel and seemed large around the stock or end of the rifle. Her impression was that the gun was a machine gun. She noticed nothing like a telescope sight on the rifle or a leather strap or sling on the rifle.

Ms. Walther said she knows nothing about rifles or guns of any type, but thought that the rifle was different from any she had ever seen. This man was standing in about the middle of the window. In this same window, to the left of this man, she could see a portion of another man standing by the side of the man with a rifle. This other man was standing erect, and his head was above the opened portion of the window. As the window was very dirty, she could not see the head of this second man. She is positive this window was not as high as the sixth floor. This second man was apparently wearing a brown suit coat, and the only thing she could see was the right side of the man, from about the waist to the shoulders.

Almost immediately after noticing this man with the rifle and the other man standing beside him, someone in the crowd said "Here they come." and she looked to her left, looking south on Houston Street, to see the Presidential Party. As soon as President Kennedy's car passed where she was standing, she and Mrs. Springer turned away and stared walking north towards Elm Street. At about the time they reached the curb at Elm Street, she heard a loud report and thought it was fireworks. There was a pause after the first report, then a second and third report almost at the same time, and then a pause followed by at least one and possibly more reports. The noise seemed to come from up in the air, but she never looked up in that direction. When the second report sounded, she decided it was gunfire, so she and Mrs. Springer started diagonally across the street toward the TSBD Building. About the time she got across the street, she heard someone yell that the president had been hit. She stopped a moment and listened to the police radio on a motorcycle, then returned to the building across the street where she works at about 12:45 PM.

Statement of Carolyn Walthers, on 12/4/1963 at Dallas, Texas File # DL 89-43 by Special Agent C. Ray Hall and Margie J. White. Date dictated, December 5, 1963.

Victoria Adams: She testified that she watched the motorcade from an open window on the fourth floor of the TSBD building (3rd set of double windows from SE corner) with Sandra Styles, Elsie Dorman, and Dorothy Garner, employees in the Scott, Foresman Co. publishing office where she worked. After the last shot, she and Ms. Styles immediately ran down the back stairs to the first floor. A statement was attributed to her that she seen Lovelady and Shelly standing near the elevator on the bottom floor. She later said that she never told authorities that. She said she left the window to start toward the stairway within about 15-30 seconds of the last shot.

She estimated it took no longer than a minute to go from the window to the bottom of the stairs on the first floor. She did not see Oswald, Truly or Baker as she ran down the stairs. (51)

Billy Lovelady's affidavit on November 22, 1963, says he heard the shots and "after it was over we went back into the (TSBD) building and I took some police officers up to search the building" He was with Bill Shelley, Sara Stanton and Wesley Frazier watching the motorcade in front of the TSBD building. (52)

Bill Shelly's affidavit stated, "I heard what sounded like three shots ......I ran across the street to the corner of the park and ran into a girl crying and she said the President has been shot.....I went back inside and called my wife and told her what happened. I was on the first floor and I stayed at the elevator".(53)

Roy Truly- Mr. Truly says he ran ahead of Officer Baker into the building and upstairs to the 2nd floor and was continuing until he realized Baker had stopped on the 2nd floor. He heard voices coming from the area of the lunch room or the inside of the vestibule and seen the police officer talking to Oswald. The police officer, with gun drawn, points it at Oswald. Officer asked me if Oswald worked there. "I said yes". The officer left Oswald and continued to run up the stairs. Truly said that Oswald remained silent. "He did not seem to be excited or overly afraid or anything. He might have been a bit startled, like I might have been if somebody confronted me. But I cannot recall any change in expression of any kind on his face". (54)

Jack Dougherty: He remained on the 5th floor during the motorcade. He did hear the shots, but heard no one on the stairway immediately after. The commission did not take to much stock in his testimony as he appeared to be uncertain and perhaps had some mental difficulty.

Officer Marion Baker, Dallas P.D. Motors

When the shots rang out (at exactly 1230 P.M.) in Dealey Plaza, one of the Dallas motorcycle escort policeman, Marion Baker, thought they came from high in the Book Depository. He drove straight to the building, dismounted and pushed his way to the entrance. Joined by the building superintendent, (Roy Truly) whom he met in the doorway, he hurried by the stairs up to the second floor. Just as he reached the landing, Baker caught a glimpse of someone through a glass window in a door. Pistol in hand, the policeman pushed through the door, across a small vestibule, and saw a man walking away from him. "As I reached the 2nd landing, I glimpsed Oswald walking away from me-about 20 feet. "I hollered at him and said "Come here". He turned and walked straight back to me. Officer Baker said Oswald did not appear to have been running, "He appeared normal" He appeared calm and collected. He did not say a word. He did not change his expression one bit". At the policeman's order "Come here," the man turned and walked back. Baker noticed the man did not seem to be out of breath or even startled. He seemed calm and said nothing. Although reports conflict, he may have been carrying a bottle of Coca Cola. At that moment, as Baker was about to start questions, the Depository superintendent arrived and identified the man as an employee. He was, of course, Lee Harvey Oswald, and the room was the second-floor lunchroom, exactly where Oswald had been last seen - almost fifteen minutes before the assassination. Baker let Oswald go, and hurried on upstairs with Mr. Truly. (55 and 56)

Geneva Hines: Ms. Hines stayed in her office on the 2nd floor during the motorcade. She heard three shots while looking out the window. She walked out into the foyer and seen no one. At this time the lights went out in the building due to a power failure in the Dealey Square area.

Doris Burns: She stayed in her office area on the 3rd floor during the motorcade. As she was walking out in the hallway, she heard one shot. She went into the office of Allyn and Bacon where she looked out the window with a Mr. Williams. She did not observe Oswald in the hallway or staircase.

Lee Oswald : When Oswald was questioned by Captain Fritz of the Dallas P.D. Homicide Division, as to his whereabouts at the time the shots were fired, Oswald told the Captain that he was eating lunch on the 1st floor of TSDB, later proceeding to the to 2nd floor dining room for a Coke. Oswald said while he ate his lunch in the 1st floor domino room he seen two black males walking thru the room. One was "Junior". After the shootings, Oswald said he was stopped by a man looking for a telephone. Oswald directed him to where the TSBD telephone was located. This man was most likely Pierce Allman, a WFAA-TV newsman, who later confirmed the contact. After leaving the depository building, Oswald got onto the bus at Lamar and Murphy Street, six blocks from TSBD. A Mrs. Bledsoe---Oswald's former landlady----, and others, saw him on bus. Oswald, when caught, was wearing long sleeve rust colored shirt over a white t-shirt. He said he had earlier had on a long sleeve reddish shirt.

A most detailed description of where Oswald was when the fatal shots were fired at Kennedy is described in Anthony Summer's book, "Conspiracy". His account has never been refuted. (57)

Remember - Oswald was seen in the 2nd floor lunch room 15 minutes before the shots and less than two minutes after the last shot. He was not seen on the 6th floor during this time frame.

ORIGIN OF FATAL SHOTS

This section indicates where the witness were standing and from what direction the shots came from - their first impression as uttered that day. Many more gave similar description of the events. There were more law enforcement eye-witnesses on the scene of this crime as it occurred that day in Dealey Square than any other major crime that we can recall. You can read of their 'first impressions' and their reactions, followed by some of the more important civilian witnesses. This information will provide the reader with a 'totality' of the immediate aftermath of the shooting of our President.

The source of this information was obtained from affidavits and statements of the witnesses that can all be found in the Warren Commission reports.

DALLAS COUNTY SHERIFF'S

The office of the Dallas County Sheriff's department was located kitty-corner across the street from the Texas School Book Depository building. Sheriff Decker had informed his investigators to assemble out in front of the sheriff's office when the motorcade passed. They had no other motorcade duties, although fourteen of the uniformed sheriff's deputies had been as assigned to the Trade Mart. The following is a summary of Sheriff Decker's twenty-plus investigators activities in the immediate aftermath of the shooting in Dealey Square. They all were standing in the block in the area of Houston Street, Main Street and Elm Street. Their complete affidavits are included in the Warren Report. These deputies, along with the Dallas P.D. officers who were on parade or traffic duty at Elm Street and Houston Street, were the first responding officers to the shooting scene in Dealey Plaza.

Deputy Henry Weatherford - Heard 3 shots and ran to the railroad yards with Deputy Sweatt, then went to the TSBD building and met deputies Ralph Walters, Luke Mooney, Eugene Broome and Sam Webster. Entered the building and accessed the roof then canvassed the 6th floor where Mooney found the three spent shells and Boone found the rifle. Weatherford was then sent to Mrs. Paine's home, where, among other things, found an address book with a telephone number that traced to Oswald's rooming house.

Deputy Ralph Walters- Heard 3 shots and ran to rail yards, then to the TSBD building. Obtained portable lights to aid in the 6th floor search. Assisted in floor search until crime scene turned over to Dallas Captain Fritz.

Deputy Eugene L. Broome - Heard 3 shots as he was with Officer Whitman, Dallas P.D. First he ran into rail yards then went to TSBD to assist in search of 6th floor. Found the rifle stashed between boxes of books. Preserved the scene until the arrival of Lt. Day, Dallas P.D. Crime Scene supervisor. Boone later obtained film from Hugh Betzner, had same developed at sheriff's office and turned pictures over to Homer Reynolds of Dallas P.D.

Deputy Jack Falkner - Heard 3 shots. Woman told him shots came from concrete arcade on grassy knoll. Heard a young black male tell a Dallas officer that a man with a gun had been in the TSBD window firing a gun. Falkner went to TSBD with deputies McCurley and Wiseman to help search the building.

Deputy C.M. Jones - Heard 3 shots while standing with deputies Sweatt and Benevides. Interviewed Plaza witnesses.

Deputy Clinton Lewis - Was home sick but responded to work after shooting. Drove to theater with newsman Scholkoef. No significant activites.

Deputy A.D. McCurley - Heard 3 shots. Ran to grassy knoll area and back through the rail yards. A rail worker advised him that the shots came from the fence area. He later went to TSBD with Deputy Falkner and helped search the building.

Deputy Charles Player - Was in window of Sheriff's department. Heard 3 shots. Drove his police car back to railroad track area and met Dallas P.D. 3-wheeler supervisor, Sergeant Harkness. They both, with radio channels for Sheriff's Dept and Dallas P.D. acted as a west command post for the next two hours until relieved by Dallas police. Search all cars leaving the parking lot by the TSBD.

Deputy L.C. Smith - Heard 3 shots. Woman told him shots came from fence area. Searched there and then went to TSBD to help search the building. Deputy McCurley and he then searched the building's roof.

Deputy W.I.Tran - Worked with Dallas PD Sgt. Jennings to gather witness, takes statements, including from Hugh Betzner, John Chism, Bob Jackson and Lee Bowers.

Deputy Buddy Walthers - Ran to rail yards. Talked to man hit in the face by bullet fragment. Found bullet strike on curb. Escorted witnesses to sheriff's office and turned them over to Deputy Elkins.

On the Tippit shooting, Walthers went to Oak Cliff with deputies J. Ramsey and Frank Vrla, where they searched library. Heard info from Deputy Courson that suspect was in the theater. He was on the scene of Oswald's arrest. Later went to Mrs. Paine's home with deputies Weatherford and Oxford and found evidence. Took Mrs. Oswald and Mrs. Paine to Dallas police headquarters.

Deputy Roger Craig - Heard 3 shots. Ran to rail yards with Buddy Walthers then went to front of TSBD. Searched for curb shot. Seen a white male running from side of TSBD building and entered a light colored Rambler station wagon, with luggage rack, which had pulled to the curb to pick this guy up. Car left scene before Craig could reach it. Craig reported same to Secret Service agent. Upon hearing of Oswald's arrest, he notified Capt. Fritz who had him come to Homicide office where he identified Oswald as the man who entered the car. (More on Craig in other chapters)

Deputy C.L. (Lummie) Lewis - Was in grassy knoll area with Craig and later took witness statements.

Deputy Luke Mooney- Heard 3 shots. Searched the rail yards. Sheriff Decker told him and Deputies Webster and Victory to cover the rear of TSBD. He secured the gates leading to TSB D loading area. Went into building and helped search. Mooney found the three shells on the 6th floor.

Deputy J.L. Oxford - With deputy McCurley, ran to picket fence area and rail yards. Talked to man who seen smoke rising from fence area. Searched rail cars with Dallas officers. Checked cars parked in rail area. Later sent to Mrs. Paine's home with deputies Walthers and Weatheford.

Deputy Allan Sweatt - (The Chief Investigator for the Dallas County Sheriff's Department.) Heard 3 shots. Went to rail yards. Then to rear of TSBD where Deputy Weatheford entered the building through a window. Quickly checked building with Weatherford and Wiseman. He had about 15 deputies on the far side of the TSBD and some Dallas officers. He then met Dallas Inspector Sawyer in front of the building to coordinate efforts. He was there when a Dallas officer brought forth a young man who "Here is the man that had done the shooting". (Unknown now who he was talking about.) Sent this man with two deputies to the sheriff's office along with a Dallas officer.

(I) took 'best' witnesses to the Polygraph room at sheriff's office for statements and interviews, along with FBI agent Heitman and Secret Service head Sorrells as well as Mrs. Allen of sheriff's office. Sent deputies Walthers, Ramsey and Vrla to Oak Cliff for the Tippit shooting. Sent copies of all witness statements to Captain Fritz of Dallas P.D. Got pictures from two girls and from Mr. Betzner. Advised all deputies to complete a report on their activities that day.

Deputy Buddy Walthers - More details on his activities in other sections. He did advise that there was a home in Dallas, at 3128 Hallendale, that has been the scene of Cuban activities for the past two months, possibly in connection to the "Freedom for Cuba Party". The Cubans apparently moved out in the week prior to the assassination.

Deputy John Weisman - Heard 3 shots. Man told him shots came from TSBD so ran there. Up to 7th floor in a few minutes. Said there were about

50 officers in the building area at that time. Helped preserve scene where gun was found. Met Mrs. Moreman who had pictures of shooting.

Got photos and turned them over to deputy Sweatt who relayed them to agent Patterson of Secret Service.

Picked up sandwiches and coffee for witness waiting at Sheriff's office.

Deputy Harold Elkins - Heard 3 shots. Went to rail yards. Then to TSBD. Obtained witnesses in street and funneled them to sheriff's department. Went to TV station and picked up two witnesses. Was there when Dallas PD came in with the '3 tramps'. Took them to Dallas P.D. and turned them over to Capt Fritz.

Deputy W.W. Maber (?) - With Officer Orville Smith of Dallas P.D. Went to rail yards to search.

Deputy Harold Strehly - In window of the I.D. section of County Jail.

Deputy L. C. Todd - Working the information desk at Sheriff's office. Heard three shots. No other activities noted.

Deputy Jack Watson, Dallas Co. Sheriff's Office: On November 22nd, Deputy Watson reported that he had received information over the police radio about a speeding car in the area. Watson reported that the Carrollton, Texas P.D. (adjacent to Dallas) called in that day that they had received a citizen's report that a car had been parked near the Henry Hines Circle for several days before November 22nd. According to the Carrollton police, very shortly after the shooting, between 1:54 and 2:11 P.M., that car had been seen traveling north on Harry Hines Boulevard "at a very high rate of speed". The car was described as a red 1963 Chevrolet Impala with Georgia license plate 52J1033. A radio bulletin was issued on the car to all area stations. The tag checked out to a 1960 Chevy in Twin City, Georgia. The owner, James Bradley, stated in an FBI interview, that in August or September of 1963 his license tag was stolen from his auto when it was parked overnight on Highway 80, between Swainsboro and Twin City with a flat tire, and that he said he had reported the theft to law officers in Twin City and Swainsboro at the time. Official records of the police in Twin City verified that Mr. Bradley had reported the theft of the tag to them. A new tag was issued to Bradley on September 10, 1963, according to Georgia authorities.

Additional reports of various law enforcement officers will be documented in the specific areas of investigative interest.

DALLAS POLICE OFFICERS

The following is a report of the Dallas P.D. officers who were on parade or traffic duty in and around Dealey Square that day.

Officer Edgar Smith -Dallas PD - Standing on Houston St, near corner of Elm St. Shots came from area of concrete structure up by railroad tracks

Officer Joe Marshall Smith - Corner of Elm Street and Houston St. Shots came from behind concrete structure in bushes toward rail tracks. Shots NW direction behind fence. He smelled smoke from gunpowder when he arrived behind the fence with Deputy Seymour Weitzman.

Officer A.J. Millican - Standing on north side of Elm Street

Heard 3 shots from up toward Houston and Elm by TSBD and 2 more shots from Arcade between Book Store and the underpass.

Officer Earle V. Brown of the Dallas P.D.: Brown was assigned to stay on the railroad overpass over the Stemmons Freeway that day. His duty was to prevent any unauthorized persons from standing on the overpass at the time of the motorcade. Brown and his partner, Officer James Lomax, had been ordered, about an hour after the shooting, to return to the area of the depository and list the license number of all cars parked in the vicinity. He was among about five officers who had the same assignment and Brown said he turned the list over to Sergeant Howard.

Brown added that soon after the Presidential motorcade passed, after the last shot was fired, he seen a man run down the stairs on the west side of the depository and then turn north away from the front of the building. Brown estimated that this occurred about 15 minutes after the shots. Brown described the man as young, fair complexion, and not having dark hair. He said the man was dressed in light blue work pants and a shirt which was similar. He did not see anything in the man's hands. The committee staff added that the view of the door mentioned was covered by foliage and the estimated distance of Brown's view was 500 yards.

Officer James Lomax: Officer Brown's partner that day. Officer Lomax was interviewed by the committee on 10/27/1968. He advised that he did not know about the assignment to record the license numbers and that he did not see anyone leaving the depository building and that Brown never mentioned it to him.

Sergeant Starvis Ellis, Dallas motor supervisor: Ellis saw a missile hit the ground in the area of the motorcade at the time of the assassination. Ellis was riding a motorcycle alongside the first car in the motorcade, about 100 - 125 feet in front of JFK's car. Ellis said that just as he started down the hill of Elm Street, he looked back toward President Kennedy's car and saw debris come up from the ground from a nearby curb. Ellis thought it was a fragment grenade. Ellis said also that JFK turned around and looked

over his shoulder. The second shot then hit him and the third shot "blew his head up".

Sgt Harkness was at the rear of the TSBD at 12:36 P.M. and had officers and a civilian train worker watch the four exits at the rear of the building.

Tom Tilson, a 17 year veteran Dallas police officer, reported that he saw a man running from the plaza immediately after the shots. Tilson, off-duty at the time, was driving east from Commerce Street and was approaching the triple overpass. He had already heard the report of the shooting on his police radio and seen the motorcade speeding away. Tilson seen a man "slipping and sliding" down the embankment on the north side of Elm street west of the overpass. Tilson said the man appeared conspicuous because he was the only one running away from the plaza immediately after the shots. Tilson said that because of his speed, the man rammed against the side of a "dark" car which was parked there. Tilson said he then saw the man do something at the rear door portion of the car, like "throw" something inside, then jump behind the wheel and take off very fast.

The car went south on Industrial Boulevard and Tilson followed. Tilson was within 100 feet and called out the license number, make, and model to his 18 year old daughter, Dinah, who was riding with him. She wrote it down on a slip of paper. Tilson said the man was white, 38-40 years old, 5-8 or 5-9, with a round face. He said the guy had dark hair and looked enough like Jack Ruby to be his "twin". Tilson said he called the homicide office about his report. He never heard anything more from the homicide squad. Tilson kept the paper for about 3 1/2 years and discarded it when he cleaned out his home after the death of his wife. Tilson explained that he never followed up on the report with the homicide squad because of his perception that the homicide office was run as a kind of "elite unit", which resented any encroachment on its authority.

Secret Service Agent Landis. "My reaction at this time was that the shot came from some where toward the front"

He was in the car behind JFK limo.

SS Agent Forrest Sorrels - In car behind JFK

Shots came from top of the terrace to my right

Secret Service Agent Lem Jones - "The first shots sounded like they were on the side of me, toward the grassy knoll.

CIVILIAN WITNESSES

The immediate observations of the more important civilian witnesses present in Dealey Square that day gave immediate written affidavits or were questioned by law enforcement in the days following the assassination. These observations were their immediate first impressions, before they had much time to reflect on their views, which are usually the most accurate of witness statements. The summary of their statements are as follows:

Arnold Rowland - Standing on east side of Houston St., facing the TSBD. Sounded if shots came from rail yards

Ronald Fischer - SW corner of Houston and Elm Street

Shots from just west of TSBD building, by railroad tracks

Victoria Adams - Window on 4th floor

Heard 3 shots from direction of the railroad tracks

Dorothy Garner - Fourth floor window of TSBD

Shots came from a point west of the building

Danny Arce - North side of Elm Street, near the TSBD

3 shots from direction of railroad tracks

J.C. Price - on roof of Terminal Annex Building

Seen man running full speed away from fence toward the railroad yards, carrying something in his hand that "could have been a gun". Shots came from behind the picket fence where it joins the underpass"

Virginia (Baker) Rackley - North side of Elm Street, near entrance to TSBD. Shots from direction of railroad tracks

Jane Berry - North side of Elm Street, just west of TSBD entrance. Shots came from a position west of where she was standing

Ochus Campbell - North side of Elm Street, 30 feet from TSBD entrance. Shots from railroad tracks

Buell Frazier - Depository employee. Front steps of TSBD

Shots came from down by underpass & railroad tracks

Billy Lovelady - Depository employee. Standing on steps of TSBD. Several shots in direction of viaduct

Jean Newman - North side of Elm Street, between TSBD and knoll. Shots came from my right

William Newman - (no relation to Jean Newman) North side of Elm, toward knoll. Shot came from the garden directly behind me

Roy Truly- Supervisor at the Depository building. North side of Elm Street, close to TSBD entrance. Shots came from vicinity of railroad tracks (concrete structure) west of TSBD

Otis Williams - Standing on front steps of TSBD

Shots came from direction of the viaduct at Elm Street.

Mary Woodward - Standing on north side of Elm St, between TSBD & grassy knoll

Shots came from over her head and possibly behind her

Faye Chism - Close to Stemmons Freeway sign on north side of Elm Street. Shots came from behind us

John Chism - with Faye - Location same as Faye Chism

I looked behind me, by the embankment

Abraham Zapruder - On pedestal on Elm St close to grass knoll- filming scene. Shots came from in back of me

Gordon Arnold - Standing close to the fence on grassy knoll (Army man) Shots came from over his head from the fence area (His late story has been disputed)

Charles Brehm - South side of Elm Street, few yards from JFK at fatal shot. See to think shots came from in front or besides JFK,

Jean Hill - South side of Elm Street

Heard 4 to 6 shots from west of the TSBD

Dolores Kounas - South side of Elm Street. Shots from triple overpass area

Roberta Parker - Standing opposite the main entrance to TSBD. Shot came from a cement memorial area, to the north of TSBD

S.M. Holland - Standing on Railway Bridge. Shots from arcade above grassy knoll-seen puff of smoke under tree.

Austin Miller - standing on Triple Overpass. Seen smoke from tree area off the railroad tracks. Austin Miller -"I saw something which I thought was smoke or steam coming from the trees north of Elm Street by the RR tracks."

Thomas Murphy - standing on Triple Overpass.

Shots from a spot just west of the TSBD

Frank Reilly - On railway bridge west end of Dealey Plaza

Shots came from trees west of the TSBD

James Tague - Where Commerce St meets Main St, by the triple overpass. Tague was hit by bullet fragment.

Shots came from my left, up by the concrete monument

Lee Bowers - In railway control tower north of the car park -top of knoll or up at TSBD or near mouth of the overpass.

Bowers "- "seen flash of 'light or smoke' from the two men behind the fence"

Ed Hoffman - Deaf mute - standing on Stemmons Freeway

Seen puff of smoke among the trees behind grassy knoll fence

Ed Johnson - In Press bus. Seen puffs of smoke from grass area in esplanade that divides the street

Kenneth O'Donnell and David Powers, two of Kennedy's top presidential aides were riding in the SS car behind the JFK limo. Both were personal friends of the President. They had a clear view of Kennedy and the grassy knoll.

Tip O'Neill, former Speaker of the US House of Representatives, in his 1968 autobiography, wrote:

"I was surprised to hear O'Donnell say that he was sure he had heard two shots that came from behind the fence. "That's not what you told the Warren Commission", I said. "You're right", he replied, "I told the FBI what I heard, but they said it couldn't have happened that way and that I must have been imagining things. So, I testified the way they wanted me to. I just didn't want to stir up any more pain and trouble for the family".

Dave Powers were with us at dinner that night and his recollection of the shots was the same as O'Donnell's".

Richard Dodd - "smoke came from behind the hedge on the north side of the plaza.

INTERVIEWS AND AFFADAVITS

Howard Brennan - Initially regarded by the police as a very important witness. He reported a man moving around "sniper's nest' window at 12:22-12:24 P.M., then seen the man fire the final shot. However, his testimony was deemed troublesome by the Warren Commission. He also did not report this immediately. When he viewed a lineup, he could not positively identify Oswald as the man he seen. There is no report showing that he actually viewed a lineup.

On the evening of November 22nd, Brennan said he was unable to make a positive identification of Oswald. He had seen Oswald's picture on television before he viewed a line-up (a line-up not recorded on any police reports). On December 17th, during an FBI interview, Brennan stated he was sure that the person firing the rifle was Oswald. In another FBI interview on January 7, 1964, he reverted back to his original statement that he was unable to make identification. Brennan later testified to the Warren

Commission that "he could at that time - at the lineup - identify him as being the same man".

The Commission stated that it was Brennan's description of the man (in the window with gun) that was the source of the police radio broadcast sent out to all units. Brennan said he originally provided that description to Secret Service Agent Sorrels. This would not have been possible as Inspector Sawyer of the Dallas P.D. was the officer who broadcasted the description prior to Sorrels return to the TSBD from Parkland Hospital. Inspector Sawyer had no memory of talking to Brennan or to anyone of his description (wearing hard hat). How many of us would condemn a man to the electric chair on vacillating testimony such as that? And, Brennan was one of the Commission's "star witnesses".

Other witnesses testified that they thought that the shots came from the School Book Depository building or the adjacent Dal-Tex building on the corner of Elm Street and Houston Street. As mentioned earlier, some witnesses observed two men in the 6th floor window, others observed one man. Several of the witnesses advised that one of the men appeared to be a Negro or Mexican. The 'other' man was described as with light hair, slightly balding. Oswald did not fit any of these descriptions. Some of the commission witnesses testified, others submitted affidavits, and still others were not called at all. Some of these witnesses were found and questioned by news media, but not by law enforcement officers.

There were many bystanders waiting along Houston Street and Elm Street to catch a glimpse of President Kennedy's motorcade. Here is the story of a few of them who seen people at the windows of the TSBD building holding rifles prior to the shooting.

Mrs. Ruby Henderson: She was standing on the east side of Elm Street just north of Houston Street. An ambulance picked up an epileptic on Elm Street before the motorcade arrived at Elm and Houston Street, so the time of this sighting is fairly accurate. Mrs. Henderson stated (FBI interview 12/5/63) that she seen two men in one of the upper floors of the TSBD just after the ambulance left the area. She said one man was dark complexioned, either Mexican or Cuban, with dark hair and wearing a white shirt. The other was taller, wearing a dark shirt. The two were standing back from the window looking out toward the motorcade. She seen these men before the motorcade reached the corner of Elm and Houston Street. She was not called to testify to the Warren Commission. Carolyn Walther: In an interview (58)) she advises that she was standing on the east side of Houston Street, 50-60 feet south of the south curb on Elm Street. After the ambulance left, she saw a man in an upper floor of the TSBD holding a rifle as he was looking down on Houston Street. The man had light brown or blond hair, wearing a white shirt. The other male was wearing a brown suit coat. She said this observation was just as the motorcade approached on Houston Street. She was not called to testify to the Warren Commission.

Arnold Rowland and wife: They were standing at the corner of Houston Street and Main Street before the motorcade arrived. Rowland said he seen, at 12:15 P.M., two men at a 6th floor window of the TSBD, one was in a west window holding a rifle. The man was standing back from the window. The weapon appeared to be a high powered rifle with scope attached. Two of the windows on the level were open and the man with the rifle was standing at port arms with barrel at a 45 degree angle, downward across his body. The man was tall and slender, 140-150; light completed dark hair, possibly Latin or white, with a close hair cut. He was wearing a light colored shirt with an open collar and with a t-shirt underneath. He had dark slacks or jeans. The subject, in his 30's, was standing 3 to 5 feet back from the window.

The second man was at the southeast window of the 6th floor, hanging out the window. He appeared to be an elderly Negro. The time was about 1215 PM. This second man remained in the window until motorcade was at Main Street and Ervay Street, about five minutes before the motorcade reached the area of the TSBD. In a 11/22/63 interview with the FBI Rowland said he seen the man with the rifle between 1215 and 1220 PM, standing 10-15 feet back from the window, about fifteen minutes before the arrival of the motorcade. Sheriff's Deputy Craig spoke to Rowland ten minutes after the shots were fired and Rowland told him that he had seen two men in the 6th floor windows.

Richard Carr: This forty-one year old combat veteran of WW2 (Rangers) advised that he was on the 7th floor of the new courthouse building across from the Book Depository building, prior to the shooting. Carr stated he seen a heavy set man wearing horn rimmed glasses, tan sports coat, on the 6th floor of the TSBD. After the shooting he observed the same man emerge from the TSBD building. The man went south on Houston to Commerce Street to Record Street and entered a 1961/62 grey colored Nash Rambler, driven by a dark skinned man. He did not testify to the Warren Commission. Carr saw three men enter the Rambler while he was watching from his perch in a building that oversees the TSBD.

After receiving many alleged threats after the assassination, Mr. Carr moved to the state of Montana. He reported that someone up there attempted to bomb his car. Later, in a confrontation in Atlanta, two men attacked him and he killed one of them. Carr did testify at the Clay Shaw trial in New Orleans after Jim Garrison tracked him down. Mr. Carr had been in serious combat during the war in both North Africa and Italy.

Amos Euins, a sixteen year old black male who had been excused from school to watch the motorcade was standing outside the TSBD and seen the shots being fired from the 6th floor window by a man with a rifle. Euins stated that the shooter had a bald spot on his head. He noted that it was a 'white' bald spot but was uncertain if the subject was black or white. Euins, whose immediate statement was recorded by a newsman after the shooting, was quite credible and precise. He prepared an affidavit the following day, was interviewed by the FBI twice in the next weeks and testified to the Warren Commission (59).

Jean Hill: Said she heard four to six shots according to an FBI interview. She said that after the shots, she saw a man "running, getting away or walking away or something - I would say he was running". She said the man was at the top of the slope near the west end of the depository building. She did not recollect seeing his hands and did not see a weapon. She advised that she ran up the hill toward the railroad tracks after the man. She said when she got in the area of the railroad tracks, she lost sight of him. At that point she thought she heard someone say: "It looks like he got away or words to that effect", she said that was consistent with the thought in her own mind that the man she saw running was involved in the assassination. She said that the man was wearing a brown hat. She estimated that he was middle-age, approximately 40 years old, and Caucasian. Mrs. Hill spoke to Mark Lane prior to her testimony to the Warren Commission. Among the things she related to Lane was she had been told by a man from the FBI or Secret Service not to mention the man she saw running in the area of the depository.

Author Mark Lane testified to the Warren Commission that Mrs. Hill told him, "She said further that after the last shot was fired, she saw a man run from behind the general area of a concrete facade on that grassy knoll, and that he ran on to the triple overpass".

Ms. Hill was watching the motorcade with Mary Moorman across from the grassy knoll. The two ladies had come to see Jean's boyfriend, a Dallas motor officer, who was working the parade that day.

Jesse Price, who was on the roof of the Terminal Annex Building, gave a statement to the sheriff's department on November 22nd stating that he also saw a man fleeing from the plaza after the assassination. After hearing the volley of shots, Price saw a man run toward the passenger cars at the railroad siding. Price said that the man was about 25 years old, with long dark hair, and was wearing a white dress shirt with no tie and khaki-colored trousers. Price said the man was carrying something in hand and that it may have been a "head piece". Two days later Price was interviewed by the FBI and that report only says he looked in the direction of the overpass at the time of the shots, but "saw nothing pertinent".

Lee Bowers, Jr.: at the time of the motorcade, Bowers was located in the Union Terminal Tower in the railroad yard. He reported to the FBI that he had observed three cars parked in the lot west of the depository building before the assassination. He said the first one arrived at about 11:55 A.M.; it was a very dirty 1959 Oldsmobile station wagon, blue over white, with an out-of-state license plate consisting of six black numbers on a white background, with a Goldwater sticker, occupied by a white male, possibly middle age. The second car arrived about 12:15 P.M. and was a 1957 Ford Tudor, black with a gold stripe on the sides, and had a Texas license tag. Bowers Thought the man was a police officer because the occupant was talking into a radio telephone or radio transmitter in the car.

Mr. Bowers described him as a white male, about 30 years old. The third car was a 1961 or 1962 white Chevrolet Impala four door and it arrived at approximately 12:22 P.M. The car license was like an out-of-state, like the first car's tag, with six black numbers on a white background. That car, too, was very dirty. The driver was a white male, about 30 years of age, with long, dirty blond hair, wearing a plaid sports shirt. Bowers told the FBI that he did not see any of these cars in the parking lot after the shooting.

Bowers told the Warren Commission that the first car first drove in front of the depository, circled the area of the tower in the railroad yard "as if he were searching for a way out, or was checking the area", and then left at the Elm Street outlet. About 15 minutes later, Bowers noted the second car; it drove in front of the depository, cruised around the area for 3 or 4 minutes, and then left. The third car appeared about eight minutes before the President's motorcade; it circled the area and probed in the area of the tower, and then slowly cruised back in front of the depository, at which point Bowers lost sight of it.

Bowers noticed two men standing between the tower and Elm Street at the underpass on the high ground, standing within 10 to 15 feet of each other. One was middle age, heavy set, and was wearing a white shirt and dark trousers. The other was in his mid-twenties, was wearing a plaid shirt or jacket. Bowers said he saw the man in the white shirt standing there at the time of the shots, but that he could not see the younger man in the plaid clothing because of the trees. After the shooting, he said that a motorcycle officer ran up the incline toward the trees in the general area of where the two men were standing.

Malcolm Summers: In a statement to the sheriff's department, Summers said he seen a car speeding from the area of the plaza immediately after the shots. Summers was located on the terrace of the small park on Elm Street when the motorcade passed him. After the shots, Summers went to the area of the railroad tracks because he "knew that they had somebody trapped there". After 20 minutes Summers returned to his truck, which was parked on Houston Street. As he began to pull away from the curb, an automobile occupied by three men, traveling in what Summers described as a "burst of speed" passed his truck on the right, which Summers thought was dangerous. He said the car then slowed when it got in front of him as though realizing they would be conspicuous in speeding. One of the men appeared to be slender and that the three men appeared to be "excited" and were motioning to each other. He thought the car was a 1961 or 1962 Chevrolet sedan, maroon in color. The car went across the Houston Street viaduct, turned off on Marsalis Street, and continued in the direction of Zangs Boulevard.

Julia Ann Mercer: She gave statements to law enforcement officers concerning the men she had seen, including one who was carrying a gun case. Her statement of 11/22/63 stated that she was driving in the area of the plaza going toward the overpass. When she got to a point just east of the overhead sign for the right entrance road to the overpass, she noticed a truck parked on the right-hand side of the road with its hood up. The truck, a green Ford pickup with a Texas plate had a sign on the driver's side in black letters which said "Air Conditioning". The driver was described as a white male, about 40 years of age, who was 'slouched" over the steering wheel. He was heavy set, with light brown hair, and wearing a green jacket.

The other man was standing at the rear of the truck, and was reaching over the tailgate into the truck and took out what Mrs. Mercer thought to be a gun case about 8 inches wide at its base, and 3 1/2 to 4 feet long. The man walked up the "grassy hill which forms part of the overpass" and she lost track of him. She described this guy as a white male, 20 to 30 years of age, wearing a gray jacket, brown pants, and a plaid shirt. He had on a wool stocking cap with a tassel on it.

Jim Garrison, the New Orleans State Attorney, wrote a letter to the House committee staff on July 15, 1977, stating that he interviewed Ms. Mercer and that she said she never claimed that the truck had "Air Conditioning" lettering on the side of truck. Further, she never said that she did not see the driver's face too clearly. Ms. Mercer said that she looked right at the man's face. She also said that "this is why I was able to recognize him when I later saw him shoot Oswald on TV". Garrison's copy included Ms. Mercers' signature at the bottom of the corrections (dated Jan 18, 1968) This account differs with a FBI report of an interview with her on 11/23/1963 which stated the truck did had the "Air Conditioning" lettering. Ms. Mercer stated to Garrison that she did not tell the FBI about any lettering on the truck. Her corrections contain this statement: "Furthermore, even before Ruby shot Oswald, when the FBI showed me pictures, I selected Jack Ruby's picture as one of those which appeared to be the driver. When one of the agents turned the picture over I saw "Jack Ruby: on the back". In The margin of the statement to Garrison she noted that it was on November 23, 1963, the day before Ruby's murder of Oswald was shown on television.

Helen Forrest: She was standing in a group of bystanders on the incline near the grassy knoll. She said she seen a man suddenly run from the rear of the depository building, down the incline, then enter a Rambler station wagon. "If it wasn't Oswald, it was his identical twin". This information was revealed during an interview with Michael Kurtz on May 17, 1974, for the book, "Crime of the Century". 1993 ()

Charles Blankenship: He was an off-duty Defense Protective Officer standing on the east side of Houston Street in front of the Records building. He heard the shots and ran to where he felt the shots had originated, this being the knoll area. He supposedly encountered two men in suits that stated they were Secret Service agents. They told him to go no further and he turned and left Dealey Square. He was not interviewed by any agency and kept this story to his immediate family until his death. His widow later told Michael Parks, a contributor to the book, "The Secret Service Agents on the Mall", by Debra Conway.()

Deputy Roger Craig, Dallas County Sheriff's Dept said that as the shots were fired he ran down the grassy incline between Main and Elm Street and saw a Dallas officer run up the grassy knoll and go behind the picket fence near the railroad yards. Craig followed, noting "complete confusion and hysteria" behind the fence. He began to question people when he noticed a woman in her early thirties attempting to drive out of the parking lot. Craig recalled, "I stopped her, identified myself and placed her under arrest". Craig advised that this was a paid lot leased by a deputy sheriff and required users to have a key to enter. "How did this woman gain access and what is more important, who was she and why did she have to leave?"

I turned her over to Deputy C.L. 'Lummie' Lewis and (he) told me he would take her to Sheriff Decker and take care of her car......I had no way of knowing that an officer whom I had worked with for four years was capable of losing a thirty-year old woman and a 3,000 lb. car. To this day, Officer Lewis does not know who she was, where she came from or what happened to her. Strange. (60)

Craig reported on 11/23/1963, that after the shots, he saw a man run down the grassy knoll and get into a light-colored Rambler station wagon with a luggage rack on its roof. Craig said in his report that his attention had been drawn to the man because as he heard a shrill whistle the station wagon pulled up to the curb. Deputy Craig described the driver as a dark-completed white male. There was no description of the man Craig seen running down the hill. Craig was unable to reach the car due to heavy traffic.

Craig said he immediately reported this information to a Secret Service agent in the area. Later that same afternoon, Craig was told to come to city hall; he said that when he arrived at city hall he identified the 'subject' they had in custody as the same person he saw running down the hill and entering the Rambler station wagon. He testified to the Warren Commission on 4/1/1964 and repeated his account. Craig said that the man was in line with the southwest corner of the depository building, and he started to run toward Elm Street and the driver was leaning to his right looking up the hill at the running man. Craig described the man running down the hill as in his 20's, 5-8 to 5-9, with medium brown sandy hair, wearing a medium blue trousers and a light tan shirt. Craig described the driver as very dark completed, with real short hair. Craig thought at first that he was a Negro. He was wearing a thin-looking white jacket like a windbreaker. Craig said the car looked white and appeared to have a Texas license plate.

Craig said about 5:30 P.M. he went to Captain Fritz's office identified the man he seen as the man in custody and talked to Capt. Fritz. The Captain later recounted that he turned Craig over to Lieutenant Baker, stating Craig was not actually in his office and must have seen the suspect through the office window. In a 1969 book by Dallas Chief Curry, a photo on page 72 did in fact show Craig within Captain Fritz's office while Oswald was being interrogated. Craig was fired by Sheriff Decker in July 1967. Some say it was because Craig would never change his story of the events of that day, still others say it was laxity and incompetence in his work.

The Warren Commission stated it "could not accept important elements of Craig's testimony". Researchers discovered in later years Warren Commission Document #5, a corroboration of Craig's story, but this was not contained in the Warren Commission's 26 volumes, but on a separate report. An FBI report stated that citizen Marvin Robinson, seen a light colored Nash station wagon driving west on Elm Street in heavy traffic, when he seen a white male walk down the grassy incline and get into the car, driving west. Deputy Craig later served as a municipal judge later and committed suicide in May, 1975.

Marvin Robinson, in an FBI interview on 11/23/1963, stated that he was traveling west on Elm Street toward Houston Street after the assassination. Just as he crossed the intersection of Elm and Houston and was in front of the depository, a light-colored Nash station wagon appeared before him. He said the station wagon stopped, and he saw a white male come down the grassy hill between the building and the street and enter the vehicle. The car then headed toward the Oak Cliff section of Dallas. No further contact was made with Robinson by authorities.

James Worrell: This witness stated he heard four shots and seen six inches of a gun barrel pointing out the window from either the 5th or 6th floor of the TSBD at 12:30-P.M. As the shots were being fired, Worrell began running toward the rear corner of the building then turning right and crossed the street. When he reached the corner of Houston and Pacific Street, he paused for a few moments. He observed the man in a dark sports coat hurriedly come out the rear door of the TSBD and run toward Houston and Elm Street where he disappeared in the crowd. A truck driver, James Romack, had been watching the rear door of the TSBD from the moment of the shots. Romack continued watching the door until W. E. Barnett, a Dallas police officer, came up a minute or two later and watched the door but then circled the building to ascertain whether there was a fire escape on the back of the building. Romack maintained a vigil on the rear door except for a few moments when he assisted a KBOX Radio car who was trying to drive up the torn up roadway that was under construction. Worrell's statement that he had seen a man exit the rear door would not be true unless the man escaped at the very moment Romack was removing the barricade to assist the radio station vehicle. Neither of the men in the radio car, Sam Pate or Josh Dowell, observed any one running from the rear door of the TSBD.

Previous observations by Carolyn Walther and Richard Carr noted that they had seen a man in a brown or tan sports coat in the 6th floor window just prior to the shots being fired.

Worrell described the man as white male, 5-8, 5-9, dark hair, dark shirt or jacket, open in front, come out of the TSBD and run in the opposite direction. "At 12:30 P.M. I was standing on sidewalk on the corner of Elm and Houston Street watching the motorcade. I heard a loud noise and looked up and seen the barrel of a rifle sticking out the window about 4 or 5 stories up the TSBD. I heard another shot and ran and then heard two more shots. I seen a W/M, 5-8, 5-9, dark hair, dark shirt or jacket, open down the front, no hat, and had nothing in his hands. He ran in the opposite direction than I. I then caught a bus to my home." Worrell went to Washington in March of 1964 to testify to the Warren Commission.

Royce Skelton: "We saw the motorcade come around the corner and I heard something which I thought was fireworks. I saw something hit the pavement at the left rear of the car, then the car got in the right hand lane and I heard two more shots. I heard a woman said "Oh no" or something and grab a man inside the car. I then heard another shot and saw the bullet hit the pavement. The pavement was knocked to the south away from the car (321) Twenty-three year old Skelton was located on the overpass directly over Elm Street at the time of the motorcade. He said that the smoke he saw rising from the cement when the bullet hit 'spread' in a direction away from the depository; he said the 'spray' of flying cement went toward the west. Skelton gave the Sheriff's department a statement on November 22nd and testified to the Warren Commission on April 8, 1964. He advised that he heard four shots. (61)

Danny Acre: Order Filler at the TSBD. Acre watch the motorcade from in front of the depository building and thoughts the shots came from back over by the railroad tracks. He testified to Warren Commission on 4/7/1964.

Howard Brennan: 45 years old: He was at the corner of Elm and Houston Street and seen an epileptic loaded into an ambulance. Brennan seen a man in the 6th floor window and also seen the 3 B/M's at the window below. He seen a man firing the rifle and heard 2 shots. He described the man as white male, 30, 160-170, wearing light color clothes. Brennan immediately reported this info to a police officer who was on foot. He said at a line-up that the man looked like Oswald but was not positive. Questioned later, he said he was positive.

John Powell: He was a prisoner on the 6th floor of the Dallas County Jail, directly opposite the book depository building. Powell was one of about 60 persons jailed on the 6th floor. He watched two men with a gun in a 6th floor window of the TSBD shortly before the motorcade drove by. Powell claims he could see so clearly that he even recalls them "fooling with the rifle scope". Powell says, "Quite a few of us saw them. Everyone was trying to watch the parade and all that. We were watching across the street because it was directly straight across. The first thing I thought, it was security guards...... I remember the guys".

None of the other 50-plus prisoners were questioned by law enforcement, to the author's knowledge.

Ronald Fischer: Seen a man in the widow on the 5th or 6th floor, but did not see a gun. He said the white male wore an open neck shirt; light colored, and had a slender face, 22-24 years old, with brown short hair.

Lillian Mooneyham: This District court clerk was watching the motorcade from the courthouse building on Houston Street. Four or five minutes after the shooting she saw a man standing behind boxes on the 6th floor.

James Simmons, was interviewed at the Union Terminal Company, 500 South Houston Street. Simmons advised that he is a car inspector and on November 22, 1963, he was standing on the Elm Street viaduct with some fellow employees waiting for President Kennedy's motorcade to come into view. Simmons stated when the President's car started down Elm Street he heard three shots ring out. President Kennedy slumped forward in his seat and appeared to have been hit by a bullet. Simmons said that he recalled that a motorcycle policeman drove up the grassy slope toward the Texas School Book Depository Building jumped off his motorcycle and then ran up the hill toward the Memorial Arches. Simmons said he thought he saw exhaust fumes of smoke near the embankment in front of the Texas School Book Depository Building. Simmons then ran toward the Texas School Book Depository Building with a policeman. He stopped at a fence near the Memorial Arches and could not find anyone. Simmons advised that it was his opinion the shots came from the direction of the Texas School Book Depository Building. He stated that immediately after the shots were fired, people were running in every direction through the whole area and there was a sense of mass confusion. Simmons was interviewed by FBI Special Agent Thomas Trettis, Jr., and E. J. Robertson on January 17, 1964.

An article by Harold Feldman, "Fifty-One Witnesses", that appeared in "The Majority of One", in March of 1965, stated that 51 witnesses thought that the shots, or some of them, came from the area of the Grassy Knoll. He noted that the police and bystanders surged toward the grassy knoll immediately after the shots were fired. Another report said that of the twenty-three witnesses that observed some sort of action in the area of the grassy knoll, only eleven of the witnesses gave testimony.

Much has been made of the "3 Tramps" that were apprehended in the rail yards behind the TSBD building shortly after the assassination. Many claimed that Frank Sturgis was one of them. Other assassination experts offered names of other persons. In 1989, the photos of the three tramps in custody of the Dallas police were released. In 1992, journalist Mary La Fontaine matched the names of the three tramps with long lost Dallas police records. The three men were Gus Abrams, Harold Doyle and John Gedney. There were no apparent connection with these men and the assassination.

With the rapid development in biometrics research such as 3-dimensional facial recognition, there may be merit in undertaking a project that attempts the identification of the people assembled in Dealey Square as the assassination occurred, by comparing these photos with known photos of all the known 'persons of interest' that have surfaced in this case. Bioscripts, Inc., is one of the firms on the cutting edge of this method of identification, as well as other well known firms. This project might identify or eliminate some of the "it looks like" theories, such as the "Umbrella Man", etc.

PART IV

INVESTIGATION BY
DALLAS POLICE

CRIME SCENE AT DEPOSITORY

The initial search of the building was conducted randomly by a combination of Sheriff's deputies and Dallas police officers. Deputy Luke Mooney discovered the sniper's nest on the 6th floor, shielded by book cartons. He also observed partially eaten pieces of chicken and a small paper bag. Dallas P.D. Sergeant Gerald Hill observed the chicken leg and a sandwich bag. Officer L.D Montgomery observed the chicken remnants and a soda pop bottle. Officer E.L. Boyd observed chicken bones about 30-40 feet west of the southeast window (the nest). Officer Marvin Johnson also observed the soda bottle and parts of an eaten chicken. Detective R.L. Studebaker photographed the evidence found on the 6th floor. A TSBD employee Bill Shelley remembered the soda bottle and the chicken remains. Officer E.D. Brewer also observed the bottle and the chicken near the rifle shells under the southeast window.

Lieutenant J.C. Day observed the same evidence, checked the bottle for fingerprints, and put aside the chicken and paper bag. Each of the officers described slightly difference positions for these items and it is obvious that these items and the cartons providing the nest were moved around prior to the time that the crime scene photos were taken. Neither the bottle nor the chicken was observed in the photos. This fact and the contradictions on the location of the evidence mentioned bring us to doubt how well the original crime scene was preserved.

Deputy Luke Mooney, at 1:12 P.M. found three empty bullet cartridges during the random search of the floor area. At that time, Mooney did not know of the floor installer's statement as to hearing the shells hit the floor as the shots were fired. Mooney stated that upon hearing the shots he ran around to the rear door and headed for the rail yards. After a few seconds, he was ordered by an unknown officer to cover the building, without being assigned to a specific area. He went to the 6th floor, where he was initially alone. Mooney did not notice the nest at first but did say he seen windows open on the south side of that floor. It should also be noted that Lieutenants Revill and Officer Dyson as well as three detectives were also conducting a systematic search of the TSDB building. Noted also, that an Inspector Sawyer, a ranking Dallas staff officer, was on the scene. A motor officer, Officer Marion Baker (mentioned earlier), stationed outside the building, began his search for a suspect as soon as he entered the front door. He was the officer who noticed Oswald in the vestibule of the lunchroom as Baker reached the second floor level.

The reports, affidavits and Warren Commission testimony noted that the search for suspects and evidence in the TSBD building was slow to begin and was conducted in a haphazard manner and the findings were not immediately documented. The author disagrees somewhat to that statement.

Regarding the search for suspects and evidence in the Depository building, it is a fact that the Dallas police had partially secured the building between 12:33 and 12:37 P.M., several minutes after the 12:30 P.M. shooting. A uniformed Dallas police Inspector with twenty-three years of service, J. Herbert Sawyer, was in charge of a portion of Main Street, for the motorcade. As the motorcade passed his position, Sawyer returned to his police car and slowly (due to the crowd) began to depart the parade route. He heard the initial police radio report by Sheriff Decker and Chief Curry of an incident at Elm Street and Houston Street, and headed to the scene. He arrived at 12:36 P.M., and personally made a quick check of the building with a police sergeant. Officer Marion Baker was already in the building with Roy Truly, an executive of the school book building. Inspector Sawyer returned to his car that was parked in front of the Depository building and ordered his officers to seal the building, allowing no one to enter or leave. He ordered a sergeant to seal the rear entrances but was advised that officers had already accomplished this task.

Regarding the evidence search, the building was quickly searched by several officers and Sheriff's deputies for a suspect. These officers then began a search of the sixth floor. Actually, the sealing of the building, the search for a suspect and the search for evidence was begun in an amazing short period of time. The author has been on hundreds of crime scenes over the years and after researching the facts of this case, concludes that there was no delay in commencing these tasks. If there was any delay at all, it was most likely due to the confusion of the location of the shots. Numerous law enforcement officers, including most of the twenty plus Sheriff's deputies standing across from the Depository when the shots were fired, headed first for the grassy knoll and rail yards before focusing on the Depository Building. It was Officer Marion Baker, riding escort for the motorcade, who immediately headed to the school building as he was riding on Houston Street alongside the press busses in the motorcade and believed that the shots he heard had come from the building and he quickly went into action.

To have a high ranking police staff officer setting up a command post seven minutes after the shooting, aided by at least two patrol sergeants and several uniformed officers, is, according to the author's experience, very rare indeed.

The search for evidence and the recording of same did not seem nearly as efficient as the initial uniform officers' response. There were Sheriff's deputies mixed with Dallas police in the evidence search (an unusual event on a crime scene) and only two Crime Scene specialists (Lieutenant Day and Sgt. Studebaker) attempting a evidence search, headed by an old time Police Captain who oversaw a flawed search and documentation process.

At 1:22 P.M., Deputy Constable Seymour Weitzman and Deputy Sheriff Eugene Broome discovered the rifle on the 6th floor near the book cartoons. It is not clear if this discovery was prior to or after the nine officers mentioned above had found various pieces of evidence, but not the rifle. One live 6.5 cartridge was found in the rifle and three shells were found on the floor near the southeast window. A homicide detective (Detective Sims) picked up the shells. Lt. Day and Detective Studebaker of the Crime Scene search team examined both the rifle and shells before they were taken to the station. Homicide Commander Captain Fritz came to the scene and also examined the rifle. There was initially some confusion with identifying the make of the rifle, with Deputies Broome and Weitzman first stating that the weapon was a 7.6 Mauser.

It was also obvious that the cartons of books that were used to erect the nest were moved several times prior to the crime scene photo being taken. One reasons proffered for this act was that the area was so narrow, the boxes had to be moved to enter that area for search purposes.

Detective Robert Studebaker, a nine year Dallas officer, assigned to the Crime Scene Office, performed most of the evidence search at the TSBD, under the direction of Captain Fritz and Lieutenant Day. Studebaker had been assigned to crime scene duties for less than two months and had no formal training in these duties.

Detective Studebaker remained on the scene at the Depository from 1:15 P.M. Friday, until 1:00 A.M. Saturday.

Lieutenant Day and Detective Studebaker, Dallas police crime scene detectives, dusted for fingerprints on the four boxes that had been moved into position as the "snipers nest" on the sixth floor by the shooting suspect. FBI Agent Sebastian Latona, supervisor of the Latent Fingerprint Section at FBI headquarters in Washington, testified to the Warren Commission that twenty identifiable fingerprints and eight palm prints were developed on the cartons that made up the "sniper's nest". One carton was 18 x 12 x 14 which had been moved from a stack along the south wall. A smaller carton, 12 x 9 x 8 marked 'Rolling Readers', was atop the larger carton. In front of this stack and resting partially on the windowsill was another 'Rolling Reader' carton. The carton on the windowsill and the large carton below the window contained no prints which could be identified as Lee Oswald's. The other 'Rolling Reader' carton, however, contained a palm print and a fingerprint that were Oswald's. The Warren Commission had considered the possibility that the carton might have been moved in conjunction with the work being performed on the sixth floor on November 22, 1963. Another carton box, separate from the above three, was dusted by Lieutenant Day and had one of Oswald's prints on it.

In evaluating the significance of the fingerprints, the Warren Commission considered the possibility that Oswald handled these items as part of his normal duties.

Henry Wade, the Dallas County District Attorney, commented on the competence of Dallas Homicide Commander, Capt. Will Fritz, in testimony to the Warren Commission, Wade stated: "he is the poorest in the getting of evidence that I know". Wade also advised that Chief Curry did not seem to be obtaining much information from Captain Fritz as to the progress of the JFK case. Wade testified that "I talked to Chief Curry on Saturday morning, November 23rd, and he knew very little of the evidence at this stage".

WEAPON RECOVERED

The Rifle: 6.5 Mannlicher-Carcerno w/scope #C2766, manufactured prior to 1941, was discovered by Dallas County sheriff's Deputy Eugene Broome and Deputy Constable Seymour Weitzman. One shell was still in chamber and three spent rounds were found nearby on the 6th floor of the TSBD near the southeast window. The FBI described the rifle as "cheap old weapon". The rifle was purchased by A. Hidell from Klein's Sporting Goods company, via mail order. The Warren Commission said suspect Oswald had not fired the gun for at least 2 months or perhaps not at all. The rifle was fitted with a 'junk' scope.

Oswald bought the rifle from Kilein's, which had been advertised in the American Rifleman Magazine. Oswald shot at General Walker on March 10, 1963 with a 6.5 cal rifle bullet. An FBI ballistic expert, Robert Frizon, and the superintendent of the Illinois Bureau of criminal identification, conclude the "fair probability" that the Walker bullet was fired by the same rifle used by Oswald to kill Kennedy.

Oswald ordered the rifle by sending in a ad clipping for a 36 inch Carcano rifle weighing 5 1/2 lbs, catalog #C20-T750. The gun was mailed to A. Hidell at Post Office box 2915, Dallas, Texas. The post office box was rented by Oswald on October 9, 1962. The rifle found on the 6th floor was a Mannlichter-Carcano, bolt action, 6.5 caliber, serial #

C2766, and was 42.6 inches long, six inches longer than the one advertised.

Army expert Ronald Summors, testified to the Warren Commission that: "Mr. Staley (one of Summors' marksmen) had difficulty in opening the bolt in his first firing exercise" "...the trigger pull is different as far as these firers are concerned. It is in effect a two-stage operative, in the first stage the trigger is relatively free, and it suddenly required a greater pull to actually fire the weapon". Summors explained that in order to achieve high accuracy, even a highly skilled marksman would have to have considerable experience with guns and also considerable experience with this weapon, because of the amount of effort required to work the bolt.

An FBI report in August of 1964....stated that the firing pin of this rifle has been used extensively as shown by the wear on the nose or striking position of the firing pin and further, the presence of rust on the firing pin and its spring... The scope itself, a Japanese product added, was out of adjustment and which would require 'zeroing' after being transported, especially if the weapon was broken down while in transit.

Lt. Col. Folsom of the U.S. Marines testified as to Oswald's accuracy with a rifle based on Marine Corps records. Oswald "his 191 score in target shooting is that of a "rather poor shot".

As said, the rifle ordered by A. Hidell (Oswald) was a 36inch rifle. The rifle found in the Depository building was a 42.2 inch rifle, which was advertised in Klein's full page ad in the November 1963 Field & Stream. The model Hidell (Oswald) ordered, the 36 inch model, was advertised in a different October 1962 magazine

Can it be assumed that Klein's made a mistake ordering by sending a different model (a 42.2 inch) rifle instead of the 36inch rifle originally ordered? Several more of the Warren Commission firearm experts characterized the rifle:

Sebastian Latona - FBI expert. "A cheap old weapon"

John Bringar -Gun shop owner in Dallas told the FBI "a very cheap rifle"

Dan Ryder - Irving Sports Shop. "Real cheap, common, real flimsy looking, very easily knocked out of adjustment"

No permit was then required to purchase the weapon and there was no requirement for a record to have been kept. The rifle was shipped to a post office box owned by Oswald. When arrested, Oswald had a fake selective service card with the name A.J. Hidell.

The Model 19 rifle is a multi-loading weapon with a fixed and central magazine. The maximum range is 2800 meters but was considered unreliable over 300 meters. The ammo for this rifle was known to be faulty and it rarely shot straight. The rifle could have been bought in lots of twenty-five at that time, for three dollars each.

The weapon found on the 6th floor of the TSBD by Sheriff's Deputies, was the only weapon used that day according to the Warren Commission. The firing pin was found to be defective or worn out. No ammo clip was found, so rifle had to be hand-loaded.

The HSCA compared the dimensions of the rifle from photographs as it was being taken out of the TSBD with that of previous 'backyard' photos of Oswald holding the rifle and concluded they are the same rifle.

A paraffin test conducted that day by Dallas crime lab personnel indicated that Oswald had no traces of nitrates on his cheek which showed that he did not fire a rifle that day. A palm print taken by Dallas Lt. Day was found under the stock of the rifle and this print matched Oswald's palm print. The FBI, in a later exam, did not find this print.

The HSCA tests linked this rifle to shots fired at the JFK limo. The three spent shells found on the 6th floor were fired from the same rifle, according to the HSCA tests.

The Dallas police turned the rifle over to the FBI at 11:45 P.M. on the 22nd. FBI tests of the rifle for the Warren Commission found that it took a minimum of 2.3 seconds to fire two shots. Three shots would require 6.9 seconds.

The bolt of Oswald's rifle could not be operated any faster than 2.3 seconds per round. Only 1.97 seconds elapsed between the firing of the shot that first struck Kennedy and the bullet that struck Connally. Therefore, two shots could not have been fired by Oswald in the time frame required to hit both Kennedy and Connally with separate bullets. So, the "magic bullet' theory was born.

Secret Service agent Roy Kellerman described the shots as a 'flurry'. Two shots were fired very close in time with each other. The first shot sounded like a firecracker but the next two shots sounded like rifle shots. Many other witnesses made this same comment that day.

Oswald, or an imposter, visited the Sportsman Gun Range in Grand Prairie, TX, 13 miles from Oswald's rooming house. Mrs. Paine's husband, Harold Paine told Hugh Farnsworth, a Dallas newsman, that Oswald had been there on Oct 26, November 9 and 10th and on November 17th, with another man in a black Ford auto whom the FBI believes was Wesley Frazier, a fellow employee of Oswald at the TSBD. Frazier has always denied this allegation.

Another witness to Oswald at the range was Sterling Wood, who was practicing with his father on November 16th. Upon seeing Oswald on Television after the assassination, Wood declared to his father, "Daddy, that looks just like the man we saw at the range when we were sighting in our rifles". Sterling had remembered at the range saying, "Daddy, it looks like a 6.5 Italian Carbine". The shooter then said, "Yes, it is".

Frazier was the young man who drove Oswald to work the morning of the 22nd and said he (Oswald) was carrying a paper sack, but advised it was not long enough to conceal a rifle. Another witness, Jack Cory, a co-tenant at Oswald's rooming house, stated one or two days prior to the 22nd, he seen Oswald carrying a package on the bus while en route to work, wrapped in newspapers. Cory said it was about 2 feet long, a foot wide and 6 inches thick. These observations leads to the theory that Oswald brought the rifle to the Book Depository building, broken down, on two or more separate days.

OSWALD'S CLIPBOARD

The Warren Commission focused on where Oswald's work clipboard was found in an attempt to fortify the testimony of witness (and Oswald co-worker) Charles Givens, who belatedly claimed to have seen Oswald on the 6th floor around noon time, thirty minutes prior to the assassination.

Another co-worker, Frankie Kaiser, advised that on December 2nd, a week and a half after the Kennedy murder, he found a homemade clipboard that Oswald had been using on the day of the killing. Kaiser had originally made the clipboard but Oswald began using it after starting on the job as order filler at the Depository. Kaiser's name was written on it the clipboard several times and it was, without doubt, the clipboard Oswald was utilizing. There were three un-filled orders still clipped to the board when found.

Kaiser, did not work on November 22nd due to dental problems. On December 2nd, while retrieving a book, he found the clipboard on the sixth floor between the elevator and the staircase, lying on the floor adjacent to some book boxes. The sixth floor was supposedly searched thoroughly the day of the murder but this clipboard was not found. Kaiser reported finding the clipboard to his supervisor, William Shelley, who in return notified the authorities. According to Kaiser, the clipboard "was lying there in the plain open...lying on the floor", said Kaiser.

Witness Charles Givens mentioned - for the first time - to the Secret Services in a interview between December 2nd and the 5th, that when he seen Oswald before lunch that day on the 6th floor, he (Oswald) was carrying a clipboard.

This statement by Givens, along with the belated finding of the clipboard, provided the Warren Commission with what they considered, the evidence that "linked Oswald with the point from which the shots were fired". Yet, in the first statement that Givens gave on November 22nd, he stated that he had last seen Oswald on the first floor, not the sixth, and that Oswald was reading a newspaper, not carrying a clipboard.

Mr. Givens was the employee who was the subject of a police BOLO (radio bulletin) provided over the police radio by Inspector Sawyer prior to Oswald being reported missing from the TSBD. Givens, with a local police record and known to the Dallas police, gave Dallas PD a statement on the 22nd and a follow-up interview with the FBI the next day, but did not mention seeing Oswald on the 6th floor that day. Givens did elaborate that fact during the Secret Service interview on or after December 2nd, and later repeated same to the Warren Commission.

In Given's testimony to the Warren Commission, the questioning lawyers mentioned the clipboard numerous times, implying that its existence on the sixth floor was critical evidence. However, Oswald's normal duties included trips to various book storage rooms in the Depository building, including the sixth floor, regardless of whether or not Givens seen him up there at 11:50 A.M. It was also mentioned in the commission minutes that Oswald had three un-filled orders on the clipboard, implying that Oswald was not doing his job that day. Other commission minutes of Oswald's supervisors pointed out that Oswald was a good worker and it would be normal to have 15 to 25 orders on his clipboard during the day. In fact, one of co-workers of Givens testified that he had seen Oswald in the book bins earlier in the morning filling orders. It does seem rather innocuous that the clipboard was found, adjacent to the elevators on the sixth floor, left by an employee heading for lunch on the ground floor. One can assume that it would be less cumbersome to just leave the clipboard where Kaiser found it, and pick it back up after returning from lunch. It appears that the commission went a long way to put Oswald up on the sixth floor at 11:50 A.M. when another Depository employee observes him (Oswald) in the second floor lunchroom at 12:15, fifteen minutes before the shots were fired.

The DALLAS P.D. - 1963

The blame due the Dallas Police Department for its ineptness on that fateful November day in 1963 can not be placed on a department that was ill-equipped to handle two homicides. The organizational structure of the department was typical of large southern or western US city at that time. The units and divisions were as proscribed by the International City Manager's Association. My department, the Miami P.D., although a third smaller than the Dallas force, had a similar structure.

The homicide division, a part of the Crimes Against Persons Unit, (Robbery and Homicide), had approximately twenty investigators including two Lieutenants, under Captain Will Fritz. The usual scheme for handling a homicide case would be to assign a two-man team as the primary investigators, under the supervision of one of the Lieutenants, supplemented by other teams of detectives. If it was a "hot case", additional teams could be assigned for 'lead chasing' from the ranks of the Robbery squad, which was also under Captain Fritz's supervision. A second 'hot case' would be assigned to another two-man homicide team, under the other Lieutenant (the Tippit case).

This was apparently not the approach Captain Fritz took. Instead, he attempted to control both cases himself, a physical impossibility, especially for a fifty-nine year old who joined the force in 1919.

The crime scene effort also appeared weak, with only Lt. Day and newly assigned Detective Studebaker involved. Exacerbating the evidence collection and evaluation tasks was the fact that Chief Curry acquisised to FBI's head Hoover request to immediately send the critical evidence to the FBI's lab during the first 24 hours of the investigation.

The homicide teams appeared to have the experience to handle the two "hot cases" simultaneously. The teams mentioned in the police reports and the investigators' tenure are as follows.

Role of Homicide Squad

Detective Elmer Boyd is an 11 year veteran of the Dallas force assigned since 1957 to the homicide squad and partnered with Detective Sims. Boyd's assignment that day was to accompany Captain Fritz to the Trade Mart where JFK was to make a speech to members of the Dallas leaders after the motorcade. Deputy Chief Stevenson called Fritz and advised him of the JFK shooting. They immediately went to Parkland Hospital and met with Chief Curry and then proceeded downtown to the Texas School Book Depository building's 6th floor where a search for evidence was already ongoing. The three spent rifle shells had already been located and the rifle was found just after Boyd and others arrived.

The supervisor of the TSBD provided Fritz with the address in Irving, Texas, where a missing employee, Lee Oswald, lived. At 2:20 PM, Boyd and Sims dropped the Captain back to his office and were about to head out to Oswald's address when other detectives advised that suspect Oswald had been arrested at the Texas Theater and was now sitting in Captain Fritz's office. The Captain began to question Oswald with Boyd, Sims, FBI agents Bookout and Hosty present. It is noted that the Dallas police did not record interviews with criminal suspects at this time, although it had become a standard practice with most American police departments in 1963. Boyd took Oswald to a lineup at 4:05 P.M. (results in later section)

Boyd mentioned in his statement that Oswald had appeared to him to be quite 'sharp' and was calm...

Detective Boyd found five .38 live bullets in Oswald's pockets and marked them each with his initials. Detectives Boyd, Sims, Hall and Dhority, then were sent out to 1026 North Beckley, a rooming house that Oswald had been living, but without a search warrant.

Detective Richard Sims: Sims is a 15 year police veteran with six years of homicide experience. His partner was Detective Boyd. Sims was assigned to the Trade Mart with Boyd and Captain Fritz that fateful Friday. When hearing of the JFK shooting, they proceeded to Parkland Hospital and conferred with Chief Jesse Curry. Boyd, Sims and Fritz then went to the

TSBD, contacting Lieutenant Revill, Detective Westphal and Deputy Luke Mooney, who had found the three spent rifle shells.

Detectives Boyd and Sims later held the first line-up, using two police officers, one jail clerk as fillers, and Oswald. They later held a third lineup using two prisoners, one jail clerk as fillers, and Oswald. Sims found the bus transfer ticket in Oswald's shirt pocket as well as an I.D. bracelet and Oswald's Marine ring. During the evening they arranged a paraffin test for Oswald conducted by Sergeants Barnes and Hicks of the Crime Scene unit.

Sims also contacted Wesley Frazier, an employee of the TSBD, who, along with his sister, had given Oswald a ride to work that morning. Frazier stated that Oswald placed a large paper sack into their car stating it was curtain rods. Frazier was then taken by Sims to the police station where a polygraph was administered to him. Sims then returned to Mrs. Paine's home with Detective Rose. While searching the garage, detective Rose found the photos of Oswald holding a rifle, revolver and two newspapers, in the garage.

Detective C. N. Dhority, 40, had been on the Dallas PD since 1946 and was a homicide investigator for eight years. Off-duty that Friday, he was called in by homicide Lt. Wells, arriving at work at 2 PM. His usual partner, H.H. Blessing, was not present so he was paired up with Detective C. M. Brown. At 6PM he picked up witness McWatters, the bus driver who said that Oswald boarded his bus soon after the Kennedy shooting. McWatters completed an affidavit and identified the bus transfer ticket that Detective Sims had found in Oswald's shirt pocket. They then escorted McWatters to a lineup.

Dhority was given three 6.5 rifle shells by Capt. Fritz, took them to the crime lab, then retuned them to the homicide office where Fritz kept one and the other two were turned over to Lt. Day. Dhority then went to the home of the two Davis sisters on 10th Street (scene of shooting) where he was given one .38 spent shell that was found in the Davis' front yard at 400 E. 10th Street.

On Sunday morning, the 24th, Detective Dhority was given the keys to Captain Fritz's car and instructed to move the car to the front of the jail door in the basement of the police station so it could be used to transfer Oswald to the County Jail.

Detective Richard Stovall, a ten year police veteran with eighteen months of homicide experience, was called into work at 2 PM on Friday. He talked to Oswald and obtained his wallet. Stovall then went to Mrs. Paine's home at 2515 W. 5th Street in Irving, Texas with Detectives Rose and Adamick. They met Dallas County detectives Weatherford, Oxford and Walthers. They searched Mrs. Paine's home after receiving permission, as they did not as yet have a search warrant.

Detective Henry Moore, 39, a fourteen year police veteran, came to work at 2 P.M. on Friday and was sent out to the North Beckley home with a search warrant for Oswald's room. At that location, Moore found a receipt for a post office box, a passport, and an application for a Texas driver's license in Oswald's name.

Detective F, M. Turner, 35, is a homicide officer who rode in the Pilot car during the motorcade, along with Deputy Chief Lumpkin, Detective Senkel of Homicide, a Secret Service agent and an Army Major, names unknown. After the Kennedy shooting, the officers went to Parkland Hospital and then to the area of the TSBD. Turner was instructed to search a boxcar located in the rail yard behind the book depository building. Turner also questioned witness Arnold Rowland, who had claimed to have seen a man in the TSBD window with a rifle in his hand, on the west side of the 6th floor. Turner also talked to witness Fischer and Edwards, who also claimed to have seen a man in the window. Turner had this witness complete an affidavit.

Officer Leslie. D. Montgomery, a nine year veteran of the force, came to the scene at the TSBD to assist Lt. Day and Detective Studebaker in searching the crime scene.

Detective Marvin Johnson, a ten year veteran,

was sent to the TSBD that Friday with his partner, L.D. Montgomery. Johnson found the long paper sack, supposedly used by Oswald to carry the rifle into the building. The sack was found near the southeast window in the corner near some heating pipes.

Detective William Potts is a sixteen year veteran of the force with seven years of experience in the homicide squad. Potts came into work that Friday at 2 PM. His partners were usually Detectives Bill Senkel and F. M. Turner. He was sent out to 1026 North Beckley with Lieutenant Cunningham and Detective. Senkel. They talked to Mrs. Johnson, Oswald's landlady and Mrs. Roberts, the housekeeper. Mrs. Roberts advised Potts that Oswald was registered at the rooming house under the name of O.H. Lee. Turner returned to this address about 3PM with a search warrant and was accompanied by Detective. H. Moore, Bill Alexander, Asst. District Attorney, and Judge Johnston. Evidence found included a .38 cal empty holster and a red notebook, which they turned over to the crime lab at the police station.

Turner also attended a lineup and later transported witness Fischer back to his home. Fischer had advised Detective Turner that the guy in the lineup "looks like him", speaking about Oswald.

Detective John Adamick, 26, reported for work at 2:00 P.M. on Friday and was sent to the Paine home at two-thirty. While there he spoke with Mrs. Randle, the sister of Frazier, who had rode to work that morning with Oswald and had seen him place a paper sack into the back seat. Adamick also talked to Marina Oswald who reported that she had seen the rifle in the blanket on the floor of the garage within the last week. Detective Adamick transported these witnesses to the homicide office and later took them back home.

On Saturday, the 23rd, Adamick came to work at 10:00 A.M., and went back to Mrs. Paine's home in Irving to assist in the search of the house and garage, along with other detectives, including Detective McCabe from the Irving police department. While at the house, Detective Adamick spoke to Mrs. Paine's estranged husband, Michael Paine, who advised that he 'thought' of Oswald being a suspect when he heard about the JFK shooting.

Major Police Mistakes

The three major department breakdowns while handling of the cases have contributed greatly to the fifty- plus years of mystery in the attempt to solve the assassination case.

One was the botched handling of the homicide cases by old Captain Fritz. He apparently failed to delegate responsibility to his Lieutenants, failed to arrange the Oswald line-ups and interrogation properly according to 'Standards', and ignored the possibility as to a conspiracy. No recording of the interrogations, either electronically or by steno, was accomplished.

Even our department (Miami) in 1963 recorded every homicide interview; some were even recorded on old Ampex video recorders at that time.

Captain John Will Fritz, 68, was described as a domineering, dictatorial officer by Attorney Travis Kirk, of Dallas. It was said that Fritz possessed a photographic memory. He had been a member of the Dallas force since 1921 and had been a Police Captain since 1936.

The second major gaffe was Chief of Police Curry allowing the police building to be over-run by the news media, resulting in a circus-like atmosphere. This could have been easily prevented by assigning Chief Stevenson or one of the non-line Deputy Chiefs to set up a news media center in the adjacent City Hall. We do not know what Mayor Cabell's instructions to Chief Curry were, but it remained Chief Curry's responsibility to take charge. It is also noted that Chief Curry, a apparent smart nice guy, lacked the experience of ever being a working detective himself. He was regarded a 'corner man' (downtown traffic officer) and seemed unaware of Captain Fritz's progress (or lack of same) in handling the two cases.

And, of course, the decision to have the Dallas P.D. transport suspect Oswald to the County Jail was not wise. By following the normal routine of having Dallas County Sheriff Decker's men do the prisoner transfer, the Ruby shooting may have been averted.

Unusual Aspect of Police Response

A quite unusual aspect of this case is that, due to the presidential visit, numerous non-line personnel (and commanders) were on field duty at the various visit locations, i.e., Trade Mart, parade routes, Love Field, etc. This fact created chaos itself by all elements attempting to use the only two police radio channels available at that time. The author can not recall a major crime in which so many officers (including Sheriff Deputies) were themselves on the actual scene of the crime, plus the fact that the crime (or portions) were photographed in real time by many citizens.

Other critical post-event situations that were screwed up were not the responsibility of the Dallas P.D. The Secret Service, swiftly and illegally removed the body of President Kennedy, depriving the Dallas P.D. of the results from a qualified autopsy team and the whisking away of the presidential limo (part of the crime scene) before any examination. These action had ramifications that still exist today.

On the plus side, the actions of the regular patrol officers and Sergeants (and some detectives) were excellent. The immediate setting up of a command post at the TSBD by Inspector Sawyer and the use of the nearby Sheriff's office for witness interviews were examples of the right action at the right time. Also, the Oswald arrest scene went quite well except for not locating the theater witness list after the fact. The Tippit scene, especially the crime scene search was not noteworthy. Much was not done.

The author read Sylvia Meagher's book and heartily applaud here for her documentation of the failures of the Warren Commission and its report. On one point, I do disagree. The radio patrol assignments that the Communication center provided during the case(s) were rational and necessary. The author has read the Dallas police archives and have listened to the police radio tapes. From my standpoint, the communication crew did as well as could be expected during the chaotic scenes and the limitations of the two-channel radio installation. The author has extensive field patrol experience at every level, including Patrol Section Commander for three years, supplemented by my communication center knowledge gained from twelve years in the military as a communication center supervisor. The patrol and communication operators performed professionally and efficiently.

On a personal note, this author was a good personal friend of a Dallas police communication center supervisor.

Jim Everett, later the Assistant Chief of Dallas police. He was on duty in the communications center on the day Oswald was shot by Jack Ruby. Jim and I have discussed these (and other assassination issues) at length. In 1970, Everett was one of my roommates at the Southern Police Institute and we had many discussions about the Dallas police response on November 22. 1963, during out four months together. Everett later became Chief of Police at Austin, Texas and another city after his Dallas retirement. Jim passed away a few years ago.

THE AUTOPSY AND THE WOUNDS

The Warren Commission reported in 1964 that there were only three shots fired, all from the 6th floor of the TSBD, one of which missed and the other two hitting JFK, One of the shots also struck Governor Connally. The House of Representatives report concluded in 1979, fifteen years later, that four shots were fired, three from the window of the TSBD and one from the area of the Grassy Knoll. An expert autopsy could have settled this critical discrepancy fairly easily.

Under Texas law, an autopsy must be - by law - performed. However, despite the insistence of the Dallas County Chief Medical Examiner Earl Rose and a Texas judge, both present at Parkland Hospital that day, Secret Service agent Roy Kellerman and Navy Admiral George Burkley, held the Dallas medical authorities at gunpoint, moved the body of President Kennedy to Air Force One, and removed it from Texas to Washington, within two hours of the assassination. The autopsy was then performed at Bethesda's naval hospital by three Navy doctors, wholly unqualified in the area of gunshot killings, in the opinion of many US pathologists.

This was a clear case of 'body snatching', contrary to Texas law. It has been pointed out earlier that, at that time in 1963, the killing of a U.S. President was not covered by federal statutes. The federal government had no justification to remove the body from Texas jurisdiction, nor did it have the authority to perform an autopsy.

The Navy's inadequate autopsy report stated that all the shots came from the rear of the presidential limo. It has since been scientifically proven that at least one shot did in fact hit President Kennedy from the front, thereby negating the 'lone assassin' theory. The famous Zapruder film, released to the public in March of 1975, confirmed this fact. In the Zapruder film it is totally clear that the President's head jerked backwards at the moment the shot visibly exploded his head. Dallas' Parkland Hospital doctors examining Kennedy immediately noticed a small entry wound in his throat. In fact, they further enlarged this wound to insert tubes in an attempt to save the President's life. It is common knowledge among autopsy doctors, police homicide investigators and millions of hunters, that an entry wound is usually small as compared to a much larger exit wound. The shot that blew out JFK's brains splattered onto two of the motorcycle officers riding as outriders in the motorcade, who had been riding slightly behind the limo.

The truth is that the President was knocked backwards by a bullet obvious originating in front of him, from the direction of a sniper in the grassy knoll.

Anthony Summers, in his book, "Conspiracy", 1991, quoted Dr. A.J. Riddle, University of California and a member of its Brain Institute, "Newton's second law of motion has remained inviolate for three centuries." (62) Basically, this law says that an object hit by a projectile will be given a motion that has the same direction as that of the projectile. Dr. Riddle further pointed out that the President's backward movement cannot be accounted for by acceleration of the car; this had not yet occurred, and the film shows no similar movements by other occupants of the limo.

Another shot, this time from the rear, allegedly entered the President's back, came through his throat, traveled on into Governor Connolly's back, and exited through his chest to cause further injuries to his right wrist and thigh. Amazing. This thesis of a "magic bullet" Magic Bullet - (63)) was born when official investigators analyzing the Zapruder film realized that a lone gunman would not have had the time to fire his rifle again between the time the President was seen to be hit and the moment Governor Connolly appeared to react to his wounds. The Commission lawyer who came up with this theory was Arlen Specter, a counsel to the commission, and later a U.S. Senator. Arlen Specter was the sole member of the Warren Commission assigned to investigate "the basic facts of the Assassination". He went to Dallas for a week and talked to 28 doctors, Jean Hill and one other witness - and that was his total investigation.

Author Summers points out that the most persistent objection to the "magic bullet" was the remarkable state of preservation. This virtually undamaged bullet was allegedly found on one of the gurneys at Parkland Hospital where both Kennedy and Connolly were taken.

Dr. Milton Helpern, former Chief Medical Examiner of New York City, (The New York Times said of Helpern, "He knows more about violent death than anyone in the world") said of the magic bullet, "the original weight of this bullet before it was fired was 160 to 161 grains". The weight of the bullet recovered at Parkland was 158.6, and not distorted in any way. "I cannot accept the premise that the bullet thrashed around in all that body tissue and lost only 1.4 to 2.4 grains of it original weight. I cannot believe either that the bullet is going to emerge miraculously unscathed, without any deformity, and with its lands and grooves intact." (64)

Dr Cyril Wecht, former president of the Academy of Forensic Science, rejects the magic bullet theory also and maintains that his fellow doctors 'judgment' is semantically sophistry and intellectual gymnastics. Wecht states that the claim that the bullet would have to swerve sharply in mid-air, "a path of flight that has never been experienced or suggested for any bullet known to mankind". These observations have been seconded by numerous experienced doctors. (65)

The retrieval of the bullet fragments was 'sloppy' and incomplete. Kennedy's brain disappeared after the naval autopsy. No 'bullet path' through JFK's body was performed, a standard practice by medical examiners in these type cases.

The autopsy at Washington, according to many eminent pathologists, was amateurish and incomplete, performed by inexperienced naval doctors, under enormous political pressure. The autopsy results were analyzed by Commission lawyers who ignored any result that did not prove that all the shots originated from the 6th floor of the TSBD and were fired by only a 'lone assassin'.

Regarding the selection of Bethesda for the location of the autopsy, Chief of Pathology Dr. Thorton Boswell statement was: He argued "That's stupid", the autopsy should be done at ARIP, the apex of military pathology", but he was told that Admiral Burkley wants Bethesda as "I was told that is what Jackie wants". (66) Dr. Humes stated in 1992, "it was true that we were influenced by the fact we have Jackie Kennedy waiting upstairs to accompany the body to the White House and that Admiral Burkly wanted us to hurry as much as possible". Dr.Piere Finck, who asserts in "The Autopsy", described the President's autopsy as only "adequate" and "not as complete as scores as other autopsies I have done". Dr. Robert Karnel was present regarding an exam of the internal organs that were not dissected. He stated flatly, "They (Boswell and Humes) were not allowed to do that.....Jim (Humes) and Jay (Boswell) were really handicapped that night with regards to performing the autopsy". (67)

The doctors (performing the autopsy) also did not consult with the Parkland Emergency room doctors who initially treated Kennedy. Dr.

Michael Baden later said JFK had a usual hospital autopsy, not a forensic one. Bobby Kennedy kept calling the autopsy room telling them to hurry. After the autopsy, JFK's brain was given to Bobby Kennedy.

Sylvia Maegher, in her outstanding book rebutting the Warren Commission's work product, wrote in 1967, "The medical conclusions of the Warren Commission are "a wealth of discrepancies, distortions, and omissions that impels one to conclude that the official autopsy is unreliable; that the description of the President's wounds is inaccurate; that the single-bullet theory is wholly unsupported by and in conflict with the evidence; that this theory represents an attempt to salvage the case against Lee Harvey Oswald as a lone assassin; that the conclusions in the Warren Report on the source, number, and perpetrators of the shots are completely invalid; and that the evidence in fact constitutes proof of conspiracy. (68)

The original autopsy report (69) appears in Appendix IX of the Warren Report. The Chief autopsy surgeon was Commander J.J. Humes, U.S Navy. For those readers interested in the minutia of the autopsy are encouraged to read -- among other reports --- Chapter 5, The Autopsy and Medical Findings, in Sylvia Maegher's book, "Accessories After the Fact", 1967, and/or Chapter 2, The Science of Conspiracy, in Anthony Summers book, "Conspiracy", 1991.

The legendary columnist, Jimmy Breslin, chronicled the story of doctors attending President Kennedy at Parkland Hospital. His story, written the day of the assassination, is about the emergency room surgeons attending the President, primarily Dr. Malcolm Perry. The story is titled, "A Death in Emergency Room One". It appeared in many newspapers the following days including the Miami News. (70)

Jimmy Breslin found that the Dallas Parkland Hospital doctors who provided the emergency treatment to President Kennedy to be open and transparent in their discussion of the treatment provided. Contrast their actions and statements to the Navy hospital autopsy personnel in Washington. The Navy physicians that performed the autopsy and reported their findings were roundly criticized by pathologists around the country as being inept. One particular fact emerged from the Assassination Records Review Board (AARB) in the 1990's that says it all. The Board, created by Congress in 1992, took depositions from nine of the original team of Navy doctors who participated in the autopsy and reported in 1997, that their were two brain autopsies, one after the President was interred into a 3,000 pound sealed casket.

The medical panel of the House of Representatives investigation (HSCA) declared that the fatal shot which struck Kennedy's skull was mis-measured by the autopsy team by about four inches which led to a confused conclusion as to the direction of the fatal shot. (71)

However, the Warren Commission failed to question Dr. George Burkley, JFK's personal physician at all. Dr. Burkley, (Kennedy's personal physician) was present during the Navy autopsy, was the doctor who signed the death certificate and verified the autopsy reports.

An exam of the brain following a fatal head shot is extremely important to any forensic investigation - damage, direction of the projectile, etc. However, in the Doug Horne report, (Assassination Records Review Board's staff investigator) dated June 2, 1998, the conclusion that the brain examination Drs. Hume and Boswell (Navy doctors) testified to the Warren Commission took place on the Monday morning of the funeral (November 25, 1963). The exam was hurried as Doctor Burkley (a Navy Admiral) had been instructed by President Kennedy's brother, Robert Kennedy, to quickly retrieve the brain so it could be interred with the President's body that same Monday afternoon.

The AARB took depositions from Doctor Humes who related that the brain exam did take place on Monday, the 25th. However, Doctor Pierre Finck testified that he was called on November 29th by Dr. Humes to participate with Drs. Humes and Boswell to exam JFK's brain. The photos taken of the brain exam of November 29th by a Navy photographer are now in the National Archives. The photographer of the brain exam on November 25th, John Stringer, testified that the National Archives' photos are not the ones he took and this was the opinion also of the person who developed Stringer's photos. (72)

The conclusion is that the brain exam report and photos in the National Archives, allegedly to be that of President Kennedy, are in fact the photos of a brain exam of some other unidentified person. Mr.Horne's full 32 page report on this issue may be read on the Internet at www.archives. gov/medical/jfk. (73)

The clear observations Dr. Perry related to Jimmy Breslin and other journalists that day, far exceeds all the subsequent 'expert opinions' from doctors and writers all over the country, then and through the years who were not present when the body was being worked on.

The President's body was observed with, "a wound in the neck was small and neat" - an entry wound. As the Zapruder film and other evidence confirmed, that the first shot Kennedy received was indeed at a time when the JFK limo was well past the school book window where it was claimed that the fatal shots were fired from. Common sense tells us that, despite the Arlen Spector spin story, that this fact is the 'smoking gun' evidence that Kennedy was hit by at least one shot "from the front". The obvious conclusion would be that there were at least two shooters, thus a "conspiracy".

Dr. Perry's observations were backed up by many of the Parkland Hospital (Dallas) emergency room doctors, including Doctors Jones, Peters, Carrico, McClelland and Crenshaw. It was Dr. Crenshaw observation that "one of the bullets entered JFK's throat from the right front while a second bullet entered his head from the side", consistent with a shot fired from the grassy knoll area. "I believe without question there were shots that came from the side, the grassy knoll". (74)

The small wound reported by the autopsy doctors in the back of the head could not have been fired by the Mannlicher-Carcano military rifle. Hardened 6.5 military jacketed rounds fired from behind would have penetrated his skull and exited through the front of his face or eye socket, it would have blown Kennedy's face off. It would be more consistent to have been from a 5.6 mm round fired by a weapon like an AR 15. (75)

A small 6 mm diameter bullet entrance wound was found in the rear of Kennedy's head. A second wound occurred in the posterior back at about the level of the third thoracic vertebra - no bullet was located.

Navy Captain (Later Admiral) Dr. David Oscorne told a congressional investigator that he saw "an intact bullet rolls...onto the autopsy table, when Kennedy was taken out of the casket. The bullet was later taken by the Secret Service. The story was corroborated by Jerrol Custer, the x-ray technician, who recalled that "a pretty good size bullet" fell out of Kennedy's back. (76)

Dr. Cyril Wecht, former head of the American Academy of Forensic Sciences has stated: "You must remember, Humes and Boswell (the Navy doctors who performed the Bethesda autopsy) had never done medical-legal autopsies in their career. It was really inept".

FLAWED LINEUPS

A police lineup is a process by which a crime victim or witness's putative identification of a suspect is confirmed to a level that can count as evidence in court. The Warren Commission concluded that the Oswald lineups "The Commission is satisfied that the lineups were 'conducted fairly'. (LOL)

Lee Oswald was placed in four different lineups over two days, November 22nd and 23rd, 1963, after being arrested in the afternoon of the 22nd in the Texas Theater. To be admissible in court, the lineups must conducted fairly and that fairness must be proved in court. The police may not say or do anything that persuades the witness to identify the suspect that they prefer. This includes loading the lineup with people who look dissimilar to the suspect.

LINEUP #1- Conducted by Detective Jim Leavelle at 4:35 PM on the 22nd at the Dallas police station. The lineup was organized for witness Helen Markham, a witness in the Officer Tippit murder. Only four individuals were in the lineup with numbers identifying them. Two Vice squad detectives and one jail clerk were selected to be the 'fillers' as well as Lee Oswald himself.

Detective William Perry, 34, Vice Division, Dallas police department. Perry was described as 5-11, 150, with brown hair and with a dark complexion.

Wearing a brown sports coat Detective Richard Clark, 31, Vice Division, Dallas police department. Clark was described as 5-11, 177, blond hair, with a ruddy complexion, wearing a white short sleeve shirt and a red vest.

Jail Clerk Don Ables, 26, Dallas City Jail employee Ables was described as 5-9, 165, with dark hair and a ruddy complexion. Wearing a white shirt and grey knit sweater.

Captain Fritz, the homicide commander had personally contacted the Vice Division for 'fillers' as he was afraid that the usual practice of using prisoners might create a danger to suspect Oswald. However, prisoners were used the Lineup #3 and #4. The 'fillers' were neat and clean but Oswald had a large bruise on his face and a hole in his shirt elbow and none of the three were very close in physical appearance to Oswald.

Mrs. Markham was very upset and crying and the detectives had to administer ammonia inhalants to her because they were of the opinion she was going to faint before the lineup was completed. Mrs. Markham later testified to the Warren Commission that "When I saw this man I was not sure, and they kept asking me 'which one', which one'.

LINEUP #2, conducted at 6:30 PM on Friday by Detective Leavelle, had the same four men in the lineup as the #1 lineup. This lineup was conducted for witness McWatters, the bus driver on the JFK case, and Callaway and Guinyard, witnesses in the Tippit case. All three witnesses were together in the line up room during the procedure. It is normal police practice to have only one witness at a time view a lineup. This was not done in this case. In this lineup, there were witnesses from two different cases, not a usual routine. Two of the witnesses were employer and employee. Callaway was the operator of a used car lot and Guinyard was a black porter working for Callaway, and of course, Guinyard followed his boss's identification of Oswald.

LINEUP #3 was held at about 9:00 PM and was conducted by Detective Sims for Barbara and Virginia Davis, witnesses on the Tippit case. Both were sitting together with a detective during the procedure and both provided an identification of Oswald. The three fillers used were prisoners Richard Borchgardt and Ellis Brazel.

And the jail clerk Abels.

LINEUP #4

This lineup was conducted by Detective Leavelle on Saturday afternoon, the 23rd, in order to show witness Scoggins and Whaley. Whaley was the taxi driver who drove Oswald home prior to the Tippit murder and Scoggins, also as taxi driver, was a Tippit witness. The three men used as fillers were prisoners John Horne, 17, and David Knapp, 17 as well as Daniel Lujan, a 26 year old Mexican.

Witness Whaley later said it was an easy identification of Oswald as he was fussing and arguing with the detectives and complaining about the unfairness of the lineup.

It was also noted that Oswald's photo had been printed in the morning editions of the Dallas newspapers that day and he had already been shown on local television.

There was no stenographic or electronic recording of any of these four lineups nor were there official photographs taken of each one, or reports by the lineup administrators, Detectives Leavelle and Sims.

There is one witness on the JFK case, a Howard Brennan, who claimed he clearly seen a man in the TSBD window during the JFK killing resembling Oswald, that may have been shown a lineup but no records exist that he did and questions to Captain Fritz by the Commission did not get a clear answer. It is still not known if Brennan was or was not able to view a lineup that contained Oswald. However, buried in the Commission files was a note on this subject; "he (Brennan) identified Oswald as the person in the lineup who bore the closest resemblance to the man in the window but he said he was unable to make a positive identification. (77)

There was no other documentation on Mr. Brennan viewing a Oswald lineup found in the Warren Commission reports or exhibits.

RAPID SOLVING OF CRIME

After the JFK slaying, the country and the author moved on after a while, albeit sadder and less optimistic about the future. But, we all had our own life to live. I was amazed however, that the FBI and President Johnson claimed within twenty-four hours, that the suspect, Lee Harvey Oswald, now dead, was the sole participant in this horrendous act. Twenty-four hours! No conspiracy! As a young police officer (and news junkie) with three years of police service, I was aware that, even in local smoking gun homicides, the solving of a case in one day was quite unusual. Of course, back during that time, most Americans had a very high regard for government authorities, especially the Federal Bureau of Investigation. (FBI).

Among the many leads not followed up as they would definitely indicate a conspiracy was the "Rambling Rose Lady". On the night of November 20th, near Eunice, Louisiana, Lieutenant Frances Frunge of the Louisiana State Police picked up an injured woman from the roadway and brought her to a hospital in Jackson, Louisiana. Her name was Rose Chermie, and she was a prostitute and a heroin addict. She told Lt. Frunge that she was on a drug run from Miami to Houston with two Italian-looking men. At a roadside bar she got drunk and was abandoned by her companions and was hit by an auto as she was hitch-hiking.

She informed Frunge that the two men were heading to Dallas after stopping in Houston and that they were going to kill Kennedy on the 22nd. She advised the police lieutenant that "word was out in the underworld that Kennedy would be killed". On hearing of the assassination two days later, Frunge went to the hospital and found that Chermie had told several nurses and two doctors the previous day that Kennedy would be killed the following day in Dallas. Frunge's account was confirmed by the nurses and by Dr. Bowers and Dr. Victor Weiss.

Frunge had his boss, Colonel Morgan, calls Captain Fritz in Dallas and provided this information. Captain Fritz said he was not interested as they had "got their man".

Again, Captain Fritz missed the boat by "blowing off" a possible good lead that might have showed the conspiracy during the first days of the investigation. Who were these two Latin men? Was Eladio Del Valle one of them?

OSWALD MISSING

After a roll call of employees by Mr. Roy Tully, at about 1:40 PM on the day of the shooting, it was reported that Lee Oswald was among the missing employees from the building. Captain Fritz informed two detectives to head out to Oswald's listed home address in Irving, Texas and attempt to contact him. Fritz was then notified that a suspect with that name had been arrested at the Texas theatre twenty minutes ago and was now sitting handcuffed in the Homicide office.

Oswald had attempted to discharge a weapon, a revolver, at Officer McDonald, in the theatre and did in fact punch the officer as he was being confronted and arrested in connection with the murder of Officer Tippit. (Details in later chapter)

NO PROBABLE CAUSE YET- JFK Case

The purpose of the author in providing this brief description of the crime is to make the point - at this time on Friday - the Dallas P.D. did not have sufficient evidence on Oswald to arrest him for the murder of President Kennedy. It certainly appears that Oswald did in fact resist arrest at the Texas theatre, so Dallas police assumed that he did in fact shoot Tippet. Then, if he in fact did shoot Tippit, then he must have, in their opinion, certainly have shot President Kennedy and Gov. Connolly. We must look much deeper before affirming Dallas P.D.'s quick conclusion.

As all of us have seen countless videos of Dealey Square on that fateful day, we acknowledge the presence of hundreds of bystanders and police officers who were watching the presidential motorcade on that nice Friday afternoon. Numerous bystanders also had cameras. Special note will be made of the cameras used by Nix, Moreland, Muchmore, and Zapruder bystanders.

A reading of the Warren Commission report and eyewitness testimonies and affidavits indicate an initial surge of witnesses toward or onto the 'grassy knoll'. This surge contained several Dallas police officers and approximately 20 to 30 deputy sheriffs. (The Sheriff's office headquarters was across the street from the Book Depository building). Many of this group of deputies testified that the shots (at least some) came from that area - which backed up to a rail yard. One witness said she saw a puff of smoke from the fence area after she heard the shot(s), another talked with a man behind the fence who identified himself as a Secret Service agent. Still others said that they seen men behind the fence prior to the shooting.

It should be noted at this time that it has been determined that there were NO Secret Service agents on duty in the Dealey Square area that day and no agents disembarked from the motorcade. The motorcade Secret Service agents continued on to Parkland Hospital with the wounded men. The Dallas based agents were either still at Love Field, at the Trade Mart or were off duty.

Other witnesses testified that they thought that the shots came from the School Book Depository building or from the adjacent Dal-Tex building on the corner of Elm Street and Houston Street. As mentioned earlier, some witnesses observed two men in the 6th floor window, others observed one man. Several of the witnesses advised that one of the men appeared to be a Negro or Mexican. The other man was described as with light hair, slightly balding. Oswald did not fit any of these descriptions. Some of the commission witnesses testified, others submitted affidavits, and still others were not called at all. Some of these witnesses were found and questioned by news media, not by law enforcement.

PART V

OFFICER DOWN

KILLING OF OFFICER TIPPPIT

On that fateful Friday afternoon, the slaying of Officer Tippit after the JFK murder led to the apprehension of Oswald at the Texas Theater. As stated previously, if Oswald, an employee of the TSDB, was the offender in the officer's killing on East Tenth Street, then it <u>must be</u> that he was JFK's assailant, according to the official investigators.

An hour or so earlier, President John Kennedy was murdered in Dealey Square in front of hundreds of witnesses, including numerous sheriff deputies and police officers as well as members of the press. The tragic event was recorded on the Zapruder film and many other photographers captured portions of the shooting. On East 10 Street, several miles away, Officer J.D. Tippit was shot and killed by a man. There was only one direct witness (Domingo Benavides) and a distraught neighbor (Mrs. Helen Markham), who witnessed most of the shooting. Several more bystanders or neighbors observed portions of the event, including the immediate flight of Oswald from the scene.

Oswald was not living with his wife Marina Oswald at Mrs. Paine's house in Irving. Instead he was renting a room on North Beckley Street in the Oak Cliff district of Dallas. Earlene Roberts, the housekeeper at

---

the rooming house, had been alerted to the assassination by a telephone call from a friend. She immediately turned on the television at about 1:00 P.M. to watch the news. Just then lodger Oswald rushed into the home. Oswald, later admitted that he changed his clothes, armed himself with his .38 revolver, and left the home about four minutes later. He was last seen by Mrs. Roberts waiting at a bus stop. Officer Tippit, the Dallas P.D. radio log revealed, was ordered into the Oak Cliff area at 12:45 P.M. Tippit reported at 12:54 P.M. that he was in that new area as ordered. The police dispatcher attempted to raise Tippit at 1:00 P.M. but received no acknowledgement. Tippit did raise the dispatcher at 1:08 P.M., but this time, the dispatcher failed to reply.

At 1:16 P.M. a citizen, later identified as Domingo Benavides, using Tippit's radio, notified Dallas P.D. that there had been a shooting and that a police officer was down on East Tenth Street, a mile or so from Oswald's rooming house. Investigator reports indicate that Tippit came across Oswald walking down the sidewalk along Tenth Street, spoke to him and emerged from the uniform patrol car. Suddenly, the suspect pulled out a revolver and shot the officer four times. The gunman ran off scattering shell cases as he went as witnessed by several persons, especially Barbara and Virginia Davis, who lived in a home across the street from the shooting.

The author has attempted to refrain from copying police and commission statements verbatim. An exception is pertinent questions and answers that resulted from the questioning of truck driver Domingo Benavides by a counsel for the Warren Commission. Benavides is the sole person that witnessed the entire shooting of the officer. Others witnessed portions of the shooting and yet others the immediate actions of Oswald during his escape from the scene. Here is the exchange between Benavides and David Belin of the Commission.

Excerpts of the statement of Domingo Benavides taken on April 2, 1964 in Dallas by Mr. David Belin, assistant counsel of the President's Commission. (78)

Q- Will you state your name for reporter, please?

A-Domingo Benavides

Q-How old are you?

A-26

Q-How long were you in the Navy?

A-Three years

Q-Who do you work for now?

A- Mr. Harris at Dootch Motors

Q-How long have you been working for them?

A-Off and on for 3 years

Q-November 22, 1963, anything unusual happen that day?

A- Yes sir.

Q-I had lunch, and then this man stalled this car in the middle of the street and asked me if I would fix it. Something was wrong with the carburetor or pump that had broken in it, and I went around to the parts house to get the part for it.

Q-Where was this car?

A- Well, on Patton Street

Q- Patton and what?

A- Between Jefferson and 10th

Q-About what time was this?

A-I imagine it was about 1 o'clock. It was after lunch. I had already eaten.

Q-What did you do? You were going to get a carburetor part, so what did you do?

A-I was in a rush and I ran off and forgot the number of the carburetor.

Q-You forgot the number of the carburetor?

A-Then I circled back. I left down the alley.

Q-Which alley is this?

A-The one directly between 10th and Patton and Jefferson Street.

Q-It runs parallel to 10th and Jefferson and it runs, the alley would run east of Patton?

A-Yes sir

Q-All right. The alley runs right behind Dootch Motors there?

A-Yes sir

Q-What kind of vehicle were you driving?

A-1958 pickup truck Chevrolet

Q-All right, what route did you take? Were you headed east or west in the alley?

A-East

Q-to what?

A-To Denver Street.

Q-Which is the next street over from Patton?

A-I turned right, which is east on 10th. Wait, Denver would be north, I imagine. I turned from the alley north on Denver.

Q-All right.

A-And East on 10th

Q-Then you turned east on ---

A-The parts house sets on Marsalis and 10th

Q-Marsalis and 10th?

A-Yes; so I got almost up to the parts house and I thought about the number, so I was going to go back and get the number off the carburetor. I turned in a drive and turned around and started back.

Q-On what street?

A-on 10th Street

Q-On East 10th?

A-I was going west on 10th Street

Q-All right

A- Then I got almost to the corner when I seen the policeman. I first seen the car up there.

Q-Now, you say you got almost to a corner. What corner was that?

A-At Denver and 10th.

Q-You almost got to Denver and 10th heading west on 10 Street when you saw something?

A-I saw this police car.

Q-You saw a police car?

A-Yes sir

Q-Where was the police car?

A-It was sitting about 4 or 5 feet from the curb and down about 2 houses from the corner of Patton Street.

Q-All right. Was it between Patton and Denver?

A-Yes sir

Q-On what side of East 10th Street, north or south?

A-On the south side.

Q-What direction was it headed?

A-It was headed east.

Q-What did you see then?

A-I then pulled on up and I seen this officer standing by the door. The door was open to the car, and I was pretty close to him, and I seen Oswald, or the man that shot him, standing on the other side of the car.

Q-All right. Did you see the officer as he was getting out of the car?

A-No: I seen as he was, well, he had his hand on the door and kind of of in a hurry to get out, it seemed like.

Q-Had he already gotten out of the car?

A-He had already gotten around.

Q-Where did you see the other man?

A-The other man was standing to the right side of the car. (riders side of the car), and was standing right in front of the windshield on the right front fender. And then I heard the shot. Actually I wasn't looking for anything like that, so I heard the shot, and I just turned into the curb. Looked around to miss a car, I think. And then I pulled up to the curb, hitting the curb, and I ducked down, and then I heard two more shots.

Q-How many shots did you hear all told?

A-I heard three shots.

Q-You heard three shots?

A-Yes sir

Q-Where were you when your vehicle stopped?

A-About 15 foot, just directly across the street and maybe a car length away from the police car.

Q-Would you have been a car length to the east or a car length to the west of the police car?

A-East of the front side of it.

Q-So your vehicle wouldn't have quite gotten up to where the Police car was?

A-No; it didn't

Q-How fast were you going when you watch the policeman getting out of his car?

A-Oh, I imagine not maybe 25 mile an hour. I never did pay much attention to it.

Q-You say you stopped the car right away? Your vehicle, I mean?

A-Yes sir. I just didn't exactly stop because I just pulled it into the curb.

Q-Then you say you heard a shot and you then ducked?

A-Yes. No; I heard the shot before I pulled in.

Q-Oh, I see. You heard the shot and pulled in and then what?

A-Then I ducked down.

Q-Then what happened?

A-Then I heard the other two shots and I looked up and the Policeman was in, he seemed like he kind of stumbled and fell.

Q-Did you see the Policeman as he fell?

A-Yes sir

Q-What else did you see?

A-Then I seen the man turn and walk back to the sidewalk and go on the sidewalk and he walked maybe 5 foot and then kind of stalled. He didn't exactly stop. And he threw one shell and must have took five or six more steps and threw the other shell out, and then he kind of stepped up to a pretty good trot going around the corner.

Q-You saw the man going around the corner headed in what direction on what street?

A-On Patton Street. He was going south.

(skipping the next directional questions)

Q-Now, the first time that you saw him, what was his position?

A-He was standing, the first time I saw him. The man that shot him.

Q-yes

A-He was standing like I say, on the center in front of the windshield, right directly on the right front fender of the car.

Q-He was not moving when you saw him?

A-No; he wasn't moving then.

Q-All right, after you saw him turn around the corner, what did you do?

A-After that, I set there for just a few minutes to kind of, I thought he went in back of the house or something. At the time, I thought maybe he might have lived in there and I didn't want to get out and rush right up. He might start shooting again. That is when I got out of the truck and walked over to the Policeman, and was lying there and he had, looked like a big clot of blood coming out of his head, and his eyes were sunk back in his head, and just kind of made me feel real funny. I guess I was really scared.

Q-Did the Policeman say any thing?

A-The Policeman, I believe was dead when he hit the ground, because he didn't put his hand out or nothing.

Q-Where was the Policeman as he fell, as you saw him?

A-I saw him as he was falling. The door was about half way open, and he was right in front of the door, and just about in front of the fender. I would say he was between the door and the front headlight, about middle way when he started to fall.

Q- Did you notice where the gun of the policeman was?

A-The gun was in his hand and he was partially lying on his gun in his right hand. He was partially lying on his gun and on his hand, too.

Q-Then what did you do?

A-Then I don't know if I opened the car door back further than what it was or not, but anyway, I went in and pulled the radio and I mashed the button and told them that an officer had been shot, and I didn't get an answer, so I said it again, and this guy asked me whereabouts all of a sudden, and I said, on 10ᵗʰ Street. I couldn't remember where it was at the time. So I looked up and I seen this number and I said 410 East 10ᵗʰ.

(other people arriving) (Benavides said he left scene for a few minutes and then returned)

Q-When you went back, what did you do?

A-Well, I started - I seen him throw the shells and I started to stop and pick them up, and I thought I'd better not so when I came back, after I had gotten back, I picked up the shells.

(Benavides seen man discarding the shells as he cut across the Davis ladies yard. He picked them up with a stick and placed them in a cigarette pack wrapper and later gave them to Dallas Police Officer Poe)

Benavides described the man as 5-10 to 5-11, wearing a light beige jacket with zipper, Dark pants, dark shirt, a little darker than average complexion (a white male) Average weight.

Q-When the officers came out there, did you tell them what you had seen?

A- No Sir

Q-What did you do?

A-I left right after. I gave the shells to the officer. I turned around and went back and we returned to work.

Benavides was contacted by two officers later about 4 P.M. and asked him if he could identify the man. He told them "I said I don't think I could (identify the man) I wasn't sure that I could or not. I wasn't going to say I could identify and go down and couldn't have".

Q-Did he ever take you to the police station and ask you if you could identify him?

A-No, they didn't.

Q- You used the name Oswald. How did you know this man was Oswald?

A-From the pictures I had seen. It looked like a guy, resembled the guy. That was the reason I figured it was Oswald.

(Benavides was joined at the police car by Ted Callaway, general manager of the used car lot around the corner, whom Benavides knew. We will pick up the story from Mrs. Markham, Ted Callaway and the other witnesses.

Helen Markham, a waitress who lived across the street, was supposedly the only other witness to see most of the shooting. Some of her statements were later proved confusing and untrue. The man in a pick-up truck (Benavides) claimed that the officer appeared dead instantly although Mrs. Markham said she talked to the officer for several minutes. She claimed it was 20 minutes before help came but this information was debunked by the other witnesses and police dispatch logs which indicated that an ambulance arrived within three minutes. In 1964, a senior counsel for the Warren Commission stated that Mrs. Markham testimony was "full of mistakes, "utterly unreliable" and characterized her as "an utter screwball".

The line-up conducted at the police department for these Tippit witnesses was quite controversial, with some identifying Oswald and others not. Some of these citizens said that, due to age and dress, it was easy to select Oswald. Four revolver cartridges were produced as evidence from the scene and Oswald was found to have a .38 revolver when arrested at the theater. Ballistics indicated that the four spent shells found had come from Oswald's gun, although there was much uncertainty about this fact in later reports. Three of the shells were of the 'Western-Winchester' type and one was a 'Remington-Peters' type. There seemed to be confusion about the finding and type of spent cartridges found. Only one bullet was handed over to the FBI that night for processing at the federal crime lab in Washington. Four months later, the remaining three shells were found in the Dallas crime lab and forwarded to Washington. (79)

A Mrs. Acquilla Clemons advised that she had seen two men near Tippit's patrol car just before the shooting. She said the man with the gun was "kind of chunky ---kind of heavy', a description that did not match Oswald. Clemons advised that the man with the gun called out to the other man, "Go on". This other man was described as thin and tall, like Oswald's description. Frank Wright, a neighbor, seen a man standing in front of the car- did not see a gun-- who ran around and entered a little grey car, possibly a 1950-51 Plymouth coupe, and drove rapidly away. T.F. Bowley came on the scene at 1:10 p.m. according to his watch. Domingo Benavides, who was the citizen who called in over the police radio at 1:10 P.M., advised that he crouched a few minutes in his pick-up after the shooting before making that call as he feared the offender was still in the area. Taxi driver William Scoggins said the man leaving the scene was walking west when Tippit approached. (West was back toward Oswald's rooming house). A soldier on leave, Jim Burt, noticed a man walking west on the sidewalk just prior to when the officer was shot. Burt said the man ran away after the shooting. Many contradictions exist on these citizen accounts, especially from Mrs. Markham.

Anthony Summers, in his "Conspiracy" book stated, "Either Oswald traveled to a point beyond the Tippit scene by some form of transportation or conceivably, Tippit's killer was not Oswald". (111) The Dallas County Assistant District Attorney Wade believes Oswald played the leading part in the Tippit murder, on the strength of ballistic evidence, but doubts he acted alone. He asks," Why was Oswald where he was when he shot Tippit"? Many of the researchers of the assassination state that the evidence against Oswald in the Tippit murder is "shaky".

We will examine the reported circumstances of the murder of Officer Tippit and the subsequent arrest of Oswald at the movie house. Officer J.D. Tippit, a ten year veteran on the Dallas P.D., was assigned to the uniformed patrol division but had no presidential motorcade assignments that day. Reports indicate, without rebuttal, that he was a devoted family man and a church-goer.

It has been determined that Oswald left the TSDB after the contact with the motor officer, boarded a bus, which then became stuck in traffic. He left the bus and hailed a taxi for a ninety-five cent ride to area of his rooming house at 1021 North Beckley Avenue in the Oak Cliff section of Dallas. He changed clothes quickly, about 3or 4 minutes, picking up his revolver and left the house. He was noticed by housekeeper, Earlene Roberts, who noted the time just prior to 1:00 P.M. Mrs. Roberts last seen Oswald waiting at a bus stop at about 1:03 or 1:04 PM. He was next allegedly noticed at the scene of the Tippit shooting at either as early as 1:07 P.M. or at 1:15 P.M. (two separate witnesses). The exact time of the Tippit shooting is of great importance in light of Oswald's alleged timetable, after the JFK murder. A citizen's call came over the Dallas police radio at 1:16 P.M. notifying that the police officer had been shot. It should be noted that Tippit attempted to raise the dispatcher at 1:10 P.M. but was not acknowledged.

Officer Tippit was killed after he emerged from his marked patrol car to engage a white male pedestrian. The suspect fired four shots, instantly killing the officer. The suspect was then noticed walking swiftly away from the scene. Another witness advised that two men were present when the shooting occurred with one walking away and the other driving away in an auto, a Plymouth coupe. We will now examine Tippit's murder in more detail:

Dallas police officer, J.D. Tippit, 39, had been on the force for eleven years and was earning $5,880 annually, supplemented by an off-duty job at Austin's BBQ restaurant. At the time of his death Tippit was assigned to a one-man uniformed police patrol vehicle (car #10) on the day shift, with an assignment to Patrol Area #78, in the residential south Oak Cliff section of Dallas. He had no specific assigned duties in connection with the presidential visit that day. Shortly after the JFK shooting, Tippit was notified at 12:45 P.M. to move to the central Oak Cliff area to cover for other patrol cars that had been diverted to the school depository building where the JFK shooting had taken place. At 12:54 P.M. Tippit advised the dispatcher that he had arrived in that new area.

According to the Warren Commission account, Tippit was patrolling slowly eastward on East 10th Avenue about 100 feet past the intersection of Patton Avenue and 10th Street. He pulled aside a man walking on the sidewalk who was of the general description of what the police radio bulletin had previously been issued for the suspect in the JFK shooting. The man walked over to the passenger side of the patrol car and appeared to be having a conversation with Officer Tippit through the open vent window of the patrol car. Tippit opened the driver's door and slowly emerged from the car and walked toward the front. At this time the man drew a revolver and fired three shots at the officer, striking Tippit in the chest area. The officer fell to the ground and the man walked up to his fallen body and fired one more shot to the officer's head, then walked away.

PRIOR MOVEMENT OF TIPPIT

7:00 A.M. - Came on duty for regular patrol. No motorcade assignment.

7:00 - 1030 A.M. Routine calls

10:30 A.M. - Tippit met fellow officer Bill Anglin for a coffee/tea break at the Rebel Drive Inn, Ledbetter Drive and South Loop 12

10:40 - 1045 AM - Out of the car for a few minutes, Annaber & Corrigan Ave

1120 - 1150 A.M. - Not clear, but indication he had lunch at his home, 238 Glencairn.

Not on Signal 5 (lunch) but his wife confirmed.

11:50 AM - Announced "Clear"

12:17 PM - Out at 4100 block Bonnie View Dr - No report made

12:30 PM - Announced "Clear" (same time as downtown JFK shooting at TSBD)

12:45 PM - Advised to move into central Oak Cliff area. He answered and advised he was at Keist and Bonnie View.

Dispatcher Officer Murray Jackson (friend of Tippit) advised Unit 87 and 78 to move their patrol over to central Oak Cliff area.

12:54 PM - Tippit announced he was in Oak Cliff, at Lancaster and Eight St.

12:54 - 1:00 PM - Tippit was seen sitting his squad car in the GLOCO gas station parking lot for about ten minutes, at 1502 Zangs Blvd. He then left "tearing down Lancaster at high speed" (this location was 1.5 miles from TSBD)

1:00 PM- 1:02 - Tippit went into the Top Ten Record Shop, at West Jefferson and Bishop, and asked to use the telephone. (away from the car radio) He was on telephone for only a few seconds - obviously getting no answer from the party he was calling) and left in a hurry, according to clerk Louis Cortinas, 18, and the owner, Dub Stark. In a 1981 interview with reporter Golz (Dallas Morning Newsman), Cortinas said that Tippit "tried to make a phone call, then left speeding across Jefferson, down Bishop, to Sunset, where he turned right".

1:08 PM - Tippit tried to raise the dispatcher twice with no avail. (Others that heard this tape say it was unit #488, not #78, that was trying to get on the radio)

1:10 PM - Near corner of Patton and 10th Street. 6/10th of a mile from the Record Shop, which was the scene where Tippit encountered the suspect and was shot dead.

PRE-SHOOTING WITNESS

Taxi cab driver Whaley dropped Oswald off near the corner of Beckley and Neely, about three blocks from Oswald's rooming house. Mrs. Earlene Roberts, housekeeper at Oswald's rooming house, seen him arrive.

Oswald was not living with his wife Marina at Mrs. Paine's house in Irving, but was renting a room on North Beckley Street in the Oak Cliff district of Dallas. As related above, Earlene Roberts, housekeeper at the rooming house, had been alerted to the assassination by a telephone call from a friend. She immediately turned on the television at 1:00 P.M. to watch the news. Just then her lodger Oswald rushed into the home. Oswald, later admitted, said that he changed his clothes, armed himself with his .38 revolver, and left the home four or five minutes later. He was last seen by Mrs. Earlene Roberts waiting at a bus stop at Beckley and Zangs, one mile from the theater.

Mrs. Roberts claimed a uniform police car tooted the horn in front of the house while Oswald was changing - sort of a signal. She made this claim a week later, but her boss, Mrs. Gladys Johnson, the owner of Oswald's rooming house, advised authorities that Mrs. Roberts was inclined to make up stories. It was proven that Officer Tippit was elsewhere when this 'horn tooting" occurred.

WITNESSES AT TIPPIT SCENE

Mrs. Helen Markham, a waitress, was interviewed at the Warren Commission on March 26, 1964. She stated, "I seen the police car stop alongside the man. I saw the man come over to the car very slowly, leaned and put his arms over the window and looked in the window....drew back about 2 steps. The officer opened his door, very slowly, and calmly crawled out of the car, walked to the front of the car and heard three shots. Tippit fell to the ground. The man walked calmly, fooling with his gun, and walked back to Patton Avenue....did not run, and then started to trot."

Mrs. Markham, who lived across the street from this scene, seen the shooting, observed the suspect walking away "fooling with his gun". She advised that it was twenty minutes before help arrived and that she was talking to the officer. This was proved untrue as it was determined that the officer was killed instantly and that an ambulance arrived on the scene within three minutes.

Mrs. Markham observed a police line-up later that day and did not recognize any one, then, after prompting, she said "I recognize #2 (Oswald). I wasn't sure, but had cold chills. He had a jacket on at the time of the shooting, a grayish tan color one". Markham claimed the suspect approached Tippit from the west, although others claimed it was from the east. Two witnesses and a photo indicated that Tippit's passenger side window was closed. Mrs. Markham said Tippit tried to talk to her, but others said he died instantly. She said that she was with Tippit for 20 minutes before help arrived and she was alone with him although other witnesses said the ambulance came within three minutes and that a crowd of about 150 people had gathered rather quickly. The other witnesses, arriving police officials, and the police conducting the line-up advised that Mrs. Markham was hysterical and crying.

In January of 1994, Joe Ball, senior Warren Commission counsel, stated that Mrs. Markham's testimony was "full of mistakes" and referred to her an "utter screwball". He dismissed her as "utterly unreliable".

Mrs. Markham was a terrified, hysterical witness, both at the crime scene and at the lineup. She stated six times that she could not recognize anyone at the lineup until prompted by counsel Joe Ball," Was there a #2 man in there? She replied "Number 2 is the one I picked.....When I saw this man I wasn't sure, but I had cold chills run all over me".

Another neighbor, Barbara Davis and her sister-in-law, Virginia Davis, heard the shots and seen the suspect crossing their lawn, shaking the empty shells from the handgun. The Davis ladies later found two of the shells and turned them over to arriving police officers. Barbara, twenty-two years old, and her sister-in-law, sixteen year old Virginia Davis, witnesses the aftermath of the Tippit shooting from their home located on the corner of 10th Street and Patton Avenue. They heard the gun shots and seen a man "unloading his gun" as he crossed their yard at the corner of Tenth and Patton. Barbara gave testimony to the Warren Commission in 1964. She said "Mrs. Markham was standing across the street over there, and she was standing over there and the man was coming across the yard. Mrs. Markham was screaming and pointing at him, and he was, I thought, was emptying the gun. He looked at her (Mrs. Markham) first and looked at me then smiled and went around the corner." He was walking a normal pace. The suspect had cut across the yard and went onto the sidewalk. She described the man as 23 or 24 years old, white, slender, medium height, light completed, with either dark brown or black hair, wearing dark trousers and a light colored shirt, with a dark coat over it. She then returned to her home and telephoned the police department.

Barbara Davis found one of the discarded spent bullet shells in her yard and his sister-in-law Virginia Davis found another later that day, and turned them over to Dallas police. Barbara and Virginia attended a line-up about 8:00 P.M. on the same day and positively identified Oswald as the shooter.

Virginia Davis lived in an apartment building at 400 E. 10th Street with her sister-in-law Barbara Davis and their family. The Tippit crime scene was right in front of their home, near the intersection of Patton Avenue and 10th Street. She states she was in the living room with her sister when she heard two gunshots. She could hear Mrs. Markham, a neighbor, so she and her sister ran out the front door. She seen Mrs. Markham as she screamed, "He shot him. He is dead. Call the police." We then saw a man cut across her lawn emptying the shells from his small gun, holding the gun in the right hand. The man was about 20, with light brown hair, slim build, wearing a light brown jacket and black trousers. I didn't take note of his shirt. The man was walking toward Patton Avenue. He was about three feet off the sidewalk on the lawn". She and her sister ran back into the house and Barbara Davis called the police. They went back outside and observed the officer lying on the ground next to the police car. A crowd gathered quickly and arriving police units began searching the area. The ambulance had arrived and left prior to the police units arrival.

The two Davis ladies were taken to the police station about 5:30 PM that day for a lineup, which they viewed together. Virginia identified lineup subject #2 - which was Oswald. She advised she was positive it was the same man she had seen in front of her house today walking across her lawn after the shots were fired. (80)

Witness T.F. Bowley had just picked up his daughter at school and was headed north on Marsalis and turned west on 10th Street. "I traveled about a block and noticed a Dallas police squad stopped in the traffic lane headed east on 10th Street. I saw a police officer lying next to the left front wheel. I stopped my car and got out to go to the scene. I looked at my watch and it said 1:10 P.M. Several people were at the scene. When I got there the first thing I did was try to help the officer. He appeared beyond help to me. A man was trying to use the radio in the squad car but stated he didn't know how to operate it. I knew how and took the radio from him. I said, Hello, operator. A police officer has been shot here. The dispatcher asked for the location. I found out the location and told the dispatcher what it was".

The call went out over the police radio at 1:16 PM that an officer had been shot. Before the arrival of the first police unit, an ambulance arrived from the Dudley Funeral Home, occupied by Clayton Butler and Eddie Kinsley, and removed Office Tippit's body to the hospital. Bowley helped load the officer onto the stretcher and into the ambulance. Bowley said, "As we picked the officer up, I noticed his pistol lying on the ground under him. Someone picked the pistol up and laid it on the hood of the squad car. When the ambulance left, I took the gun and put it inside the squad car. A man took the pistol out and said, "Let's catch him." He opened the cylinder, and I saw that no rounds in it had been fired. This man then took the pistol with him into a taxicab and drove off. The police arrived and I talked to a police sergeant at the scene. I told him I did not witness the shooting and after questioning me, he said it was all right for me to leave. I then went to the Telephone Company office at Ninth and Zangs to pick up my wife". (81) Witness William Scoggins, eating his lunch in his parked taxi, noticed a man and the approaching police car, heard shots and saw Tippit fall, then saw the man run south on Patton. The following day he picked Oswald out of a lineup, not as the killer, but as the man he had seen running past him. The suspect walked past Scoggins, within 12 feet. All witnesses claimed that they never did see Officer Tippit draw his gun.

Domingo Benavides, driving his pickup truck in the area, stopped and watched the shooting. He saw the police car and the officer getting out and apparently talking to the man toward the front of the car. The suspect then shot Tippit. "I was sitting in my truck. The man turned from the car, took a couple of steps, and was unloading the gun. He threw the empty shells in the bushes or grass on Davis's lawn".

Benavides advised that the suspect, after shooting the officer, walked away while shaking the empty bullet hulls.

This witness crouched down in his truck for a few moments to insure that the suspect had left, and then went to the officer's car and attempted to notify the police dispatcher of the shooting. He attempted to use Tippit's radio, to notified Dallas P.D. that there had been a shooting and that a police officer was down on East Tenth Street, a mile or so from Oswald's rooming house. Investigator's reports indicate that Tippit came across Oswald walking down the sidewalk along Tenth Street, spoke to him and emerged from the uniform patrol car. Suddenly, Oswald pulled a revolver out and shot the officer four times. The gunman ran off scattering shell cases as he went, which was witnessed by several persons. Benavides first said he could not identify the killer, and, incredibly, Benavides was not taken to a police lineup. When Benavides testified before the Warren Commission, he would only say that a picture of Oswald "bore a resemblance" to Tippit's killer, and he seemed to identify a dark jacket as the one the assailant had worn, whereas the Commission claimed the killer wore a light gray jacket. Only years later did Benavides make a "positive identification" of Oswald as the gunman. When Benavides was contacted a few years ago, he was hesitant to talk about the case, in part because he said he believed federal agents were monitoring his phone conversations.

Frank Wright lived across the street at 501 E. Tenth Street and heard the shots while in his home. He seen Tippit roll over and lie still. Wright seen a man standing in front of the police car, looking at the officer on the ground. He did not see the gun. Wright described the man as medium height, wearing a long coat. The man ran around the police car and got into a grey car, driving away fast.

Frank Wright statement is as follows:

"As soon as I heard the shots I went out the front door. I could see the police car in the next block, facing me. I saw a man fall down under the left fender. He didn't move anymore. Seen a man standing in front of the car, medium height, and long coat. I did not see a gun. He ran around the passenger side of the PD car and got into a grey, old coupe, maybe a 50-51 Plymouth and drove away from me, down 10th Street. I seen a woman come down from her porch, steps toward the PD car and shouts, "Oh, he's been shot". She and I were the only ones there when I got there. By the time the ambulance arrived there were about 25 people there; then the police arrived. I tried to tell two or three people what I seen but they didn't pay any attention. I've seen what came on TV and in the papers but I know that's not what happened. "I know a man drove off in a grey coupe just as clear as I was born. I know what I saw. They can say all they want to about a fellow running away, but I can't accept this because I saw a fellow get in a car and drive away".

Wright's wife said she heard the shot and seen the man lying in the road. "I ran to the telephone and dialed "O" and said, call the police, a man has been shot. After that I joined my husband outside and the ambulance arrived a minute later. The police operator took Mrs. Wright's address and connected immediately by way of a direct line to the Dudley Funeral Home, which handles ambulance calls for southern Dallas. The funeral home operator stamped the incoming call at 1:18 P.M. The funeral home was only two blocks from the scene of the shooting. The director sent employees Clayton Butler and Eddie Kinsey to the scene, siren screaming. Butler radioed his arrival time as 1:18 P.M., less than 60 seconds from the call from the police. Butler noticed about 10 persons on the scene when he arrived. He pulled the blanket away from the body and realized that the victim was a police officer. He thought the police officer was dead. On the way to the hospital he called in that a police officer was the victim. The ambulance arrived at the hospital at 1:26 P.M. Butler talked to an officer at the hospital but was not contacted by anyone after that. Mr. Wright was not contacted by any law enforcement authorities after leaving the shooting scene. About two months later, two men came to Mrs. Wright's home and talked to her briefly. They took no notes nor were any report located. They did not talk to her husband.

Mrs. Acquilla Clemons, a neighbor, told independent investigators much later that she saw two men near the police car just before the shooting. The man with the gun was 'short and heavy', wearing khaki and a white shirt. The second man was tall. The FBI talked to her after the shooting but did not take a statement due to her poor health. When questioned several years after the shooting, she stuck to her original story. Mrs. Clemons advised that she had seen two men near Tippit's patrol car just before the shooting. She said the man with the gun was "kind of chunky ---kind of heavy', a description that did not match Oswald. Clemons advised that the man with the gun called out to the other man, "Go on". This other man was described as thin and tall, similar to Oswald's description.

Mrs. Clemons, sitting on the porch across the street, claimed she saw two men during Tippit's shooting, one with a gun. It is possible that she had noted two young men who had pulled up to the scene just after the shooting.

Mrs. Clemons later advised that she was visited by an unknown apparent law enforcement officer about two days after the assassination who told her it was just as well for her not to say anything more about her observations.

Mr. Warren Reynolds testified at the Warren Commission on July 22, 1964. "Our office was up high. I heard the shots and went to the front porch. I saw man coming down the street with the gun in his hand, swinging it just like he was running. He turned the corner of Patton and Jefferson going west, and put the gun in his pants and took off walking. I heard 4 or 5 or 6 shots. The first time he was interviewed by law enforcement was on Jan 21, 1964. In talking to friends before that, he said it was Oswald. Witness Warren Reynolds was on the south side of Jefferson Boulevard east of Patton Avenue, in a used car lot. He said the man he seen was not Oswald. He was shot several weeks later and after recovering, now claimed that the man was Oswald.

Mr. Ted Callaway is a witness from the nearby used car lot. His statement on 11/22/63 follows: "I am the manager of the Used Car lot at 501 E. Jefferson. I was working today when I heard some shots. This was about 1 pm. I ran out into Patton Street and looked to see what the shooting was about. I saw a white man running South on Patton with a pistol in hand. I hollered at him and he looked around at me, and then kept on going. I rar. around on 10th Street and saw a Police officer lying in the street. He looked dead to me. I got the officer's gun and hollered at a cab driver to come on, We might catch the man. We got into his cab, number 213 and drove up Patton to Jefferson and looked all around, but did not see him. The number 2 man in the line up that I saw at City Hall is the man I saw with the gun in his hand."

Sam Guinyard, a porter at a car lot, seen the suspect running from the Tippit scene. He gave an affidavit on November 22, 1963 that reads as follows: "I worked as a porter at the used car lot at 501 E. Jefferson. Today, about 1 P.M. I heard some shooting near Patton and 10th Street. I ran out and looked. I saw a white man running south on Patton Street with a pistol in his hand. The last I of this man he was running west on Jefferson. I went around on 10th Street and saw a policeman lying in the street. He was bloody and looked dead to me. The #2 man in the lineup I saw at the city hall is the same man I saw running with the pistol in his hand". Guinyard provided an affidavit.

Another witness, William Arthur Smith, 20, was visiting at 505 E. 10th Street. He and friend Jimmy Burt were one block from Tippit shooting. He saw the suspect running and the police officer falling. He told James Markham (Mrs. Markham's son) that the suspect at the line-up had lighter hair than the suspect at the shooting, which was brownish-black hair, wearing dark pants and a sort of sports coat.

Jim Burt, an AWOL soldier living at 505 E. 10th Street, Dallas, stated in an December 16, 1963 FBI interview, that he and a friend, William Smith, were sitting in his brother's house at the corner of Ninth Street and Denver Street. They heard two gunshots and ran from the house to his car, a 1952 two-tone blue Ford, which was parked facing south on Denver Street. As they ran from the house they heard four more shots, making a total of six. Burt says he drove his car to the next intersection which is Denver and 10th Street, and turned west on 10th Street. He immediately saw a police car parked at the curb in the middle of the block. It was parked facing east on 10th Street. A police officer was lying on the street near the left front wheel. Burt later recognized him as being an officer who frequented that neighborhood. This particular officer was known by the name "Friendly" to the residents of that area.

Burt parked his car in front of the police car on the east side of the street with the front end facing the west. He and Smith jumped out of the car and as they did so looked west on 10th Street. At that moment he caught a glimpse of a man running on the sidewalk on the south side of the street. The man, at this point, had reached the intersection of 10th Street and Patton Avenue. He described this man as a white male, approximately 5-8. He was wearing a light color jacket. Burt says he could not describe the man further as he was never closer than 50-60 yards from this man. He said at one point that he did notice the man had a pistol in his right hand. Although he is familiar with hand weapons, he said because of the distance, he could not describe the pistol.

At the intersection of 10th & Patton Ave, the man ran south on Patton. Burt said he ran to 10th & Patton "when he was close enough to Patton to see the man running into an alley located between 10th and Jefferson on Patton. The man ran into the alley to the right and ------".-

Burt advised that he and Smith hung around the shooting scene for about 45 minutes but did not provide his name to the police due to his Army AWOL status. (82)

Jack Tatum was questioned on February 1, 1978, by House of Representative investigators, fifteen years after Tippet's murder. His statement follows:

"I was driving north on Denver Street and stopped at Tenth Street where I first saw the squad car and man walking on the sidewalk near the squad car. Both the squad car and the man, hands in pockets, were coming in my direction. (East on 10th Street) At the time I was just approaching the squad car, I noticed the young man with both hands in the pockets of his zippered jacket leaning over the passenger side of the squad car. The young man was looking into the squad car from the passenger side. The next thing I knew I heard something that sounded like gun shots as I approached the intersection. I went through the intersection and stopped my car and turned to look back. I saw the officer lying in the street and saw the young man standing near the front of the squad car. Next, this man with a gun in his hand ran toward the back of the squad car, but instead of running away, he stepped into the street and shot the officer who was lying in the street. At that point this young man looked around him and then started to walk away in my direction and as he started to break into a small trot running in my direction, I sped off in my auto. I saw him to the intersection and run south on Patton toward Jefferson. I did not report anything as there was more than enough people there and I did not think I could contribute anything".

Jack Tatum was the Chief Medical Photographer at Baylor University, at the time he was contacted in 1978.

Harold Russell - This information obtained from an FBI statement that Russell, an employee at Johnny Reynolds Used Car Lot, 500 Jefferson St, Dallas, gave. Russell was standing on the lot with L.J. Lewis and Pat Patterson, when they heard shots come from the vicinity of Patton and Tenth. A few seconds later they observed a young white man running south on Patton Avenue carrying a pistol or revolver which the individual was attempting to either reload or place in his belt line. Upon reaching the intersection of Patton and Jefferson, the individual stopped running and began walking at a fact pace, heading west on Jefferson. Russell advised that he and Patterson proceeded to the area of Tenth and Patton and that Lewis went into the office to call the Dallas Police.

Russell advised upon arriving at the intersection of Tenth and Patton he observed a Dallas uniform officer lying on the ground in front of a Dallas police car, and from all indication the officer was dead. Russell advised the officer's weapon was lying on the front seat of the police car. At this point an unknown individual stated to Russell, "Lets take the police officer's gun and go get the S.O.B. who is responsible for this". Russell advised he informed this guy that he would remain at the police car so he could advise the other police officers upon their arrival of the direction in which the person responsible for the shooting had gone.

Russell advised approximately five minutes later Dallas police officers arrived., at which time he informed them of the general direction in which the person responsible for the shooting had gone and also the fact that Reynolds and Patterson had attempted to follow the individual as he headed west on Jefferson Street. Russell said he gave this same info to the Dallas PD on the afternoon of Nov. 22nd. Russell advised he was not a witness to the actual shooting of the officer and could only testify to the fact that he had observed an individual whom he now knows as Lee Harvey Oswald leaving the scene. Russell positively identified a photo of Oswald, New Orleans PD #112723, taken August 9, 1963, as being identical with the individual he had observed at the scene of Officer Tippit's shooting.

Note: Harold Russell was killed by police in a bar fight in 1967

In a statement to the FBI on 1/22/1964, L. J. Lewis, 7616 Hums, Pleasant Grove, Texas, advised he is presently self-employed as a wholesale car dealer. Lewis advised that on the afternoon of November 22, 1963, he was on the used car lot of Johnny Reynolds Used Cars together with Harold Russell and Pat Patterson, during which time they heard approximately three or four gun shots coming from the vicinity of Tenth and Patton Avenue, Dallas, Texas. Approximately one minute later he observed a white male, approximately thirty years of age, running south on Patton Avenue, carrying either an automatic pistol or a revolver in his hands, and while running was either attempting to reload same or conceal the weapon in his belt line. Upon reaching the intersection of Patton Avenue and Jefferson Street, Dallas, Texas, the individual then proceeded west on Jefferson, at which time Lewis advised he went into the office of the car lot and called the Dallas Police Department to advise them of the fact that the shooting had just occurred just north of the intersection of Jefferson and Patton Avenue.

Lewis advised that Pat Patterson and Warren Reynolds attempted to follow the individual, and to the best of his knowledge, Harold Russell had gone in the direction of Tenth and Patton Avenue to determine what had happened. Lewis advised he later was informed that a Dallas uniform police officer had been shot at the intersection of Patton and Tenth Street in Dallas, and that in all probability the individual they had seen running south on Patton Avenue with a gun in his possession was the individual responsible for sane. Lewis was shown a photograph of Lee Harvey Oswald, New Orleans PD No. 112723, dated August 9, 1963, at which time Mr. Lewis advised due to the distance from which he observed the individual he would hesitate to state whether the individual as identical with Oswald.

Robert Brock, a mechanic at Roger Bellew Texaco gas station, 800 Jefferson, at about 130PM 11/22/63, observed a young white male pass him and his wife and proceeded north past the Texaco gas station into the parking lot but disappeared. About five minutes later, Warren Reynolds and another guy from Johnny Reynolds Used Car lot informed him that a police officer had been shot about 2 blocks away and that the suspect was seen turning north off Jefferson past the Texaco station.

Brock, Reynolds and some police officers searched the parking lot without finding the suspect. Brock did advise that one of the officers found a jacket under an auto on that lot that probably belonged to the suspect. Brock, shown a photo by the investigators, said he could not positively identify the picture shown him as the man that passed him the day of the Tippit shooting. Brock gave a statement to the FBI on January 22, 1964.

TIPPIT BULLETS

The House Select Committee on Assassination (HSCA) assembled a Firearms Panel. The panel concluded that all four cartridges cases found at the scene of the Tippit shooting were fired from the pistol that Oswald had in his possession when arrested in the theater.

Since Oswald's revolver (85) had been partially modified to shoot different ammo than the type it was manufactured to fire, it was not possible for the panel to determine whether the bullets that killed Tippit were fired from it. The panel did determine that the characteristics of the bullets were consistent with their having been fired from Oswald's revolver. (84)

The four cartridges found at Tippit scene were marked as Warren Commission Exhibit #CE594. The four bullets removed from Tippit at the autopsy were marked as Exhibit #CE 604- a Remington-Peters round, and Exhibits # CE602, CE603 and CE 605, manufactured by the Western Cartridge Co.

The panel was unable to conclude that the Tippit bullets were fired from Oswald's revolver, nor could they eliminate that possibility.

The HSCA Firearms Panel took note of a discrepancy between the brand of the bullets removed from Tippit's body and the brand of the cartridge cases found at the scene of the shooting. Three of the recovered bullets were Western Cartridge Co bullets and the fourth was a Remington-Peters bullet. Of the recovered cartridge cases, however, two were Remington-Peters and two were Western Cartridge.

The panel gave two possible explanations.

1- One Western Cartridge casing was not recovered and one Remington-Peters bullet missed Tippit and was not recovered.

2- One Western Cartridge casing was not recovered and one Remington-Peters bullet was in the revolver prior to the Tippit s murder.

(As he ran from the scene, the shooter was seen by the Davis sisters to be shaking out the revolver's empty cartridges onto the front yard of their home, two of which were found by witness Benavides soon after the shooting and were given to Officer Poe; and the other two were found by the Davis sisters later in the afternoon and given to Dallas police.)

The report noted that the hypotheses about the discrepancies in the physical evidence were beyond its scope of responsibility. (85)

In the realm of could of-should of-would of; if the Dallas police had noticed that brand discrepancy early on during the investigation they could have returned to the Davis home on 10th Street and searched their small front lawn with metal detectors in search of another shell casing. Instead, much of the evidence was rushed off to the FBI the evening of the assassination and not examined or analyzed correctly by Dallas authorities. So it remains unresolved.

Some assassination researchers have proffered another theory about the mixed brands of Oswald's bullets, claiming that due to two different brands of bullets in his revolver and in his pocket equated with two different shooters being involved. The author keeps his HR#218 carry permit (Active and retired national permit) active by going to the local sheriff's range annually. I recently dug into my cloth ammo bag and examined what brands the loose bullets I had accumulated over the years, any one of which could have ended up being loaded into one of my two .38 revolvers.

There were over 60 loose .38 caliber bullets in the bag that were of three brands; Super Vel, Winchester and Remington-Peters. They were of seven different types of bullets, some 110 grain, others 158 grain. Some of the bullets were lead round nose, some flat, a hollow point or two, some semi-jacked hollow point, others nickel case. One was a Winchester silver tip with a copper jacket. In the author's opinion, the carrying of different brands of cartridges by Oswald was not sinister or an indication of multiple shooters.

Another point not clear in the reports is what happened to the remaining cartridges in Oswald's revolver which he was seen 'shaking' out on the lawn in front of the Davis home on 10th Street. To unload cartridges (live or spent) from a revolver, it is only necessary to open the cylinder and press one's thumb on the ejector pin and all the cartridges will be pushed out of the revolver. It seemed remote that Oswald would hand pick spent cartridges while jogging away from the shooting scene when he had a pocket full of spares ((13 spares). Six he used to reload the revolver and five extra rounds were found in his pocket after his arrest.

POLICE ACTIVITY AT TIPPIT SCENE

Kenneth McCroy, a Dallas P.D. reserve officer and witness, gave testimony to the Warren Commission on February 21, 1964. McCroy, a police Sergeant in the Dallas police reserves since 1959, arrived on the Tippit scene after hearing the initial call on the police radio. McCroy, in uniform in his own vehicle, said he arrived on Tippit scene as they were loading Tippit into the ambulance. McCroy remembers speaking to Mrs. Markham, taxi driver Scoggins, and other witnesses. McCroy said he received Tippit's gun from Ted Callaway and turned it to the arriving police units. He also steered the shooting witnesses to the on-duty officers. He advised that he was on the scene a few minutes before other officers arrived. He did not talk to the FBI or any other agency until today. During the earlier motorcade, he on duty working at a Main Street assignment.

McCroy also was working the jail basement detail Sunday morning when Oswald was shot. (This will be covered in the Ruby section)

Officer J.M. Poe, a nine year veteran Dallas police officer, testified to the Warren Commission on April 9, 1964. Poe was assigned to Patrol Section duty with Officer L.E. Jez, on the day of the assassination. His beat was district #105 and #106 that day. When the JFK shooting occurred, they initially went to the TSBD to assist in crowd control. When word went over the radio that Tippit was shot, they proceeded to the Oak Cliff address, arriving on that scene at between 1:50 and 2:00 P.M. Tippit had already been transported to hospital by the ambulance. Poe spoke to witness Mrs. Markham who described a white male, 25 years, with medium brown hair, wearing a white jacket. Poe then talked to Domingo Benavides and the Davis sisters who provided a similar description. The Davis ladies said that after the shooting, the guy cut across their lawn, emptying shells from gun. Benavides gave Officer Poe two shells that he had found on the grass. Although Officer Poe was told by Sergeant Hill to mark the shells with his initials, Poe testified to the Commission that he was unsure if he did mark the shells. Poe turned the two shells over to a crime scene officer, Sgt. Pete Barnes. The bullets were of the Western brand. Officer Poe noted that Mrs. Markham very excited and confused at the scene.

Sgt Bud Owens, the supervisor of patrol officers for that area, arrived and took charge of the Tippit scene. Officer Poe and his partner, Officer Jez, then participated in the area search for the suspect. When the report was broadcast that a suspect was seen entering the nearby Texas Theater, Poe headed to the theater by way of the back alley. After leaving the theater scene, Poe went to the hospital where Tippit was taken and met Captain Cecil Talbert. The Captain was heard by Poe telling the doctor to remove a slug from Tippit. Sergeant Owens had remained at the 10th Street scene when the others went to search for the suspect. While there, he contacted Captain Westbrook, and met the crime scene team led by Captain Doughty. It is noted that Sgt. Owens was the acting Lieutenant that day in charge of the patrol officers in the Oak Cliff area, including Tippit.

Officer Poe advised that Sgt H.M. Hunt of the Intelligence squad of Dallas P.D. was on the scene and that Motor officer J.T. Griffin was present at the scene where the jacket was found near the gas station. Poe reported that he heard Deputy Chief of Dallas P.D., N.T. Fisher, asks the communications center over the radio if the two homicide cases were tied together.

Officer C.T. Walker, a uniformed accident investigator was also on the Tippit scene at that point and issued the description of the suspect over the police radio.

Detective Bob Carroll -Was on scene at the theater and assisted in the arrest of Oswald.

Sergeant Gerald Hill was an eight year veteran of the Dallas police assigned to the Personnel Section conducting background investigations on recruits. When hearing of the JFK shooting, Sgt. Hill responded to the TSBD to assist. When the report of the Tippit shooting came over the police radio, Hill asked Inspector Sawyer to be relived and headed out to Oak Cliff along with Patrol supervisor, Sergeant Bud Owens and the Dallas County Assistant District Attorney, Bill Alexander. Upon his arrival at the Tippit scene on E. 10th Street, Hill ordered Officers Poe and Jez to guard Tippit's car. Taking Poe's patrol car, Sgt. Hill then responded to the nearby ga station along with two uniform accident investigators, C.T. Walker and Bob Apple, where a jacket supposedly discarded by the Tippit suspect, was found and turned over to Captain Westbrook. Sgt. Hill and his crew then responded to the Texas Theater where a suspect had allegedly entered. Hill searched the balcony area with Detective Bentley, a uniformed Dallas officer and a uniformed Deputy Sheriff. Returning to the main floor of the theater he met several officials including Captain Talbert, 3-wheel officer Hutson, Officers C. T. Walker, Ray Hawkins, Bob Carroll, Paul Bentley, and K.E. Lewis. Sgt.

Hill assisted in arresting Oswald after the confrontation between Oswald and Officer McDonald.

Officer Ray Hawkins, an 11 year veteran of the force, was a uniformed accident investigator that day and was paired with Officer Elmer Baggett. They were joined by 3-wheel officer Hutson and responded to the theater when word was received that the suspect may have entered same. Hawkins was also present when Officer McDonald marked Oswald's gun with initials.

Other Dallas police at the scene of the chase and/or arrest of Oswald were:

P/O BAGGETT - At the theater

P/O BILL ANGLIN - Tippit close friend in an adjacent squad car that day.

P/O J.T. GRIFFIN -Operating Unit 279

P/O HUTSON - A 3-Whell motorcycle officer on scene

P/O SGT STRINGER -On scene of the shirt find

P/O/ MURRAY JACKSON- Police radio Dispatcher

SGT BARNES - Crime scene technician on Tippit scene

P/O C.T. WALKER - Riding Unit 85 that day

P.O R. W. WARNER - Present during chase and theater arrest.

P/O H.W. SUMMERS - Assigned to Unit 221that day in the area of the
Tippit shooting.

OWALD ROUTE TO THEATER

Citizen Elcan Elliott, who lived a few blocks from Oswald's rooming
house, observed a suspicious looking character 'relieving himself' in some
bushes, in full view. Curious and concerned, Elliott followed the man,
circling around streets, to catch up with him. "I watched as he would
walk down a block, stop, look around, and (then) reverse direction", says
Elliott. "He did this three or four times. He looked lost, bewildered" As
he approached Lancaster Street, Elliott sees the man, face to face, from
about 10 feet away. When Elliott seen Television later that day, he instantly
recognized him. "There's absolutely no doubt about it", Elliott insists.
Elliott was unsure if his sighting was before 1:00P.M. or after the 1:16
P.M. shooting.

After rigorously planning his escape from the attempt on General
Walker, Oswald obviously did not bother to plan his escape from the JFK
assassination.

Oswald initially entered a bus, exiting shortly thereafter as the bus became
snarled in traffic. He hailed a taxi, a very unusual mode of transportation
for him. He had the cabbie take him past his rooming house and drop

him off several blocks further. We can only speculate that he wanted to ascertain if there were police units or other dangers already waiting for him at the rooming house. None were noticed.

Prior to the Tippit shooting, Oswald walked back to his rooming house and quickly changed clothes, picking up his revolver and continued on his way, apparently without a preplanned destination. After shooting Officer Tippit, he fled on foot prior to the arrival of police units. He next was noticed passing the shoe store next to the Texas Theater, several blocks from the shooing scene. It can only be speculated that, after discarding his jacket in the gas station parking lot, he traveled on foot along the alleyways in the rear of the residential area that he fled. (A common tactic of fleeing criminals in residential areas such as Dallas (and Miami) where the existence of alleys is common) The time element from the shooting scene to the theater was much longer than one could walk the few blocks so it must be assumed that Oswald secreted himself en route to the theater, moving only when the police sirens seem to be moving away from him. We will never know exactly.

The following description is what the searching officers had after the JFK hit.

"Attention all squads, Attention all squads. The suspect in the shooting at Elm and Houston Streets is reported to be an unknown white male, approximately 30, slender build, 5-10, 165, reported to be armed what is thought to be a .30 caliber rifle". (86)

One of the most glaring discrepancies in the Tippit case can be seen in the accounts of the direction in which Tippit's killer was walking just before Tippit stopped. William Scoggins, a cab driver who was an eyewitness, testified that the gunman was walking west toward Tippit's car prior to the shooting. Another witness, Jim Burt, reported similarly. Reports from the Dallas police as well as the first reports of the Secret Service reflect the same impression. Despite the preponderance of evidence that the killer and Tippit's car were moving *toward* each other, the Warren Report concluded the killer was walking in the opposite direction. The commission version held that Tippit's car overtook the pedestrian killer. (87)

The witness may all be correct. It is quite possible that Oswald spotted the uniform police car approaching him as he was walking on the sidewalk, spun around and began walking toward the opposite direction. It is the author's experience and common knowledge among police patrol officers that often times, to avoid a face to face position with an approaching officer, a suspect will often spin around and proceed in the opposite direction. The author recalls numerous encounters while on routine patrol that a subject who takes evasive action upon spotting a uniform officer will definitely be the cause of an inquiry by the officer. In fact, on quiet days, my riding partner and I would troll the business districts of our beat looking for the person in the crowd that takes evasive action. Many good arrests have resulted from the paranoia of a suspect.

Another well known tactic of uniform officers will be for the officer/passenger to watch sidewalk suspects in the rear side mirrors as the patrol car passes them to see which of them jerks their head around after the patrol car passes to ascertain if the police unit continues routine patrol. This action of a subject always got a quick turn-around of the patrol car and a field inquiry - again resulting in many good arrests. Very few ordinary law-abiding pedestrians bother with a passing patrol car, but crooks certainly make it a habit.

It is entirely reasonable to assume that Officer Tippit's attention was alerted by an evasive action by Oswald.

If Oswald had been tried for the murder of Officer Tippit, the eyewitness testimony against him by Mrs. Markham would have been jeopardized under competent cross-examination. She was one of the Commission's star witnesses in this case. Helen Markham markedly contradicted herself and made false statements, not to mention the fact that initially she described the killer in terms that did not resemble Oswald. None of the Commission's other witnesses actually saw the shooting. One of those witnesses initially said he could not positively identify Oswald as the assailant, but then later changed his story after being shot in the head. This same witness gave a description of the killer's jacket that differed from the jacket that Oswald allegedly discarded in the vicinity of the crime scene. (The story surrounding the jacket itself is rather cloudy. For one thing, to this day no one knows who discovered it, and the coat was initially described as being "white," whereas the coat in evidence was clearly gray.)

ARREST AT THE THEATER

It was shortly after Officer Tippit was killed that shoe store employee, Johnny Brewer, looked out his store window as police sirens were heard in the neighborhood.

Brewer, an alert shoe salesman, observed a man ducking into the store alcove as a police car passed by. The man was then observed by Brewer entering the Texas movie theatre, bypassing the ticket taker who was manning the booth at the theatre entrance. The female clerk, Julia Postal, after being notified by Brewer of the man's actions, notified the police by phone, relative to a suspicious man.

Brewer proceeded to the movie house and spoke with Ms. Postal, the ticket seller and Butch Burroughs, the concession operator, who claimed not to have seen the suspicious man enter. Brewer requested the ticket seller to contact the police, who arrived in moments, some with drawn guns. Arriving Sergeant Gerald Hill, who had commanded the search previously at the TSBD building, then had the theater lights turned on.

Just minutes later, approximately fifteen police officers arrived at the theatre. The lights were turned on and officers started searching the almost empty movie house, both the balcony and the main seating area.

Officer M.N. McDonald was standing on the side of the movie screen, noting about fifteen or so people sitting spread out in the theater. A patron tipped Officer N.M. McDonald off that the man he was seeking was sitting near the middle rear. McDonald confronted Oswald sitting alone. Oswald struck the officer with his fist and attempted to withdraw a .38 revolver from his jacket. McDonald approached the man who stood up and declared, "It's all over now". The man then struck the officer in the face with his fist and attempted to draw a weapon from his clothes. The officer grabbed the butt of the gun as the man pulled the trigger but the shell did not fire. (See Warren Commission Report and Officer McDonald's statement to the Associated Press) Several other officers then joined Officer McDonald in subduing the suspect. After the struggle with McDonald and several other police officers, Oswald was subdued, handcuffed, and rushed out to a police car. He was immediately transported to the Homicide office at the Dallas police headquarters.

The concession operator at the Texas Theater, Butch Burroughs heard someone enter the theater shortly after 1:00 PM and go up to the balcony. At 1:15 P.M., Oswald came downstairs and bought popcorn from Burroughs, then took a seat in the main seating area.

Burroughs, in a 1987 interview, stated that Oswald had actually entered the theater earlier, about 1:00 P.M., fifteen minutes before the suspicious man entered. An 18 year old Jack Davis also confirmed Burroughs story in an interview with the author Jim Marrs of "Crossfire" years later. These accounts remain a difficult contradiction.

The man arrested at the theater about 2:00 P.M., Lee Harvey Oswald, was taken to the Homicide office on the third floor of the Dallas P.D. and turned over to Detective Guy Rose. The detective removed Oswald's handcuffs and searched him for identification. Detective Rose found two identifications, one with the name Lee Harvey Oswald and the other with the name Alek Hidell. Oswald was not cooperative, refused to identify himself, and only produced 'lies' according to Detective Rose. About 2:20 P.M. Rose was contacted by Homicide Division commander, Captain Will Fritz, who asked Detective Rose to get help and proceed to an address in the Dallas suburb of Irving to locate a man named Lee Harvey Oswald. Rose then advised Fritz, "Captain, I think this is Oswald, right in there.

WE HAVE OUR MAN(?)

It was at this point, the focus of the investigation changed. Author Jim Marrs, "Crossfire", later wrote, "Dallas police and federal authorities quickly lost interest in any information that did not fit in with any presumed activities of Lee Harvey Oswald". (88) An FBI document by J. Edgar Hoover was released in 1977 stating, "I called the Attorney General (Bobby Kennedy) at his house and told him I thought we had the man who killed the President down in Dallas…" Oswald, for his part, made no admission or provided any other incriminating information to the police during this questioning or any subsequent interviews, a total of 12 hours of questioning during the following two days.

Oswald's main cry was "I am a patsy".

CHARGING SUSPECT OSWALD

The Dallas police radio logs and other observers clocked the time of the TSBD rifle shots at 12:30 P.M., that Friday, November 22, 1963. Suspect Oswald was arrested at the Texas Theatre less than two hours later, for the murder of Dallas police officer J.D. Tippit that occurred on East Tenth Street less than a half hour earlier, two miles or so from the scene of Kennedy's murder. A preliminary hearing was held in the Dallas police station that evening by a Justice of the Peace for the killing of Officer Tippit, with the charge sheet being signed by Homicide Captain Will Fritz. A similar hearing was held, by the same official, at 1:30 A.M. Saturday morning in the police identification section of the Dallas P.D., charged Oswald with Kennedy's murder.

RAELIGH TELEPHONE CALL

While Oswald was in custody of the Dallas police, he requested to call an attorney in New York, but was unsuccessful in reaching him. He attempted another interesting contact. He tried to reach a man in the Raleigh, N.C. area.

John Hurt, was the person in North Carolina that Oswald tried to telephone on November 23, 1963, while in custody, Oswald requested to call a John Hurt in Raleigh, North Carolina, of which researchers later found two. The phone number he wished to call was 834-7430 or 833-1253, both of which are in area code 919.

The two ladies working the switchboard that evening were Alvetta A. Treon and Louise Swinney. The supervisor told them to assist two Secret Service agents in monitoring the call. Oswald called the switchboard at 11:45 P.M. (Saturday). Swinney told Oswald, "I'm sorry, the number doesn't answer. She then unplugged the call. Afterward, Swinney threw the call slip in the waste basket and left work for the night.

Ms. Treon retrieved the slip from the basket, copied the information on a standard call slip, and kept it as a souvenir. The slip noted "John Hurt, Raleigh, N.C.".

Author Canfield, "Coup D'Etat in America", traced the numbers and found that one was listed to a John W. Hurt and the other to a John D. Hurt, both of Raleigh.

Canfield stated that nearby at the time was the Illusionary Warfare Training Base at Nags Head, N.C., where idealistic sailor recruits were instructed to be fake defectors.

Dr. Grover Proctor, Jr., a historian and an expert on the Kennedy assassination summarized the documents on this John Hurt, from the declassified documents of the House Select Committee on Assassinations. His full summary may be seen in HSCA files or viewing Proctor's summary on the Internet.

PART VI

WHO IS OSWALD

WHO WAS THIS OSWALD GUY?

Who was Lee Harvey Oswald? With the death of his father before he was born, he was raised by his mother, Marguerite Oswald, living in numerous cities, including New Orleans, Dallas, New York City, and Fort Worth, Texas. Oswald had two brothers, Robert Oswald and John Edward Pic (his half brother). Three days after his 17th birthday, Oswald joined the U.S. Marines, serving for almost three years, after dropping out of high school in Fort Worth, getting his mother to sign permission for him to join. Oswald attended radar operator's military school in Mississippi, and was assigned to Atsugi Air base in Japan. This base was adjacent to a top-secret U-2 airplane facility that had a mission to monitor the activities in communist China. At one point, he was temporally assigned to the Philippines but soon returned to the Atsugi base in Japan.

As his enlistment was nearing the end, Oswald requested and was approved for a hardship discharge for the purpose of taking care of his ill mother in Fort Worth. Several weeks later Oswald headed to the Soviet Union where he attempted to renounce his U.S. citizenship and obtain Russian citizenship. Oswald married a Russian woman, Marina Prusakova, from Minsk, on April 30, 1960, whom he had met at a dance in March of 1961. At the time, Marina advised that Lee was proficient enough to converse

---

135

in the Russian language that one might believe he was from a different area of Russia, instead of being a North American. On February 15, 1962, Marina gave birth to a daughter June. On June 2nd, 1962, Oswald and his family returned to America. On October 20, 1963, five weeks before the JFK killing, Marina gave birth to a second daughter, Audrey.

Reports have been attributed to a CIA Finance officer who claimed a CIA case officer told him on November, 23, 1963, that Oswald was a CIA agent. In September of 1959 Oswald was discharged from Marine Corps. In October of 1959 he was at the American Embassy in Moscow. Oswald came thru Helsinki on 10/14/1959 en route to Moscow. On 10/16/59, Oswald applied for Soviet Citizenship. He said he had important information for Soviets. Embassy officer Snyder immediately notifies his superiors at the Embassy.

Other than two minor scrapes in the military, not involving personal violence against another, Oswald had not demonstrated any violent tendencies toward anyone in his life, according to all known reporting, until the attempt on General Walker. Oswald reported to be very intelligent despite being a high school dropout was well read and appeared to be verbally articulate. He was not known to be an abuser of alcohol or any type of narcotics. Known as a loner in the military, keeping to himself when off duty, and spending time attempting to learn the Russian language. He was also known to be an avid reader of Soviet newspapers, magazines and books.

A reading of the statements and affidavits of the White Russian community in Dallas who had befriended the Oswald family upon their return from Russia show that they all generally agreed that Lee Oswald was smart and rational but that his social skills left a lot to desire. He was a loner, an abuser of his wife Mariana, rude to acquaintances and very cynical. He displayed no appreciation of the efforts of the community to help him and his family; with some saying he seemed to expect the help.

As previously noted, Oswald purchased the rifle and the revolver in the spring of 1963. There was no prior information that he possessed any firearms earlier than March of 1963.

However, after the assassination, George DeMohrenschidt and his wife were interviewed by U.S. Embassy officials in Haiti on December 4, 1963. Both were very cooperative and gave a full statement of their past relationship with the Oswald's. In the State Department summary telegram to Washington, released in 1995, one statement caught my attention. DeMohrenschidt stated, "In the fall of 1962, Mrs. Oswald remarked to his wife that her husband had bought a gun". I found no other indication of this action by Oswald or of its purpose.

POSSIBLE OSWALD MOTIVE

The search for a motive to attribute to Lee Oswald is still elusive after all these years, or have we overlooked it in the haze of too many theories? I don't have one either but do want to offer a possibility. A 1993 interview that Frontline had with Oswald's brother, Robert Oswald, proved interesting to me when it revealed Lee Oswald's almost obsession with the book and television series involving Herb Philbrick.

In 1952, a book was written by Herb Philbrick, "I Led Three Lives, 'Communist Counterspy", followed by a popular television series of the same name. The subject was the story of a Boston area advertising executive who became a counterspy for the FBI in the Communist Party of the USA. Philbrick, in the 1940's, joined a peace group in a Boston suburb and discovered that it was a communist front. He talked with the FBI who urged him to remain involved as a government source. Philbrick worked himself up to a rather high rank in the Communist Party during World War II. In 1947 he was outed as a result of him being a witness in the famous 'Smith' trial, which exposed the communist infiltration of US government agencies.

The author, who is close to Oswald's age, was himself enthralled with the Philbrick story back then, as a teenager. I read the book several times and eagerly watched the television story faithfully. The story was fascinating to me, a mid-teen. We all have heroes and Philbrick and baseball great Ted Williams were mine. I later moved on to a non-Walter Mitty life, dropping the desire of being a counterspy: nor did I replace Williams in left field at Fenway (I couldn't hit),

As a teenager, Oswald was shuttled from school to school in various cities and had no father at home. Maybe this was not only his escape, but grew into a goal of being a counter-espionage agent who would become famous like Philbrick. It could very well be the impetus for Oswald to cooperate with the Office of Naval Intelligence and the CIA/FBI group that was introducing 'fake defectors' into the Soviet Union. It would not be far-fetched for Oswald to continue his 'stringer' work with the CIA and FBI after his return from Russia.

Author Philip Melanson's in his book, "Spy Saga", devoted extensive theories that Oswald was a CIA agent.

Oswald's brother Robert expressed that Lee being engrossed in Philbrick's story was: "It was a training ground for his imagination". Robert further stated that Lee's views were: "He wasn't political. He was what's convenient to be"

Far fetched? You be the judge.

OSWALD'S MEXICO CITY TRIP

A few weeks before the assassination Oswald travelled to Mexico City. The CIA may have had Oswald under aggressive surveillance in Mexico City during the six-day visit. There were reports years later that there were photographs of Oswald in Mexico City that the CIA had taken. There were tape recordings of his telephone calls in Mexico City. All of that evidence would later disappear. The tapes, the CIA would say, were erased; the photographs, they would claim, never existed, even though there's a fair amount of evidence to suggest that they did.

Both the FBI and the CIA seemed determined not to get to the bottom of what Oswald did while in Mexico. Oswald apparently has encounters with Cuban spies and Cuban diplomats and Soviet spies and Mexicans who are sympathetic to Castro's revolution. The FBI and the CIA seemed determined not to find those people that Oswald was dealing with, and the question becomes: Was Oswald, in this

time period, just several weeks before the assassination, told by anybody, or encouraged by anybody to do what he would do in Dallas? Both the FBI and the CIA seemed determined not to get to the bottom of what Oswald did in Mexico.

In January of 1964, Author Peter Dale Scott wrote "Much of the government's failure to investigate thoroughly and honestly the murder of President Kennedy can be traced, it appears, to highly embarrassing secrets buried in the CIA files. Indeed a central part of the cover-up can be attributed to one such secret alone. This secret, found in pre-assassination CIA cables, is that Oswald had been falsely linked to a senior Soviet KGB agent in Mexico, Vareriy Kostikov, in such a way as to create a misleading impression of a sinister KGB assassination plot". (89)

Records finally released by the CIA as a result of the Assassination Record Review Act of 1992, relate details (still murky) of Lee Harvey Oswald's trip to Mexico City in late September and early October of 1963, seven weeks prior to the JFK assassination. In 1963, the Mexico City CIA Station surveillance was conducted at both the Cuban and Soviet compounds, electronically and photographically. The CIA station received daily transcriptions of the telephone surveillance and results from the photographical surveillance twice weekly. Between September 27 and October 1st, there were nine Oswald related telephone calls and five physical visits in question, either to the Soviet compound or to the Cuban facilities.

On September 27th, an unidentified man called the Soviet Military Attaché looking for a visa to Odessa. He was referred to the Consulate office. A few minutes later the man called the consulate and was told to call back later in the day. Late in the afternoon, Sylvia Duran, employee of the Cuban Embassy called the Soviet Embassy. She told them that an American was at the Cuba Embassy seeking a visa (to Cuba). Sylvia had sent the American to the Soviet Embassy stating that his acquiring a Cuban visa was contingent on his previously acquiring a Soviet visa. On Saturday, Silva Duran called the Soviet Consulate advising that there was an American at the Cuba facility who had previously visited the Soviet Consulate. More calls were exchanged on October 1st and 3rd.

It took years for the Mexico City CIA story to partially emerge. Two of the US House Assassination Committee investigators, Edwin Lopez and Dan Hardaway, went to Mexico City in 1978, questioning every possible source and examining whatever files still existed. They prepared the now famous "Lopez" report, (412 pages) which was finally released in 2003, still partially redacted. Many of the CIA officials questioned were forthright, others had foggy memories. Ann Goodpasture, a supervisor in station at Mexico City since 1960, was vague in some of her recollections. Also, an experienced clerk, Elsie Scaleti, routinely handled much of the material sent to and received from CIA headquarters. Her supervisor stated to the Lopez team that Scaleti was a real whiz with a photographic memory, who was a 'major domo'in the office, 'in the know' about virtually everything. When Scaleti was questioned by Lopez, she played "Sgt Schultz" - I know nothing". When asked specifically what she remembered about November 22, 1963, she drew a blank. She advised that she could remember nothing of the Oswald information and that she only recalled that when she returned home that day her husband was watching assassination related broadcasts on the television.

The points of contention were primarily whether Oswald did in fact make which of these (recorded) phone calls to either the Soviets or to the Cubans; and what became of the photos of persons who visited either of them countries' Embassy and consulates. Was Oswald photographed? If so, what happened to the photos? Was Oswald voice recorded (as part of the normal protocol for persons going to them facilities and where the tape was? Did the Mexico City CIA provide the opportunity for the Dallas based FBI to listen to the tape(s) (as reported), and if so, where are the tapes and/or the transcripts.

Win Scott was then CIA Station chief in Mexico City. He had the habit of secreting top secret material in his own office safe rather than in the regular filing system at the CIA station. When he retired, he took much of this material home with him. Upon his death several years later, CIA's Jim Angleton went to Scott's home and carried away the contents of the home safe, according to Scott's widow.

The 2013 book, "Oswald, Mexico and Deep Politics", written by Peter Dale Scott, brilliantly examined the "Mexico City Visit" of Oswald. The long "Lopez Report", prepared for the House Assassination Committee (1978) opened the door to much of what the CIA was covering up down there. It is a long report but worth the read for interested assassination researchers.

JFK ASSASSINATION RECORDS, 1993

The "Lopez" report, Oswald, CIA & Mexico City",

By Eddie Lopez and Dan Hardaway of the House

Select Committee on Assassinations

INTERROGATION OF OSWALD

Oswald was questioned by Dallas police six times between his arrest on Friday afternoon and his death on Sunday morning. Captain Fritz, the homicide commander, conducted most of the questioning, all of which occurred in Fritz's small third floor office in the Dallas P.D. headquarters between Friday and Sunday. Many others law enforcement officers participated in the questioning or were witness to the Captain's questioning. These included FBI agents Bookout and Hosty, Inspector Kelly and Agent Marshall of the Secret Service, Postal Inspector Holmes and various Dallas homicide detectives. None of the interviews were recorded nor were there any stenographers. Captain Fritz did not make reports on the individual interviews, but instead, completed a cumulative report several days later. However, there were written reports made summarizing specific questioning by the Secret Service, FBI, and Postal authorities.

The interviews were conducted under chaotic conditions at the police department, with hordes of media representatives clogging the third floor corridor. Each time Oswald was moved from the jail to the small 9 X 12 room where the questioning was conducted, he had to run a gauntlet of yelling newsmen. In addition, the Dallas police was still trying to conduct their normal operations in the other third floor offices, such as the Forgery, Robbery, and other units. One may still watch 1963 videos on the Internet of the wild unorganized scene at the department.

The fact that came out of these interrogations is that Oswald never wavered in his denial of committing either the assassination of John Kennedy or the killing of Officer Tippit. He openly admitted that he struck the arresting officer, McDonald, at the theater and was carrying a concealed .38 revolver. He denied owning a rifle and said the package he carried to work that morning only contained his lunch. Oswald was arrogant in his denunciation of the charges but was rational and calm. The only incident where Oswald displayed real anger arose when he was questioned by FBI agent Hosty, whom Oswald claimed had been harassing his wife. He did answers many questions and appeared to be fully aware of his 'rights". He would only stop answering questions when the subject matter was the killing of Kennedy or Tippit.

Oswald advised his interrogators that, at the moment of the shooting of President Kennedy, he was sitting in the lunchroom eating. He denied being the person in the famous photo which showed him holding a rifle and revolver and some communist newspapers. He said the photo was a fake and that the Dallas police had pasted his photo onto the picture. Oswald also proclaimed many times that the police lineups were very unfair as his clothing was different and the physical characteristics of the lineup 'fillers' were completely unlike that of him, a correct observation.

Oswald did admit taking a bus, then transferring to a taxi cab, to transport him to the area of his rooming house in the Oak Cliff section of Dallas. He said he went to his room, changed clothes, and put his revolver in his pocket. When questioned as to whether or not he was a Communist, he replied that "No, I am not a Communist but am a Marxist". He admitted handing out leaflets in New Orleans earlier in the year for the "Fair Play for Cuba" committee, a group that he was the only New Orleans member.

Oswald submitted to three different fingerprinting and photo sessions that first night and underwent a paraffin test. Officers advised that Oswald appeared alert and mindful of what was transpiring during the interrogations and testing. He made no secret of his disapproval of what the detectives were doing but kept his cool except for the one outburst toward FBI Agent Hosty.

Detective Sims of the homicide squad, said of Oswald's demeanor during the questioning, "He conducted himself, I believe, better than anyone I have ever seen in interrogations. He was calm and wasn't nervous". Detective Boyd, Sim's partner, said," I never saw a man that could answer questions like he could". FBI Agent Bookout stated, "He spoke very loudly....he gave an emphatic denial". Captain Fritz remarked that, "Oswald frantically denied shooting Tippit or shooting President Kennedy". Officer Marion Baker, who was the police officer who confronted Oswald in the book depository building, asked Oswald "Did You kill the President?" Oswald replied, "That's absurd, I want a lawyer. I want a lawyer".

Postal Inspector Holmes wrote, "Oswald at no time appeared confused or in doubt as to whether or not he should answer a question. On the contrary, he was quite alert and showed no hesitancy in answering those questions he wanted to answer, and quite skillful in parrying those questions which he did not want to answer...."

When questioned by the Warren Commission regarding the chaotic interrogations of Oswald, at the police department during them three days, Police Chief Jesse Curry stated "that the interrogation of Oswald at the Dallas police department was just against all principles of good interrogation practice".

ATF Agent Frank Ellsworth recalls Oswald with "a smug look on his face" he was surrounded by fourteen agents and officers and he didn't look disturbed. He had the cat-that-ate- the-canary look on his face the whole time".

In mid-afternoon Friday, the day of the JFK assassination, Oswald was brought into the Dallas P.D. office of Captain John Will Fritz. This began the first of three different interviews over the next two days. The Dallas Police Chief, Jesse Curry, advised the assembled news media that, during each session, there was at least one FBI agent and one Secret Service agent present, as well as several Dallas detectives. The interviews were led by Captain Fritz, the 68 year old head of the Robbery-Homicide Division, who had joined the department in 1921. Oswald, between interviews, was also placed in line-ups, read his rights, and was given a paraffin test to determine if he had fired a gun that day. Oswald did not, in any of these sessions, admit any guilt in either murder. As pointed out earlier, these homicides were a State of Texas crime, but -----at that time ---- were not a federal violation as the statute of killing a President was not enacted until some time later.

As the investigators bored into Oswald's motive for killing President Kennedy, President Johnson appeared on the verge of panic, as evidence indicating Soviet Union or Cuban involvement might be a catalyst that would start World War III, which most likely would be a nuclear conflagration. Initially there were no reports of Oswald harboring or expressing homicidal intentions toward JFK. It was known soon however, that he was a declared Communist or Marxist.

Author Sylvia Meagher, in her later excellent expose of the inadequateness and disorganization of the Warren Report, pointed out that "The complete absence of any motive was a main factor in the doubt of Oswald's guilt that flourished all over the world after the assassination. (90) She noted that "the Warren Commission has not resolved the problem despite its microscopic research into Oswald's life". President Johnson felt it necessary to spread the word quickly that Oswald was indeed a loner who committed this crime by himself and that there was no conspiracy. Oswald did, very emphatically, expresses his antipathy toward General Walker and the John

Birch Society but did not state any hatred for Kennedy. With views such as this, it is "an affront to logic to suggest that Oswald would shortly after, attempt to kill John Kennedy, the President of the United States -- unless to show that he was insane". (91)

The Warren Commission did not look deeply into Oswald's mental balance after his death. His Marine (1956-59) service medical records indicated no sign of emotional problems, mental abnormality, or psychosis. Even his wife, who was not shy in providing negative information on her husband, considered Oswald "mentally sound, smart, and capable, not devoid of reason. His friends also shared a similar view.

During the interrogation (as well as during the arrest) Oswald steadfastly maintained that he was innocent. He indicated fear of a frame-up and said explicitly and publicly that stance, even as he laid near death in the police basement on Sunday morning. He freely admitted his Marxist connections but, time and time again, denied being the killer of Kennedy.

OSWALD'S LETTER TO THE FBI

It appears that the FBI's attempted to cover up their connections with Oswald has since been revealed. Dallas-based FBI agent James Hosty had received and later destroyed a letter from Oswald protesting the FBI's questioning of Oswald's Russian-born wife, Marina. Under orders from his Dallas superior, Hosty destroyed the letter by ripping it into pieces, then flushing the pieces down the toilet at the Dallas FBI office, two days after the assassination, when Oswald was killed by Jack Ruby.

A former press secretary to President Johnson described Oswald's letter to the FBI as "a note threatening to blow up the Dallas office of the FBI, the building, if the agents did not cease trying to interview Oswald's wife Marina."

The House Committee confirmed this act (of evidence destruction) during its interview with John Gale, of the FBI Inspection office.

"The decision was made two days after the assassination to destroy this note. In truth, we'll never know exactly what was in that note, and it's been described in different ways," author Philip Shenon told television host Bob Schieffer. "The Warren Commission knew absolutely nothing about it.

Despite the intentional destruction of evidence, Clarence Kelley, who succeeded Hoover as the head of the agency, came to see Hosty as a victim when he later conducted a private search of the FBI's own files about the investigation. "He was convinced that if Hosty had been told everything that FBI headquarters knew about Oswald's Mexico trip, he would have alerted the Secret Service to the obvious threat that Oswald posed," Author Phil Shenon writes. "The FBI, Kelley said, would have 'undoubtedly taken all necessary steps to neutralize Oswald.' And that was Kelley's larger conclusion - that President Kennedy's assassination could have been prevented, perhaps easily."

PART VII

OSWALD IS DEAD

MURDER #3 - VICTIM OSWALD

Chaos in the Jail

The American public watching television that Sunday, was appalled at the chaotic scenes of hordes of newsmen clogging the hallways of the Dallas Police Department on November 22 and 23, 1963, as the homicide detectives paraded suspect Oswald thru the hallways to and from between the jail and the interrogation rooms. What a circus. A big city police department forgot all the basics in interrogating and booking a suspect in a major crime. Newsmen were interviewing police officers of every rank on any and all aspects of the investigation in the hallways. The Chief of Police, Jesse Curry, himself gave at least six on-air interviews, providing details of the on-going investigation that never should have surfaced at that stage of the investigation. The Chief, trying to cooperate with the local and national press, tried to be the Police Information Officer instead of supervising his elderly homicide commander, Captain John Will Fritz.

What has not been publicized very much was the fact that Chief Curry's career began by rising up through the ranks of the Traffic Section of the police department and that he had little or no experience in being a detective. Chief Curry did attend the Northwestern Traffic Institute, the

---

curriculum of which was almost totally traffic orientated and attended the FBI Academy, not known at that time for the pursuit of intellectual law enforcement studies, but instead concentrating on firearms training and hearing what a great man Hoover was. (been there, done that!) Curry's homicide chief was a sixty-eight year old police veteran who had been on the force since 1921 when the President of the United States was Warren Harding. The performance of both of these lawmen during the JFK assassination case investigation was definitely not sterling.

The failure of Chief Curry to order the police building to be cleared of all but departmental members carrying out police duties was outrageous. The chaos of the first two days of Oswald's confinement continued into Sunday. The normal protocol then of prisoner transport between the city jail and the Dallas County jail was for the county officer to pick up the prisoners in the city jail basement and transport them to the county jail twelve blocks away, to be held for court proceedings. In this case, most certainly for the publicity, the Chief decided to have the Dallas department deliver the prisoner them self.

The transfer of Oswald was due to occur at 10:00 A.M. that Sunday morning. Chief Curry went to the homicide office where last minute questioning of the suspect was being conducted by Fritz, Postal Inspector Holmes and Inspector Kelly of the Secret Service. He was advised by Captain Fritz that they were almost finished with the last interview. The prisoner was to be taken from the third floor interrogation office down to the basement of the jail. An armored car and escort car was to be used as a decoy and that Oswald was intended to be actually transferred in Captain Fritz's unmarked police car.

Jack Rubenstein, alias Jack Ruby, a fifty-two year old Dallas night club owner, shot suspect Lee Oswald on Sunday, November 24th, 1963, while Oswald was being transferred from the city jail to the county jail. On the day of the assassination of Kennedy, Ruby whereabouts placed him near the book depository building and later at Parkland Hospital, where President Kennedy's body was taken. Ruby was also seen in the hallways of the Dallas police department by numerous people during a several hour period on Friday. Again on Saturday, Ruby was at the police department while Oswald was being interrogated. In late morning, Sunday, Ruby showed up in the jail basement as Oswald was about to be transferred.

At 11:21A.M., on Sunday morning, Dallas police detectives were escorting Oswald through the jail basement to a waiting car. Ruby stepped out behind a gaggle of newsmen and fired one shot at Oswald, striking him in the stomach, and fatally killing suspect Oswald. Ruby was armed with a snub-nosed Cold Cobra .38 caliber revolver. Ruby was immediately pounced upon by Dallas detectives and arrested. Ruby's act ended any hope of discovering any real facts from the suspect in the killing of the President, and possibly unearthing a motive and identify of any co-conspirators. Who was Jack Ruby? What was <u>his</u> motivation for killing Oswald? Was Ruby directed to kill Oswald by organized crime figures or others as part of a conspiracy to silence Oswald?

Ruby moved to Dallas from Chicago in 1947 at age thirty-six. He managed several night clubs and strip joints and, in 1963, was the owner of the Carousel Club and the Vegas Club. Both of these joints were also the hangout for numerous Dallas police officers, who were well treated by Ruby. During the years since the assassination of JFK, many accounts of Ruby associating with organized crime figures have surfaced. These associations were not discovered by the Warren Commission and the House Commission as each concluded Ruby was not involved in mob activities. Were they naïve or were they stonewalled by the FBI and other law enforcement agencies, local and national?

Much speculation arose on how Ruby managed to gain access to the jail basement. Was it because of coordination with his 'friends' at the Dallas department, was it chance or luck, or did Ruby know that access could be made without assistance by way of an unlocked door.

In March of 1964, Ruby was convicted of murder with malice and sentenced to die. His attorneys appealed to the Texas Court of Appeals who agreed that Ruby could not get a fair trial in Dallas. The conviction was overturned and a new trial was scheduled to begin in Wichita Falls, far away from Dallas. While in jail awaiting a re-trial, Ruby was diagnosed with cancer and died on January 3, 1967, at the age of fifty-five.

RUBY'S TIES TO ORGANIZED CRIME

Santos Trafficante, Jr., was the owner of casinos in pre-Castro Havana and the boss of the Florida Gulf Coast Mafia, including the cities of Miami and Tampa. Carlos Marcello was the long-time Mafia head for the areas of Louisiana and Texas. Much more will be discussed relative to these two mobster leaders in the following chapters. For now, let's examine Jack Ruby's connections to the mob which the Warren Commission said did not exist.

When Fidel Castro took control over Cuba, he cracked down on the casinos, closing many immediately. These casinos were owned and operated by American mobsters such as Meyer Lansky and Santos Trafficante. Castro at first allowed the Capri Hotel, operated by Trafficante, to continue operating. Soon, however, Trafficante was picked up by Castro forces and incarcerated in the minimum security prison at Trescornia. The inmates here were allowed visitors and were able to have meals brought into them from nearby hotels. Immediately after Ruby murdered Oswald, an Englishman by the name of John Wilson went to the American Embassy in London and advised that he had been in Trescornia in 1959 and had met Trafficante. Wilson advised that an American gangster named Ruby had visited Trafficante on several occasions. (92) Wilson himself had been involved in gun-running with a Miami gun dealer, Eddie Browder, a close associate of Trafficante's. When Wilson provided this information, it was not known otherwise that Ruby had visited Trescornia during that period. Wilson further advised that Ruby, in company with Lewis McWillie, would bring meals to Trafficante from the Havana hotels.

Ruby's travel documents from that time period, revealed that he stayed at the Capri hotel, where Trafficante held a major interest in the casino. Trafficante and McWillie, a lieutenant at the Capri, gave testimony to the House Assassination Committee. McWillie said that "maybe" Ruby had accompanied him to the Trescornia prison when he visited the Mafia boss, although Trafficante said he did not remember Ruby. Trafficante stated he wasn't sure McWillie had either but did admit that McWillie had visited him at his Miami home in later years. The Assassination Committee reported flatly, that that there was considerable evidence that there were meetings between Ruby and Trafficante. The Committee further stated that Ruby had been connected with Trafficante associate, Russell Mathews, who had worked at Trafficante's Deauville Hotel in Havana; James Dolan, described as "one of the most notorious hoodlums in Dallas; and Jack Todd, a Dallas resident described in the commission's report, whose telephone number was found in Ruby's car after Oswald's murder. (93) Neither the FBI nor the CIA fully informed the Warren

Commission of the alleged Ruby-Trafficante connections and that John Wilson was not called as a witness.

The FBI did concede beginning in 1959, that FBI Agent Charles Flynn had meetings with Ruby as a "potential criminal informant". Nine meetings between the two were documented. It was noted that, after meeting with agent Flynn, Ruby went out and purchased a large variety of modern sophisticated eavesdropping gadgets.

Another tip received after the Oswald murder was from a CIA operative, William Gaudet, whose name was listed next to Oswald's on the visa list during Oswald's Mexico City trip, in the fall prior to the assassination. Gaudet also admitted being with Guy Bannister, a New Orleans private investigator (and former head of the Chicago FBI office) in 1959, who was heavily involved with the anti-Castro Cubans in the summer of 1963.

Author Anthony Summers, in his book "Conspiracy", raised a good question: Why would a CIA operative in New Orleans have been interested, as early as 1959, in the mundane activities of a Dallas huckster called Jack Ruby? (94)

Jack Ruby had been reported to be in the Cuban gun-running operations of Dallas and the CIA and Mr. Gaudet had a keen interest in the trafficking of Eddie Browder and Santos Trafficante. The Warren Commission received information that Ruby first took part in the gunrunning for the pro-Castro groups, later switching to the anti-Castro side.

In June of 1963, the Dallas police intelligence was aware that a number of Chicago gangsters had a serious of meetings relative to controlling local prostitution and gambling, at Ruby's Carousel Club. Telephone records also showed Ruby calls to the motel that the hoods were staying during these meetings.

In September of 1963, a telephone call went out from Ruby's Carousel Club to a number listed to the ex-wife of Russell Matthews, another Trafficante associate from the 1959 Cuba days. Ruby followed up with calls to Jimmy Hoffa associate, Irv Weiner, and just two weeks before the Kennedy hit, Ruby received a call from top hoodlum, Barney Baker, Hoffa's personal strong man. The following day, Ruby exchanged calls with Murray (Buster) Miller in Miami, a Hoffa associate, and yet again he calls Barney Baker. Ruby also had two personal meetings with Alex

Gruber, an ex-con with Hoffa connections as well as Paul Jones, a one-time emissary of the Chicago mob.

These contacts came at a time when Bobby Kennedy was putting extensive pressure on Hoffa. Jimmy Hoffa was already on record of threatening the lives of the Kennedy brothers. Hoffa, of course, was closely tied with Santos Trafficante and Carlos Marcello.

Three weeks prior to the killing of President Kennedy, Ruby called the office of Nofio Pecora, at the New Orleans Tropical Court Transit Park. Pecora was a top lieutenant in Marcella operations. Marcello himself, normally shy of making telephone calls, called the same number (Pecora) in the summer of 1963.

During this period of the early 1960's, the Dallas organized crime leader was Joe Civillo, an underboss of Marcello. Civillo was one of the Mafia leaders who were rounded up at the Appalachian summit in upstate New York in 1957. His top lieutenant was Joseph Campisie, the owner of the Egyptian Restaurant in Dallas, where Ruby dined often. Campisie acknowledged to the FBI that he had a long standing relationship with Carlos Marcello. One of the few visitors to Ruby at the Dallas jail after he killed Oswald was Joe Campisie.

On the evening of the assassination, Jack Ruby dined with Ralph Paul, an owner of a Dallas drive inn. The location of this late meal was Campisie's restaurant. Earlier that evening Ruby had a meeting with Lawrence Meyers of Chicago, at Ruby's Carousel Club and Ruby later joined Meyers at his motel after the meeting. The Cabana hotel was where Ruby stayed until after midnight. Another interesting guest at this hotel that night was Eugene Brading, a real interesting figure in the JFK case.

Brading was using the name Jim Braden at that time. Under his real name, Eugene Brading, he had accumulated a long rap sheet of crimes all across the country. As Assassination Committee report noted that, in 1951, Brading was observed in the company of James Dolan (noted earlier as knowing Jack Ruby) and has been described as an acquaintance of both Carlos Marcella and Santos Trafficante.

Brading was nabbed the day of Kennedy's murder, fifteen minutes after the assassination, for acting suspiciously at the Dal-Tex building, adjacent to the school book depository building from which the fatal shots had been fired at President Kennedy. Brading's explanation to the police at that time was that he entered the Dal-Tex building and took a freight elevator to the third floor looking for a telephone. The third floor of this building, at the corner of Elm Street and Houston Street, overlooked the entire Dealey Square area, the scene of the assassination. Brading was released by the police because the criminal record under his real name was not then known. A check by researchers discovered that Brading at that time was using a New Orleans address of room #1701, Pere Marquette Building. This room was just down the hall from an office that David Ferrie was using while performing defense work in behalf of Carlos Marcello's upcoming trial.

Another strange "coincidence" was that Ferrie, eight weeks earlier, had made a telephone call to a Jean West in Chicago. It just so happened that West, on the night of November 21st, was staying at the Cabana Motel in Dallas and her companion was Lawrence Meyers, the friend Jack Ruby visited that midnight.

It turned out that Lee Harvey Oswald had been under surveillance by the FBI for months before the assassination, and the question becomes: Did the FBI have information to suggest what a threat Lee Harvey Oswald might be? And didn't it have an obligation to warn the Secret Service in advance of President Kennedy's arrival in Dallas? ... The decision seems to have been made by Hoover very early on to portray Oswald, whatever the evidence, as a lone wolf whose plot to kill the president could never had been detected by the FBI in advance — there was no conspiracy that the FBI could've stopped and saved the president. ... The extent of the knowledge that the FBI had of Oswald before the assassination seems to be something that the FBI wanted to hide from the Warren commission.

Russell Matthews, born in 1920, lived in Havana from July 58-Jan 59, and in the mid -1959 to Nov 1959. He owned two bars in Havana, living for a while at the Deauville Hotel where Trafficante had an interest. Matthews worked for mobster Benny Binion in 1978 and had known Ruby for 12 years. Dallas County Sheriff Decker says he knew Matthews all his life. Matthews had a long criminal record, including bookmaking, etc. In 1971 he moved to Las Vegas. When testifying to the US House Committee he displayed an arrogant and non-cooperative demeanor.

A 1964 FBI report states that James Dolan and R.D. Matthews were "notorious hoodlums". Dolan was described as a strong-arm man who worked for Trafficante. Another associate of Matthews was Dallas hood Jack Todd.

James Dolan, an associate of Eugene Brading, knew Ruby from the mob controlled AGVA association. He was also associated with Charles Harrelson, the sniper killer of Federal Judge Wood.

Joe Campisie was reported to be Carlos Marcello's man for the Dallas area. Campisi owns the Egyptian Lounge in Dallas. He had known Ruby since 1947 and visited Ruby in jail in the days after Ruby's arrest. Campisi was reported to be associated with R.D. Matthews, Ralph Paul, Jack Todd, Benny Binon and others Dallas criminals, although he had no convictions on his record.

Ruby, although allied to many Dallas racketeers, was regarded by organized crime leaders as TOO ERATIC and closely associated with the police and was not given any organized crime leadership position.

Can you now imagine the statement of the Warren Commission that Jack Ruby "did not have any ties to organized crime"?

PART VIII

PRIOR ATTEMPTS ON JFK

ATTEMPT ON JFK AT
CHICAGO, NOV. 2, 1963

In 1975, Edwin Black, a Chicago author, received information relative to a proposed 'hit' on Kennedy when the President would be in Chicago for the Army-Navy football game. The FBI had received a tip that a Homer Echevarria, an anti-Castro Cuban was overheard stating, "They will take care of JFK". A tip from a landlady also was received who rented rooms to four 'dark looking men' and that the lady observed two rifles on a bed. She got suspicious and called the Secret Service as Kennedy's trip was coming soon. The Secret Service attempted to conduct surveillance on these men but, during the stakeout two of the suspects spotted the agent. The two suspects were allegedly picked up and taken into custody. The other two suspects were not to be found. The author painstaking searched for records from the FBI, Secret Service and Chicago police but all paper traces of this contact had disappeared. (95)

Black's informer also identified a former Marine, Thomas Vallee, as one being set up to be the 'patsy' in the murder of the President, just as Oswald was in Dallas. Author Black traced down this Vallee and interviewed him, receiving confirmation of much of the story. Author Black's story appeared in November of 1975, in the Chicago Independent, but the informer's identify was not revealed.

In 1997, former Secret Service agent, Abraham Bolden, revealed that he knew about the 1963 Chicago plot and confirmed Black's story. It was most probable that he was the original informer. Bolden, the first black Secret Service Agent, was later charged with bribery and served two years in prison. Bolden claimed that he was framed because he was too vocal about the laxness of the Secret Service in handling this JFK plot, as he felt that if the probe was conducted properly, Kennedy would not have been killed in Dallas. Bolden backed up Black's story and elaborated in his book, (96)

One can read the entire story on the Internet by entering 'Edwin Black JFK'. (95)

PLOT ON JFK AT TAMPA, NOV. 18, 1963

In 2005, authors Lamar Waldron and Thom Hartmann published a book, "Ultimate Sacrifice", that claims JFK was to be murdered in Tampa during a motorcade. The hit was to be made from either a highway overpass or from the tall Floridian Hotel, and was allegedly order by Florida Mafia chief, Santos Trafficante, in conjunction with fellow Mafia members John Rosselli and Carlos Marcello. After an informant tipped off the Tampa police, Trafficante called off the hit as he was informed by a police buddy that Tampa was assembling a force of 600 officers, from their agency and others in the Bay area, which well protected Kennedy during the long motorcade. There were no records remaining in neither the Tampa police files nor the Secret Service files at the time the authors followed up on this story. All references to the plot had been removed or deleted. The plot however, was confirmed by the then Chief of Police of Tampa J. P. Mullins, now 82 years old and retired. (97)

Trafficante died in 1987 of natural causes. In 1989, Trafficante's attorney, Frank Ragano (and a next door neighbor to Trafficante in North Miami) published a book that said Trafficante had told him (Ragano) that he had something to do with JFK's murder in Dallas. Ragano testified under oath to the Assassination Records Review Board in 1997 and repeated this information.

PLOT ON JFK AT MIAMI, NOV. 18, 1963

After leaving Tampa that same day, President Kennedy flew into Miami International Airport. He was to be escorted by motorcade over to Miami Beach for a speech. A Miami P.D. Intelligence team of Lieutenant Charlie Sapp and Sergeant Everett Kaye had received information from an informant, Willie Somersett, that JFK would be killed by a sniper perched on a high building during his Miami trip. At the time, the author was an aide to the Assistant Chief of Police, Glen Baron and Patrol Commander Bill Harries. It was decided in a staff meeting with Secret Service that the Miami P.D. highly recommended that the motorcade be replaced by helicopter for transit to Miami Beach from the airport. A rally was held at the airport and Kennedy was flown by helicopter to a Miami Beach hotel for this speech. With otherwise tight security, there were no incidents. The author has heard this chilling tape recording between Somersett and right wing militant, Joseph Milteer, several times over the years, the theme of which was that killing Kennedy would be accomplished soon by use of snipers from tall buildings as the president traveled in a motorcade. This recorded meeting occurred two weeks prior to President Kennedy's murder in Dallas.

The FBI Miami office also received a call from Willie Somersett on November 10, 1963, informing them that the Miami P.D. had recorded Milteer's conversation about the JFK hit. They also acknowledged receiving a teletype from the Miami police department on November 9th, concerning this recording. Lt Sapp, Miami commander of the Intelligence Unit sent FBI Agent Lenny Peterson a copy of Milteer tape on November 12, 1963.

A year earlier, (1962), this same Intelligence squad of the Miami Police department received information from informer Willie Somersett about the details of an ongoing terror operation against Miami area Jewish leaders. Bombs had been thrown against the homes of Miami newspaper executives who were Jewish. Police Chief Walter Headley of the Miami police force pulled German speaking rookie officer Steve Plumacher from the police academy and placed him into the workforce of the Miami Water Department where the bombing suspect worked. After a several week investigation, a suspect, Donald Branch, was arrested for the bombings and was sentenced to two terms of six years in Florida's state prison. Remember now, this information came from the same informer, Willie Somersett that provided the tip on the proposed Kennedy killing.

156

The taped copy of the conversation between informer Somersett and Joseph Milteer of Quitman, Georgia, on November 9, 1963, was turned over to both the Secret Service and the Miami office of the FBI. Lieutenant Charles Sapp and Sergeant Everett Kaye met with Secret Service officials on November 12, 1963, ten days before the assassination, at the Miami police station.

Harry Williams, Attorney General Bobby Kennedy's liaison with the Cuban émigrés, and a close personal friend, recalled in 1993, certain security measures he took for JFK's November 18, 1963 visit to Miami. "I was given a list by the Secret Service with the names of five people on it. These were members of a group of Cuban anti-Castro groups who said they were going to kill Kennedy. I didn't know the guys. I got into a car, picked them up, and took them to Key West, where we rented a motel and kept them there while Kennedy was in Miami. The Kennedys were definitely worried about the Cubans in Miami".

Incidentally, this same Miami Intelligence trio of Lieutenant Charlie Sapp and Sergeants Everett Kaye and Gene McCracken, were the officers who broke the famous Star of India jewel robbery case that occurred on October 29, 1964. The crime was characterized at the time as "the biggest jewel theft in American History", and resulted in the arrest of Jack "Murph the Surf" Murphy.

One can read the details of that case in my previous book, "Miami Police Worksheet", available from Amazon.com, or on-line at www.mpdvets. org/history.

PART IX

WASHINGTON VISIT

AUTHOR'S VISIT TO WASHINGTON

In the mid 1960's, the author initially accepted the findings of the Warren Commission Report on the assassination after reading the paper back version. That assessment changed dramatically in 1976 as a result of attending a Dignitary Protection Seminar in Washington, D.C., hosted by the F.B.I. and U.S. Secret Service. The F.B.I. overdid the presentations detailing their conclusion that Oswald was the lone assassin to such a degree that many more questions arose than were answered. The bureau spent that entire week in March 1976, attempting to brainwash the seminar attendees into believing that Oswald alone, was the one and only participant of this crime of the century, completely ruling out any possibility of a conspiracy. I suspect that some of the older attendees swallowed the bait but several of the others asked very penetrating questions that went unanswered. The author's opinion at that time was that the FBI spokesmen (instructors) were lying through their teeth abut the Kennedy assassination and the story they were feeding us was simply a load of baloney. I was a bit shaken and disillusioned. (And still am)

One humorous note on our FBI visit was upon arriving at the FBI Academy on Sunday evening, we attendees were escorted to an area where we had a social gathering (a cocktail party of sorts). The following morning the class members were asked by the FBI to cough up a few bucks to pay for the booze consumed. What class!

The following week, the seminar class moved over to the Secret Service headquarters in Washington, and we were presented much detail to back up the Warren Commission and the FBI's assertions on the JFK case. However, the Secret Service did say that they were open to the possibility of a conspiracy. The class attendees screened the famous Zapurder film several times and asked many questions, some of which were answered and others not.

In later years, I toiled with Secret Service agents in other events and remain to this day in awe of the professionalism of their organization at that time, but do pray that the F.B.I. establishment has finally rid itself of 'Hooverism'. (I did, however, have the pleasure to work with many fine individual FBI agents over the years who were great cops, especially the Miami FBI bank robbery team investigators of the early 1970's, led by Agent Gene Flynn.

One key question a couple of attendees asked at the seminar was why the Secret Service (the U.S. government) did not reimburse local governments for the cost of providing the requested manpower for presidential type visits. I remember a black Police Major from Detroit backing me up on this point. The federal government was coming into our department at that time demanding, that on one hand we hire a certain percentage of minorities regardless of qualifications and to implement silly and wasteful programs, but would not provide the reimbursement for the hundreds of man-hours expended during each presidential-type visit.

The Secret Service agent instructor stopped the class at one point, took a short break, and an Assistant Director was brought in for a follow up. I inquired of him where in the federal statute on Presidential protection did it state that Miami or Detroit or any other local agency being required to provide any manpower support without being compensated. The Assistant Director finally agreed that we were correct, there is no legal obligation to provide support, and he hoped that some legislation would be offered that would solve this financial problem in the future. (I doubt if it ever has come about)

This brings me to another point where the reader, if unfamiliar with how our federal intelligence agencies cultivate local assistance, will find a partial answer.

Just prior to attending this seminar, which I did not apply for, I was the Major (Commander) in charge of the Patrol Section, which was then staffed by over 500 field patrol officers. A presidential candidate, by the name of McCormick from Philadelphia, was coming to the Dupont Plaza in Miami for a campaign event. The Secret Service relayed a request to my office for thirty of so officers to be assigned to this event. After reviewing the event plans and discovering that most of the event was inside the hotel and not on public property, I advised that one sergeant, two officers (for traffic) and a K-9 officer would be assigned as well as putting a bomb technician on call. If they desired more officers than that, to produce a crowd photo shot for the campaign, I suggested that they arrange with our off-duty office for the hiring of whatever more officers they would like, at their expense.

The following Monday morning I was advised by the Chief's office that I was selected to attend a Dignitary Protection seminar in Washington the following week. I did not apply to attend, but certainly enjoyed the trip and seminar. At one point during the week with the Secret Service, the class toured the White House. During the tour, an Assistant Director tapped me on the shoulder and took me - just me - on a tour inside the 'inner sanctum' areas of the White House. We passed Susan Ford walking down the hall and then entered the Oval Office and observed that President Ford was conducting a cabinet meeting just outside, in the Rose Garden area. I observed Henry Kissinger and others sitting around a table. While in the Oval office, my guide offered me to sit behind the President's desk, which I declined, as I thought it would be a sacrilege to do so. (this was before Clinton's tawdry actions in that same office.) I appreciated the 'extra' tour and can say nothing but the best for the Secret Service. But, why the special courtesies?

My later involvement with the Secret Service during a 1987 Pope John Paul II visit to Miami (after my retirement from Miami P.D.) increased the admiration I had (and have) for the professionalism of the Secret Service. I was even graciously assigned a desk at their office for several months for liaison purposes despite not being an active police official who could no longer return favors. I observed them in action daily and was duly impressed by their performance, integrity and professionalism.

This Washington trip prompted me to review, through the eyes of an experienced law enforcement officer, and to apply common sense logic, to the entire Kennedy case. I became totally convinced that the FBI was lying through their teeth regarding the Kennedy investigation. I am convinced of my opinion that conspirators were present in Dealey Square that day and that the leaders and plotters of this conspiracy were most likely Mafia bosses Carlos Marcello and Santos Trafficante, and the actual field assassins were quite likely from the Anti-Castro Cubans/Organized Crime element, possibly aided by elements of the CIA.

PART X

INVESTIGATIONS BY
FEDERAL AGENCIES

SECRET SERVICE

James Duffy and Vincent Ricci wrote in their book, "The Assassination of John F. Kennedy, 1992, "The reason for the Secret Service neglect remains one of the intriguing mysteries of the Kennedy assassination". (98)

Robert Groden and Harrison Livingston wrote in "High Treason", 2nd ed. 1989, "Kennedy was killed by a breakdown in a protective system that should have made the assassination impossible". (99)

David E. Wilkes, Jr., wrote in "Intriguing Mysteries - The Secret Service and the JFK Assassination", (100) "Based on the information available nearly 50 years after the assassination, there is a consensus among those who investigated Kennedy's Secret Service protection. The consensus: JFK's protection was inadequate. Indeed, the protection was so defective that it dangerously insured the likelihood that an assassination plan involving one or more concealed snipers firing into the presidential limousine would succeed. By making the murder easier and the undetected escape of the assassins more likely, this Secret Service bungling contributed to the assassination".

The Warren Commission merely faulted the Secret Service for not conducting a prior inspection of the buildings along the motorcade route. Had the Secret Service made the meticulous protection it should have, President Kennedy would not have been slain that day in Dallas. The US House 'Select Committee on Assassinations final report in 1979 concluded that the Secret Service was deficient in the performance of its duties:

1- The Secret Service possessed information that was not properly analyzed, investigated or used in connection with the Dallas trip.

2- The Secret Service agents in the motorcade were inadequately prepared to protect the President from a sniper.

3- There was a failure to arrange for prior inspection of buildings along the motorcade route.

4- The Secret Service reduced the number of motorcycles from eight to four and had the four remain to the rear of the presidential car.

The Secret Service did not heed the warnings created by the threats at Chicago, Tampa and Miami, in the weeks prior to the Dallas trip. The information on the Milteer threat was not passed on to the Secret Service in Dallas prior to the trip. In Tampa, after a threat was received, six hundred police officers were used in the motorcade that day, with the Tampa police using officers from the surrounding cities and sheriff departments. In Miami, travel from the airport to Miami Beach was made by helicopter, after the threat in that city. It seemed to David Talbot, as stated in his book, "The Hidden History of the Kennedy Years, 2007, "Kennedy was in fact being methodically stalked in his final weeks of life. No building inspection was made along the Dallas motorcade route by the Secret Service nor was the Dallas police asked to perform that task. The head of the Dallas Secret Service office, Mr. Sorrels, was quoted to say they would do the motorcade as they did for President Roosevelt in 1936. (That was twenty-seven years earlier).

The Secret Service did not have the 'first team' on duty in the Dallas motorcade. Jerry Behn, the Special Agent in Charge of the White House detail was on vacation. He normally would have been in the right front seat of the presidential limo. His top assistant, Floyd Boring, was off-duty that day in Washington. This resulted in Roy Kellerman, then 48, being in Agent Behn's usual position. The driver of Kennedy's car that day was William Greer, a 52 year old agent. Greer, upon hearing the first shot, slowed the car down from 11 miles an hour to an almost stop. After the third shot, he finally accelerated down Dealey Plaza onto the Stemmons Highway. This hesitation allowed the shooter(s) ample time to zero in on Kennedy to make the fatal shot.

There was also confusion in the Secret Service back-up car. This car was staffed by agent-driver Sam Kinney, ATSAIC Emory Roberts, presidential aides Larry O'Donnell and Dave Powers, and agents George Hickey, DRS agent Glen Bennett, Clint Hill, Jack Ready, Tim McIntyre and Paul Landis. Other than Agent Clint Hill and Vice President Johnson's agent, Rufus Youngblood, the agents seemed to be in shock when the shots rang out and were slow to react. Hill bravely jumped onto the rear of JFK's car at great risk to his own life and threw himself over JFK and Jackie Kennedy. Agent Youngblood pushed Johnson down and covered him with his own body. Both moved quickly and bravely. Usually, the local police homicide squad had a car placed in presidential motorcades just to the rear of the Secret Service back-up car. Agent Winston Lawson, who planned the motorcade, deleted this squad from the motorcade.

The head of the Secret Service, James Rowley, testified at the Warren Commission that nine of the Dallas trip agents were drinking at a Fort Worth joint called "The Cellar", and several of the agents then went, after 2AM, to a private club, staying close to 5:00 A.M. the night before the assassination. Four of theses agents were in JFK's detail the following morning, November 22, 1963.

Secret Service Chief Rowley did not tell the Warren Commission anything about the Milteer tape that advised that "Kennedy would be killed by a sniper from a high building when he traveled south". This tape recording between a Miami police informant, Willie Somersett and Joseph Milteer, a violent right-wing leader, was made by Sergeant Everett Kaye of the Miami Police Department and was promptly passed on to the Secret Service and the Federal Bureau of Investigation. The Secret Service, in 1995, destroyed copies of their 1963 reports - despite the existence of the JFK Assassination Materials Disclosure Act of 1992, which prevented this destruction. The Secret Service personnel were also advised not to destroy these reports by National Archive personnel.

Chief Rowley report of the assassination was completed on December 18, 1963. It did not include any investigative activities of the Secret Service to ascertain the identify of the assassin as this type of information was instead passed on to the specified investigators of the assassination, the Federal Bureau of Investigation, who had the overall responsibility for the investigation.

FEDERAL BUREAU OF INVESTIGATION

Immediately after the assassination and the arrest of Lee Oswald, the Asst. Attorney General, Nick Katzenbach, wrote a memo at the urging of FBI Director Hoover.

"The public must be convinced that Oswald was the assassin, that he did not have confederates who are still at large....Speculation about Oswald's motivation ought to be cut off". (102)

The FBI then proceeded to carry out about 25,000 interviews and submitted 2,300 reports totaling 25,600 pages to the Warren Commission to prove that theory.

William Sullivan, the number three man in the FBI in 1963, stated, "Hoover's main thought was always how to cover, how to protect himself". (103)

Agent Laurence Keenan was sent to Mexico City by FBI leaders Hoover, Belmont and Sullivan. Many years later he said -among other things, "Any idea that Oswald had a confederate or was part of a group or a conspiracy definitely placed a man's (FBI agent) career in jeopardy". Keenan received NO help from Mexico City's CIA personnel or the US Ambassador to Mexico. (104)

FBI Agent Hosty visited Marina Oswald twice, on November 1st and the 5th, 1963. Oswald, when told of these visits, proceeded to the Dallas FBI office while on a lunch break, and left a note to Hosty that if he (Hosty) wanted to learn about Oswald, come talk to me directly, and cease bothering my wife. The Warren Report stated that Hosty should have notified the Secret Service. As a result, Director Hoover of the FBI suspended Hosty and other agents and transferred Hosty to Kansas City.

U.S. Ambassador Mann at Mexico City, "I had no knowledge of Kennedy's anti-Castro plots"

"I think the FBI can look back and feel that this one investigation disgraced a great organization".

In mid-afternoon of the 22nd, the Dallas P.D. became aware that Oswald had at thick FBI dossier and was currently being handled by FBI Agent Hosty of the Dallas bureau. It became known that the FBI had not informed the Dallas police or the Secret Service, of Oswald's presence in Dallas or his employment at the Book Depository building.

Don Adams, a retired FBI agent, wrote a book on his involvement in the Kennedy case, "From an Office Building With a High-Powered Rifle", (101) Adams was a Georgia based FBI agent who was assigned on November 13, 1963, to locate militant Joseph Milteer, who had been secretly recorded describing how President Kennedy would be shot. Adams, who served twenty year in the FBI, was assigned in November 1963 to the Thomasville, Georgia FBI office. He was told to investigate Milteer, a racist extremist from Quitman, Georgia. Adams was not told at that time that Milteer had been recorded describing just how Kennedy would be shot while traveling through the south later that month.

A day after the killing of JFK, Adams was again assigned to locate Milteer. The agent could not locate Milteer for several days although official FBI reports inaccurately stated that Milteer had indeed been in Quitman on the day of the assassination. Adams, later a police chief in Ohio, waited fifty years to reveal this explosive information.

Former Secret Service agent, Bolden, mentioned earlier, wrote an interesting review of Don Adams's book on Amazon.com Mr. Bolden congratulated Mr. Adams for his book and expressed belief that any thinking person will be convinced "that there was more to the Kennedy assassination than certain force wanted the American people to be aware of". Bolden observed that "the book clearly shines the light on the behind the scene machinations that were in operation by high authorities and supervisors within the United States Secret Service and the FBI to conceal from the

American People many of the facts and persons suspected to have been involved in the assassination"

Former Agent Bolden expressed disappointment in the writing the fact that the Adams had this information for the past nearly 50 years and did not come forth. "I needed your book then Don....The American People and the researchers trying to solve the mystery of the assassination right after it happened in 1963 needed Adams's book then......not nearly 50 years later. I hope that it is not too late. God Bless America".

"The author (Don Adams) had this information, these documents, and these provable inconsistencies for an extended amount of time and chose to keep silent and become a participant in the conspiracy to mislead the American People as to the facts surrounding the assassination".

On December 9, 1963, the FBI produced a 384 page, five volume report concluding that Lee Harvey Oswald was the sole assassin and that no evidence of a conspiracy existed.

CENTRAL INTELLIGENCE AGENCY

There were at least nine assassination plots by the Central Intelligence Agency to kill Fidel Castro. Allen Dulles, former head of the CIA, never told the Warren Commission, which he was a member, that the United States had been trying to kill Castro.

Winston Scott, CIA station chief in Mexico City said:

"In fact, LHO (Lee Harvey Oswald) became a person of great interest to us during the 27 September-2 October period". (1963) "Every piece of info concerning Oswald was reported immediately after it was received....These reports were made on all his contacts with both the Cuban consulate and the Soviets".

FBI Director Clarence Kelly said: "Had our intelligence community pooled their information on Oswald.....had the Secret Service Protective Research Section been aware of all the Oswald data, and had the information been distributed to New Orleans and Dallas FBI offices in time for them to act, then, without a doubt, President Kennedy would not have died in Dallas on November 22, 1963"

We will now look at some of the 'CIA players' that had some connection to the JFK case because of their assignment or actions taken during that time.

Howard Hunt, 1918-2007, worked for the CIA from 1949 to 1970. In World War II he was in the Navy and was attached to the OSS. Hunt was one of the White House plumbers squad during the Watergate era and was convicted of Burglary, Conspiracy and Wiretapping. He served thirty-three months in prison for these crimes. He helped in the overthrow of President Arbenz of Guatemala. After the Bay of Pigs he was a personal assistant to Allen Dulles, former head of the CIA from 1961 to 1963. Hunt was chief of the CIA Covert Action group in the Domestic Operations section for four years, in charge of "subsidizing and manipulation of the news.

In 1963 Hunt was acting CIA chief in Mexico City during the period of Oswald sightings in August and September of 1963. He later worked for the CIA front, the Mullen Company, and was hired by Charles Colson to work on White House matters. He had retired from the CIA in May of 1970. Hunt was also one of the burglars who broke into Ellsworth's psychiatrist office.

After the Kennedy assassination Hunt was in charge of the assassination related dis-information program for the CIA. After getting caught in Watergate he actually tried (with some success) in shaking down the White House for funds to handle attorney fees and living expenses.

A 1966 CIA memo related that Hunt was in Dallas on the day of the JFK assassination according to Vincent Marchetti story in the Liberty Lobby law suit file.

In later years Hunt lived in the Miami suburb of Biscayne Park. A colleague of mine, MPD Charlie (C.I.) Smith was his neighbor and we often speculated if Hunt would talk to us about the assassination if we stopped by, but we never got up the courage to knock on his door.

Vincent Marchetti, a high-ranking CIA official who left the agency in disgust, later made a career writing about the CIA. In a 1978 article he charged that the CIA was about to frame its long-time operative, E.

Howard Hunt, with involvement in the JFK assassination. A libel suit resulting as a consequence of Marchetti's article resulted in a climactic finding by a jury that the CIA had been involved in the assassination of the president.

David Atlee Phillips, 1922-1988, was a CIA employee for twenty-five years. He was chief of all operations in the Western Hemisphere. He was connected to the well known Alpha 66 anti-Castro Cuban group and used the alias "Maurice Bishop". Cuban activist Antonio Veciana claimed that he met with Phillips and Lee Harvey Oswald prior to the assassination. Phillips was Mexico City chief of Cuban operations in September of 1963, just before Oswald's visit to that city. Phillips retired from the CIA in 1975.

Other CIA operatives that had activities relating to the JFK assassination are:

Bernard Barker, CIA operative who assembled the Watergate burglars, Richard Helms, Deputy CIA Director, James Angleton, Chief of Counter-Intelligence, George Joannides, Chief Psychological Warfare -worked at JMWAVE with David Phillips. Recalled from retirement to be liaison between the CIA and the HSCA in 1978.

Birch O'Neal - Counter Intelligence -Tracked Oswald from 1959 to 1963. Chief of Special Operations Group, reporting to Jim Angleton. David Morales, Asst. Chief, JMWAVE. William Harvey, CIA assassination expert. Theodore Shackley - Chief of Station, JMWAVE, Miami, and Grayson Lynch -Trainer-Agent, JM Wave, among other operatives.

The Mary Ferrell Foundation website posted a very informative story titled, "The CIA and the JFK Assassination" which must be read by any student of this case. The story reveals the inner workings of the CIA in the JFK case, before, during and after the fact. The website address is: htps://www.maryferrell.org/wiki/../The_CIA_and_the_JFK Assassination

After joining the CIA, David Morales became an operative for the CIA's Directorate for Plans. It's alleged that he was involved in "Executive Action", a series of projects designed to kill foreign leaders deemed unfriendly to the United States. Morales reportedly was involved in Operation PBSUCCESS, the CIA covert operation that overthrew the democratically-elected President of Guatemala, Jacob Arbenz Guzmán. [2] Through the 1960s and mid-1970s, Morales was involved at top levels in a variety of covert projects, including JMWAVE (The huge Miami

CIA station), the ZRRIFLE plot to assassinate Fidel Castro, the Bay of Pigs Invasion operation, the CIA's secret war in Laos,[3] the capture of Che Guevara, and the overthrow of Salvador Allende. He worked closely with Tracy Barnes, William D. Pawley, David Atlee Phillips, John Martino, Johnny Roselli, and the infamous Ted Shackley, who was Morales boss in the giant CIA station in Miami (JMWAVE). The team of Shackley and Morales during the period of the Cuban Missile Crisis, as well as the Cuban Project (also known as Operation Mongoose), which Shackley directed, has been become well known.

Ted Shackley is perhaps best known for his involvement in CIA "black ops". During the period (1962–1965), Shackley was station chief in Miami, Florida. While heading the CIA office (known as "JMWAVE") shortly after the 1961 Bay of Pigs Invasion, Shackley dealt with operations in Cuba (alongside Edward Lansdale). JMWAVE employed more than 200 CIA officers, who handled approximately 2,000 Cuban agents. These included the famous "Operation Mongoose" (aka "The Cuban Project"). The aim of this was to "help Cubans (exiles) overthrow the Communist regime" (of Fidel Castro Ruiz). During this period as Miami Station Chief, Shackley was in charge of about 400 agents and general operatives (as well as a huge flotilla of boats), and his tenure there encompassed the Cuban Missile Crisis of October 1962.

PART XI

WHO ORDERED HIT

What prompted me to look deeper into the Kennedy case some twenty years ago was a private investigation of the Detroit Mafia I conducted in my post retirement years while operating a private investigation (P.I.) agency in Miami in the late 1990's. That investigation expanded from the Detroit Mafia and Jimmy Hoffa to the Kennedy killing. I drafted a report, drawing upon many public sources (newspapers, magazines, and books), some very factual and logical and others a bit questionable. I am a few of the statements made back then might melt under today's spotlight, but the overall theory will stand tall. (105)

It is the author's opinion that the Kennedy assassination was planned and plotted by organized crime leaders, (principally Carlos Marcello) utilizing Oswald, Dallas area gangland figures, and rouge CIA agents with the crew of anti-Castro Cubans from Miami, New Orleans and Dallas, as likely accessories. In addition to studying the various public literatures on this case, I have visited Dealey Plaza, interviewed FBI agents, Secret Service agents, Louisiana State police officers, high ranking Dallas P.D. officers and a kin of Attorney Jack Wasserman. I also had numerous discussions with Lieutenant Everett Kaye, Captain Gene McCracken, and Sgt Andy Giordano, all of the Miami Police Department. (As well as other MPD detectives) Sergeants Kaye and McCracken were Intelligence officers and later testified to Senate Committees on the Kennedy case and Detective Giordano was the initial lead investigator in the Eladio Del Valle murder case in Miami. All three of the officers worked for me at the Miami Police Department. They were also personal friends and top-notch investigators.

ORGANIZED CRIME INVOLVEMENT

Carlos Marcello (born Calogero Minacore) joined the Mafia in 1936 and became boss of the Mafia in Louisiana on May 5, 1947, upon the deportation of Sam (Silver Dollar) Carolla. His territory included Louisiana, Mississippi and Texas. Marcelo, born in Tunisia of Sicilian parents in 1910, came to America as a baby and never did become a citizen of the USA. He married Jackie Todaro, daughter of a Mafia underboss in 1936. He formed the Jefferson Music Co. in the late 1930's and began distributing pinball and jukeboxes, pool tables and various gambling paraphernalia to area bars and restaurants. When reform Mayor LaGuardia was elected in New York City, Frank Costello began moving his 'Chief' slot machines down to New Orleans area, with the permission of Huey Long and Louisiana Mafia chief Sam Carolla. Costello's rise to the "prime minister of the Mafia" started in 1929 when he faced down Al Capone at the famous Mafia meeting in Atlantic City. Costello claimed he was in a loose partnership with Joe Kennedy, as attested to by various people including Joseph Bonanno (in his autobiography), Doc Stracher and author Peter Maas. After the repeal of prohibition, each went separate ways. Costello setup Alliance Distributors handling King's Ranson and House of Lords Scotch and Kennedy setup Somerset Liquors to distribute Haig and Haig scotch, Dewars's scotch and Gordon's gin. This competition fostered intense animosity against the Mafia by the elder Kennedy. Author John H. Davis, in his book, "Mafia Kingfish", 1989, Signet Books, provided a detailed description of Carlos Marcello's life.

The Jefferson Music Co. spread the 1,000 plus Costello slots throughout New Orleans under the direction of Marcello, 'Dandy Phil' Kastel and 'Diamond Jim' Moran. In 1944, Costello opened up a plush Las Vegas style gambling house in Jefferson Parish, the Beverly Country Club, on the East Bank. Marcello was made a part owner as was Meyer Lansky. Phil Kastel, Costello and Freddie Rickerfor owned the remainder. Marcello gave Sheriff Clancy a 2 1/2% slice and let him hire all non-administrative help, an arrangement approved by then Governor Jimmie Davis. Marcello also ran the racing wire, Southern News Co., and bought his own casino, the New Southport Club, as well as the Nola Printing Co., a mid-west gambling wire service.

On January 25, 1951, Senator Kefauver's Special Committee to Investigate Organized Crime in Interstate Commerce held hearings in New Orleans with Marcello as the main witness. Marcello took the "5th" 152 times as advised by his attorney, G. Wray Gill. In 1953, the government issued its first deportation order against Marcello.

That same year (1953) Marcello bought the Town and Country Motel on Airline Highway between New Orleans and the airport. His two assistants, Nofino Pecora and Joe Poretto, his brother Anthony Marcello and one of his lawyers, Phil Smith, also had offices at the motel. In the mid-1950's, Marcello acquired a 6,400 acre bayou ranch called Churchill Farms. The only local thorn in Marcello's side was Aaron Kohn, head of the New Orleans Crime Commission. The F.B.I.'s Special Agent in Charge for New Orleans, Regis Kennedy, consistently maintained that Marcello was "only a tomato salesman" and not an organized crime chieftain. In 1959, Kohn provided information on Marcello to a U.S. Senate committee to investigate corruption in labor and management chaired by Senator John McClellan. Senator John Kennedy was a committee member and Robert Kennedy was appointed the chief counsel of the committee. On March 24, 1959, Carlos Marcello was called as a witness. Next to him was the brilliant Harvard trained lawyer, Jack Wasserman.

FBI Director J. Edgar Hoover had denied the existence of a national organized crime organization until the New York State Police broke up the famous Appalachian conclave of over 60 organized crime leaders, including Marcello's representatives, brother Joe Marcello and his Dallas associate, Joseph Civello. Bobby Kennedy asked Marcello 68 questions, each one of which was answered "I decline to answer on the ground that it may tent to incriminate me". Senator Sam Ervin interrupted the questioning to ask how Marcello had managed to stay in the US for almost six years after being ordered deported. Marcello answered, "Senator, not being an attorney, my attorney (Wasserman) could answer that question". Senator Mundt then asked that the Attorncy General be queried as to why Marcello had not been deported as ordered. No clear answer was forthcoming.

In 1960, Jack Kennedy became President and appointed his 35 year old brother Bobby as Attorney General. Although both possessed extraordinary leadership qualities and high degree of political responsibility, there was a secretive, reckless side to both the brother's private and public lives that bore little resemblance to the chivalric sprit of the legendary Camelot. Jack had the propensity to enter into liaisons that were so dangerous as to strain credulity. His most reckless extramarital adventures were with starlet Judith Campbell, who was also Sam Giancana's girlfriend and with actress

Marilyn Monroe. Fred Otash, a private detective working with Jimmy Hoffa, had installed listening devices on Monroe's telephones and in her home. Bobby also proved equally reckless in entering into a relationship himself with Marilyn Monroe, at a time when other private detectives hired by Jimmy Hoffa, (Bernard Spindell and Earl Jaycox), was keeping Monroe under close electronic surveillance. Complicating the Kennedy's plot against Cuba, their campaign against the Mafia, and the recklessness of their private lives was the strange and sinister alliance with certain Mafia bosses entered into, perhaps unbeknownst to the Kennedy brothers', for the purpose of assassinating Castro.

Legendary criminal Meyer Lansky was thrown out (he flew out the night Castro rode into Havana) of Cuba's casinos (and country) and he promptly put a price on Castro's head of one million dollars. Cuban exile groups sprang up, especially in Miami, Tampa and New Orleans (some funded by Carlos Marcello). Upon taking office, Bobby Kennedy increased the Justice Department's organized crime section four-fold. Kennedy was aware that Carlos Marcello had obtained by bribery, a false Guatemalan birth certificate under his real name, Calogero Minacore, and an entry permit describing Marcello as a citizen of Guatemala.

On April 4, 1961, Carlos Marcello, accompanied by lawyer Phil Smith, went to the Immigration and Naturalization office in New Orleans to make a required quarterly alien registration. Marcello was handcuffed, hustled out to the airport and put on an INS (Immigration and Naturalization Service) airplane. Marcello demanded that he be allowed to call his immigration attorney, Jack Wasserman, in Washington, but was refused. He was flown directly to Guatemala and dumped out. It should be noted that Bobby Kennedy was quoted in a Louisiana's States-Item article in December, quoting Kennedy as vowing to step up deportation proceedings against Carlos Marcello once he assumed the Attorney General's position.

Marcello's attorney, Smith, finally got through to attorney Wasserman in Washington, who filed suit in federal court the next morning, demanding Marcello's immediate return to the U.S. While Wasserman was filing suit, Bobby Kennedy publicly announced that Marcello had been deported to Guatemala and that he was taking full responsibility for the expulsion of the New Orleans crime boss. Carlos Marcello was joined in Guatemala four days later by Mike Maroun, Marcello's Shreveport attorney. After two months, Marcello snuck back into Miami. Some say he was flown in by a Dominican Republic Air Force jet (this info allegedly obtained by a wiretap) and others say that David Ferrie, a private investigator of one of Marcello's attorney's (a pilot) flew him back.

Meanwhile, on April 10th, in New Orleans, the Internal Revenue Service filed tax liens of $835,000 against Carlos Marcello and his wife, an action instigated by Bobby Kennedy. It has been said that when Jack Wasserman telephoned this news to Marcello, he went into a rage. Attorney Wasserman advised Marcello that he would immediately file suit to remove the liens. After a month in Guatemala, Marcello and family were provided a visa to return to the U.S.

At the airport, Marcello was advised that the U.S. denied his visa, but the others could return to New Orleans. To get the heat off the Guatemalan government, Carlos Marcello and Mike Maroun were driven into El Salvador, and then finally worked their way to Tegucigalpa, Honduras, where Maroun flew home commercially and Marcello flew two weeks later into Miami, allegedly in an Dominican Air Force jet. At that time, General Rafael Trujillo, the President of the Dominican Republic, was a good friend of Santos Trafficante and that Irv Davidson, Marcello's friend, was a Capitol Hill lobbyist for the Dominican Republic. (Two days later, Trujillo was assassinated by CIA backed Dominican forces, and applauded by Bobby Kennedy, who knew that the elimination of Trujillo was a necessary move in Bobby's war against organized crime)

This fact (of US officials assisting Marcello's return) was not made public until 1975, when the Senate Intelligence Committee released it, although the FBI reported in 1961 that a "high ranking US government official, Senator Russell Long, (Huey's son) may have intervened to allow Marcello to land in Florida.

Bobby Kennedy then sent 20 agents to Shreveport to try to find Marcello who then turned himself in to the INS office in New Orleans. On July 11, he was ruled an undesirable alien and once again ordered him deported, a ruling that Wasserman immediately appealed. In the meantime, Marcello was released on bond. While Marcello was in exile, Wasserman filed two lawsuits in his behalf. One was against the IRS 835K lien and the other was against Bobby Kennedy over the circumstances of Marcello's deportation to Guatemala.

In the fall of 1961, Marcello was again summoned to testify at new McClellan hearings but Attorney Wasserman showed up and claimed that Marcello was still ill and injured as a result of his deportation travels. Carlos Marcello later appeared and claimed the "5th" again. Bobby Kennedy was said to have been particularly annoyed at attorney Jack Wasserman's reference to the "cruel and inhumane way" Kennedy had deported Marcello. It should be noted that J. Edgar Hoover also chided Kennedy for wasting his time on a "hoodlum" and had gotten into a mess by his kidnap-style deportation of Marcello.

On October 30, 1961, Kennedy had Carlos Marcello indicted on conspiracy charges in falsifying a Guatemalan birth certificate and committing perjury. On December 30, 1961, a Board of Immigration Appeals upheld the deportation order against him, denying Jack Wasserman's appeal that it be declared invalid. It has been widely reported that Marcello and family's hatred for Bobby Kennedy was tremendously strong, but Marcello still tried to get straight with Kennedy by appealing to Santos Trafficante and Sam Gianciana to have Frank Sinatra intercede with Kennedy's father. This story was picked up by a FBI wiretap on July 27, 1962, between Mafia member Russell Buffalino (another client of Wasserman) and Angelo Bruno, boss of the Philadelphia Mafia. This attempt by Carlos Marcello only goaded Bobby Kennedy to step up his efforts against Marcello. In the late summer of 1962, Marcello was overheard on two occasions to loudly state that he was going to take care of the Kennedy's. One of these men who overheard the remarks was private detective, Edward Becker.

Becker was questioned by the FBI on November 20, 1962, and told them of the meeting with Marcello but did not pass along Marcello's threat. Also, this same week, Santos Trafficante was discussing Kennedy and Hoffa with Jose Aleman, a Cuban exile Miami millionaire. Trafficante told Aleman that Kennedy' were putting extreme pressure on Hoffa and "Mark my words, this man Kennedy is in trouble, and he will get what is coming to him". Aleman argued with Trafficante that Kennedy was doing a good job and would get re-elected. Trafficante remarked, "No Jose, you don't understand me. Kennedy's not going to make it to the election. He is going to be hit". (Aleman was a FBI informant for several years up through 1963. Ninety-five of his FBI files, FBI #109-584, are posted on the Mary Ferrell Foundation website, six of the which files are still restricted. Aleman also testified to the HSCA (House committee that Trafficante did indeed make this statement to him.)

Also this summer (1962), Louisiana Teamster official Ed Partin claimed that Jimmy Hoffa was seriously thinking of killing Bobby Kennedy and perhaps also his brother, Jack.

In October of 1962, the Immigration and Naturalization Service's order to deport Carlos Marcello as an "undesirable alien" because he was convicted of a felony in 1938 was appealed by attorney Jack Wasserman, by filing a writ to set the 1938 conviction aside. The federal court ruled against Carlos Marcello on October 30th. Jack Wasserman then petitioned the Supreme Court to review the deportation order.

It should be noted that the stories coming out of the Marcello camp at that time about Marcello's threats against the Kennedy(s) were numerous. Also, Bobby Kennedy was hounding Director Hoover about infiltrating Marcello's organization, but New Orleans FBI head, Regis Kennedy, kept insisting that Marcello was only a "tomato salesman". Since the 1957 Appalachian crime boss meeting, the FBI was able to penetrate each and every Mafia organization in the US except Marcello's (they finally did in 1979) and were able to plant electronic bugs in the headquarters of every Mafia boss in the US, except Trafficante and Carlos Marcello.

In early 1963, two people heard specific threats against Kennedy while working or visiting in Marcello's area. One was a FBI informant, Eugene De Laparra, who worked in the Lounnor Restaurant on Airline Highway, owned by Bernard Tregle, an associate of Carlos Marcello. Tregle stated that there was a price on Kennedy's head and somebody will kill Kennedy when he comes down south. About the same a businessman named Summer from Darien, Georgia, was having dinner at Marcello's Town and Country restaurant with Ernest Insalmo, Sal Pizza and Benny Capeana. During dinner he observed a heavy set man sit down with a young couple and hand the young man a wad of cash under the table. After President Kennedy was killed, Summer claimed that the young man at the table that night was Lee Harvey Oswald and the older heavy set man who Summer thought was the owner of the restaurant actually fit the description of the manager, Joseph Poretto, a high ranking member of Marcello's organization.

Oswald, it should be noted, was living in New Orleans the later part of April, 1963. He left Dallas on April 6th and six days later someone took a shot at Major General Edwin Walker, member of the John Birch Society. Oswald's wife claimed that it was her husband. Oswald showed up on the 24th of April in New Orleans and moved in with his aunt, Lillian Murret and her husband, Charles "Dutz" Murret, a middle-level bookmaker in the Marcello gambling network.

On May 27th, 1963, the U.S. Supreme Court declined to review the Marcello deportation action and upheld the earlier decision of the U.S. Court of Appeals that the INS order to deport Carlos Marcello remain in effect. At that time, attorney Wasserman had only one chance to avoid Marcello's deportation. That was he had to beat the charges of conspiracy and perjury in regard to the falsification of his Guatemalan birth certificate Kennedy had brought against him after his illegal reentry in June of 1961. The case was due to be tried in November of 1963. Marcello's New Orleans attorney was G. Wray Gill. Gill had a client named David W. Ferrie, a former Eastern Airlines pilot fired in a dispute with Eastern. Gill was so impressed with Ferrie that he hired him as a legal aide in March of 1962. In 1963, Gill assigned Ferrie to work on Marcello's defense against the government's conspiracy and perjury charges. During the summer of 1963, Ferrie was working with Marcello at the Town and Country Motel in New Orleans. During the same period of time, Ferrie was also meeting with a former student of his in the New Orleans Civil Air Patrol, Lee Harvey Oswald.

It should be noted that Ferrie was a former gun runner for Castro in his fight against General Batista but once it became clear Castro was a Communist, Ferrie turned against him in a fury and was soon piloting bombers to Cuba on sabotage raids on behalf of various Cuban exile groups. Ferrie joined the violently anti-Castro CRF, an organization heavily fronted by Carlos Marcello and became a sworn enemy of President Kennedy, whom he accused of betraying the Cuban exiles Bay of Pigs assault. In addition to working for Marcello's attorney, Ferrie was also employed by Guy Bannister Associates, a private detective agency at 544 Camp Street in New Orleans. Witnesses had observed Oswald and Ferrie, Bannister and Sergio Smith, leader of the Cuban Revolutionary Front (CRF) during the summer of 1963 meeting at this address. Oswald was also seen with Bannister at several places around New Orleans during the summer. Bannister had done work for Marcello previously and was an ex-FBI agent (actually he was the FBI S.A.C. in Chicago) and a former deputy superintendent of the New Orleans Police Department, and an officer in Office of Naval Intelligence.

In mid-September of 1963, Oswald was seen with David Ferrie in Clinton, Louisiana, during a voter registration drive for blacks of that area. Oswald obtained his Mexican visa and moved back to Dallas, and then, on the 26th of September, made the trip to Mexico City.

Dallas, Texas was a Marcello city controlled directly by his underboss, Louisiana born Joe Civello and his assistants Joe Campisie and Frank LaMonte. Marcello also allegedly had paid enormous amounts of money at that time to Texas politicians for protection through John Halfen. Much, it was said, was funneled to U.S. Representative Albert Thomas, Supreme Court Justice Tom Clark and U.S. Senator Lyndon Johnson. (Legal political contributions?). It was claimed that over $50,000 annually went from Dallas gambling rackets direct to Johnson's political machine. Civello was with Marcello's brother at the infamous Appalachian crime confab in 1957. Three days after Civello's return from New York state, he was observed having lunch with Sergeant Pat Dean of the Dallas P.D. Dean, it should be noted, was in charge of basement security at Dallas P.D. on the Sunday that Oswald was to be transferred to the Harris County Jail in Dallas. A Dallas nightclub operator, part-time narcotics dealer, bookmaker, slot machine operator and pimp, Jack Ruby was alleged to be under the overall control of Joe Campisie.

An informant named Moore stated that Ruby was a frequent visitor to Civello and LaMonte at their importing company in Dallas. Jack Ruby had been born to Jewish immigrants and had been raised in Chicago's West Side ghetto. Ruby had visited New Orleans in June and October of 1963 and had visited Frank Caracci, a middle level player in Marcello's organization, at his bar in New Orleans. Ruby had also visited Harold Tannebaum, an associate of Carlos Marcello assistant, Nofio Pecora. Tannebaum lived at Pecora's Tropical Tourist Court Motel and that between May and November of 1963, Ruby made 18 telephone calls to Tannebaum from Dallas.

During October of 1963, David Ferrie met with Carlos Marcello several times at the Town & Country Motel and traveled to Guatemala on Delta Airlines on October 11th through the 18th and again from October 30th to November 1st. Ferrie spent the weekends of November 9th and 10th and again from November 16th and 17th, with Marcello at Churchill Farms. Marcello's trial was due to start on November 4th, 1963. Ferrie had been fired by Eastern Airlines in 1961. One reason was that Ferrie was a homosexual; another was the fact that he often loudly expressed his violent hatred against Jack Kennedy for calling off the Bay of Pigs air cover. Marcello testified to House Committee on Assassinations in 1978, that he had paid David Ferrie $7,000 in cash for his legal assistance in October of 1963 while preparing for trial.

In the 1950's, Carlos Marcello heard that Italy would take him in if the U.S. booted him out of the country. Marcello then obtained a fraudulent birth certificate from Guatemala as he would rather go there if deported, than Sicily. He hired Carl Noll, a friend of one of his brothers. Noll went to Guatemala and struck a deal with Antonio Valladares, a former law partner of Guatemala's prime minister. Valladares, for a fee, came up with a Guatamalen birth certificate for Marcello. Marcello was then able to obtain citizenship papers from Guatemala. Jack Wasserman then provided a copy of these papers to the Italian government. Ten years later, the Justice Department made this one of the charges against Marcello. To do battle against the government, the Marcello brothers had assembled a crack defense team. G. Wray Gill of New Orleans, Mike Maroun of Shreveport, and Jack Wasserman of Washington, D.C. Gill, who would represent Joe Marcello, was Carlos Marcello's attorney during the Kefauver hearings; Maroun had joined the deported Carlos in Guatemala and had endured the ordeal in El Salvador and Honduras at Marcello's side; and Wasserman, who, as the former INS counsel, who knew U.S. Immigration law better than anyone in the INS itself, had fought the government's efforts to deport his client since 1953.

Wasserman was the principal defense attorney in Carlos Marcello's November trial and no stone was left unturned to obtain a not guilty verdict. Marcello's principal partner in the Pelican Tomato Company, Joe Mantassa, arranged through a friend to bribe one of the jurors, Rudolph Heitler. Jack Wasserman, the former Chief Counsel for the United States Immigration and Naturalization Service, spent the first three weeks of November in New Orleans for Marcello's trial, taking the role of leading attorney and David Ferrie was with both Marcello and Wasserman daily. On Thursday, November 21st, 1963, the defense rested its case and closing arguments were heard Friday morning, November 22nd. Judge Christenberry announced President Kennedy's death to the courtroom as he was delivering the case to the jury. The verdict was reached by 3:15 PM, and it was Not Guilty on both charges. Ferrie immediately left for Texas by auto after the trial. On Saturday, the 24th of November, Carlos Marcello received a call from David Ferrie in Houston.

It should be noted, that a man arrested in the Dal-Tex building moments after the Kennedy shooting was a California businessman named Jim

Braden. Seven years later, it was revealed that Braden was in fact, Eugene Hale Brading, a courier and liaison man for the mob with ties to Marcello. During the summer and fall of 1963, Brading used an office in the Pere Marquette Building, only a few doors down from the office of G. Wray Gill, Marcello's New Orleans attorney where the Wasserman/Gill/Maroun/Ferrie defense team was preparing for Marcello's federal trial. It was speculated by the 1979 House Assassination Committee that the leaders of the conspiracy had made preparations to kill Oswald immediately after the Kennedy shootings, but this part was somehow bungled, thereby necessitating Jack Ruby's open action to silence Oswald.

Ferrie returned to New Orleans on Sunday afternoon and, accompanied by Attorney Gill, reported to the New Orleans District Attorney's office on Monday morning, November 25th. Shortly after the shooting of Kennedy, Jack Martin, an employee of Guy Bannister the private detective, notified authorities that David Ferrie was involved with Oswald in the conspiracy to kill Jack Kennedy. Ferrie's interviews with the F.B.I., the Secret Service and the New Orleans police on the 25th and 26th of November, 1963, were immediately classified and buried in the National Archives. They were not mentioned in the FBI summary report nor were they turned over to the Warren Commission. Both interviews are now posted on the Internet. In the November 25, 1963 interview, Ferrie denied knowing Oswald. (XI-1)

Jim Garrison opened his investigation of the Kennedy conspiracy on February 16, 1967, and named David Ferrie as one of the chief suspects. Garrison had Ferrie in protective custody until the 21st of February and then released him. On February 22nd, David Ferrie was found dead in his apartment, of an apparent suicide.

During that same year, several revelations surfaced on the same subject. Eugene DeLaparra advised the Newark FBI office of Ben Tregle (associate of Marcello) knowing about the Kennedy hit before it happened, having heard it from Marcello's brother, Tony. President Johnson became aware of possible organized crime involvement in plots to slay Fidel Castro, asked FBI Director Hoover for a report, and found out that Sam Giacana and John Rosselli were going to arrange, through Santos Trafficante, a hit on Fidel Castro at the request of the CIA. This move, if accomplished, would be of great benefit to the Mafia as they would have a chance to re-establish casino gambling in Cuba. Pulitzer Prize winner Ed Reid's book came out with the chapter on Ed Becker's story of Carlos Marcello's threats against the Kennedy's that were made at Marcello's Churchill Farms.

It should be noted that Jimmy Hoffa entered prison on March 7th, despite the Teamsters and the Mafia (especially Carlos Marcello) efforts to prevent him from going to Lewisburg prison. Fixer D'Alton Smith (brother-in-law of Marcello's lieutenants, Joseph Poretto and Nofio Pecora) and Washington lobbyist Irv Davidson attempted to use the Garrison investigation to frame the government's chief witness against Jimmy Hoffa, Edward Partin. That failing, they tried to bribe him with $1 million of Marcello's money, but the offer was turned down. John Rosselli was also in prison on extortion, etc., charges and through his attorney, Edward Morgan, got columnist Drew Pearson to approach Chief Justice Warren on the charge that agents of Fidel Castro in association with Santos Trafficante, had made the hit on President Kennedy, and Carlos Marcello (via his investigator, David Ferrie and Jack Ruby) helped by setting up the 'nut' Oswald, who in turn was supposed to get hit that day. Failing that, Jack Ruby was told to do it himself - which he did.

The day after David Ferrie was found dead, an associate of his in the New Orleans delegation of the Cuban Revolutionary Council (CRC), Eladio Del Valle, was found executed in the Central Shopping Plaza parking lot, NW 7th Street and 37th Avenue, Miami. His head was cracked open and a bullet was in his heart. Del Valle, a former Batista Congressman in Cuba and an associate of Santos Trafficante, Jr., had paid Ferrie $1,500 for each 'bombing' mission over Cuba shortly after Fidel Castro took power. Three months after Del Valle's murder, a close friend of Ferrie, Dr. Mary Sherman, was murdered in her New Orleans apartment.

On October 6, 1964, Carlos Marcello was indicted for paying off jurors in his November 1963 case where he was found not guilty. Marcello went to trial on August 17, 1965, represented by none other than his brilliant Washington-based deportation attorney, Jack Wasserman. Wasserman succeeded in demonstrating that, although a conspiracy to bribe Juror Heitler did occur, there was absolutely no proof that Carols Marcello was behind it.

On September 22, 1966, two New York P.D. officers noticed several black limos in front of La Stella Restaurant in Forest Hills, Queens. In a basement dining room they found thirteen men, five of whom turned out to be among the most powerful Mafia leaders in the nation. Included were four men from New Orleans; Carlos Marcello, his brother, Joe Marcello, Anthony Carolla, son of former Louisiana mob boss, Sam "Silver Dollar" Carolla, and Frank Gagliano, son of a deported mobster. Others included

Mafia boss Carlo Gambino, Joseph Gallo and Aniello Dellacroce, his two capos from the Gambino 'family'; Joseph Columbo, another Mafia boss, and four members of the Genovese family, Thomas Eboli, Michael Miranda, Dominick Alongi and Anthony Carillo. The thirteenth man was Santos Trafficante, Jr, friend of Marcello, boss of the Florida Gulf Coast mob, and former conspirator with the CIA to murder Fidel Castro. The men were charged with "consorting with known criminals", and held in $100,000 bail each. The following afternoon, Carlos Marcello, his lawyer Jack Wasserman, brother Joe Marcello, Carolla, Gagliano and Santos Trafficante, Jr., and his lawyer returned to the La Stella restaurant for lunch to celebrate their freedom.

The original meeting was allegedly for the purpose of settling a dispute on the 'rights' of Anthony Carolla in mob business in Louisiana.

Upon Marcello's return to New Orleans he slugged FBI Agent Patrick Collins. Marcello was arrested the next day and tried on May 20th, 1968 for Assault. The trial was moved to Laredo, Texas with the result being a hung jury. He was re-tried in Houston in August of 1968 and was given two years in prison (Only served six months).

During this period of time, Jimmy Hoffa was released from Lewisburg prison and was making noises that he was going to try and take back the Teamsters if President Ford would lift the restrictions on his parole. Hoffa also made many rash statements to Oscar Fraley (in Fraley's' book on Hoffa) concerning Hoffa's planned crusade against the folks that took over 'his' Teamsters Union while he was in prison. However, the mob was well satisfied with the way they were now milking the Teamsters and Anthony (Fat Tony) Salerno started arranging a 'hit' on Hoffa. He allegedly had Tony Jack Giacalone call Hoffa to come to a meeting with Tony Provenzano (whom Hoffa had problems with in Lewisburg prison) to settle their differences. On July 30, 1975, Hoffa arrived at the Red Fox restaurant on Telegraph Road in Bloomfield Township (near Detroit) and was supposedly met by his adopted son, Chuckie O' Brien and Salvatore (SallyBugs) Briguglio. They drove Hoffa to a house in Mount Clemons, Michigan, and as soon as Hoffa walked into the house he was shot by three hired hit men.

These men, according to the story, were paid $25,000 up front and promised $175,000 when the job was completed. After the shooting, Hoffa was cut up and placed in a series of plastic trash bags. His body parts were then placed in a huge trash compactor at Central Sanitation Services, 8215 Moran St, Hamtramck, (112) a Michigan suburb of Detroit, which was owned at the time by Raffael (Jimmy Q Quasarano and Peter Vitale, Detroit Mafia under boss, and later by Domenic (Fats) Corrado.

Among other discredited versions of the disposal of Hoffa's body was that the three men opted not to run Hoffa's remains thru the Central Sanitation compactor as they feared the FBI was watching. Instead, they dumped the body in a construction site at the Meadowlands in New Jersey. This was indeed a far fetched version. One would have to transport the body parts hundreds of miles away with the risk of being detected by police.

In 1978, Tony Provenzano was sentenced to life for the 1961 murder of Anthony Castellito, a Teamster Local #560 man who was going to run against 'Tony Pro'. Provenzano died in prison in 1988. Some, including government informer Charles Crimaldi, claim Hoffa was killed because of his knowledge of the whys and how of the JFK killing but considerably more weight would have to go to the theory of protecting the vast flow of funds going into Mafia coffers by having complete control over the Hoffa-less Teamsters.

Perhaps one of the reasons of body disposal is the similarity to that in the John Roselli case. It was Roselli and Chicago Mafia boss Sam Giancana who met with the CIA's representative, Robert Matheu, in September of 1960, at the Fontainebleau Hotel on Miami Beach to plot the assassination attempts against Fidel Castro. A second meeting shortly thereafter included the men who had the knowledge of Cuba and the people in place to get the job done, Santos Trafficante, Jr., Florida Mafia boss and close associate of Carlos Marcello. Trafficante had run the Sans Souci and other casinos in Havana and was very powerful. When vicious Mafia boss Albert Anastasis attempted in 1957 to muscle in on Cuba's casinos and other rackets, he died riddled with bullets while sitting in a barber's chair in New York. Castro had incarcerated Santos Trafficante for a short while after the Cuban revolution. It has been said that while he was in jail he was visited by Jack Ruby.

John Rosselli disappeared in July of 1976 after leaving his Florida home to play golf. His car was found at the Miami International Airport. Ten days later, Rosseli's body was found floating in Biscayne Bay, rammed into an oil drum. The drum was weighted with chains and punctured with holes, apparently intended to ensure that the gases from the corpse escaped and did not bring it to the surface. Rosseli had been garroted and stabbed and his legs had been sawed off and squashed into the drum along with torso and head. At the time of his death, Rosselli had testified to the Senate Intelligence Committee and was due to appear again. Roselli, who had dined with Trafficante just two weeks previously, had been last seen alive on a boat owned by an associate of Trafficante. As for Santos Trafficante, Jr., he died in 1987 following heart surgery, at the age of 72.

The FBI provided a wiretap tape to the House Assassination Committee which, following the murder of Sam Giacana, Santos Trafficante was overheard to say "Now only two people are alive who know who killed Kennedy. And they are not talking". It is strongly speculated that the two were he and Carlos Marcello. Sam Giancana was killed in June of 1975, in his own Chicago home. He was shot six times - in a neatly stitched circle - around the mouth. When he died the Senate Intelligence Committee was preparing to question him about the CIA plots to kill Fidel Castro. The only clue in the Giancana killing was a sawed-off 22.cal pistol, which police traced to a gun shop in Florida operated by Eddie Browder

The U.S. House of Representatives 1979 "House Assassination Committee" pointed out all kinds of fingers at Carlos Marcello on the Kennedy killing, and suggested that the Justice Department pursue several good leads. It wasn't until 1988 that the Justice Department responded. Assistant Attorney General William Weld stated that the Department of Justice "has concluded that no persuasive evidence can be identified to support the theory of conspiracy in the assassination of President Kennedy".

Carlos Marcello's reaction to the House Assassination Report was to assign Jack Wasserman, his most trusted attorney, with an investigation of his own. Wasserman immediately set about obtaining the available FBI files on the Kennedy assassination, which included the extensive files on David Ferrie and some documents on the allegations of DeLaparra and SV T-1, as well as the Edward Becker story of Marcello's threat to kill Kennedy. These files amounting to well over 220,000 pages of documents, had been obtained through a lengthy and costly Freedom of Information Act lawsuit brought against the Justice Department by Harold Weisberg, noted Kennedy assassination researcher and author of several books relating to the assassination. They were the files the Assassination Committee should have had at the beginning of its investigation but did not receive until too late. Now they were being put at the disposal of Carlos Marcello's attorney.

Throughout the summer and fall of 1979, Jack Wasserman searched through the recently released FBI files in an attempt to retrieve every FBI document that could relate to the possibility of his client's having been involved in the assassination. One wonders if Marcello was expecting an indictment on the Kennedy case. If so, he was putting his entire trust in Wasserman. Jack Wasserman successfully defended him against the Immigration and naturalization Service for over thirty years, in what had been the longest and costliest deportation case in US history. But Jack Wasserman never got to defend his client against the charge that he had conspired to murder President Kennedy, for shortly after Wasserman began preparing for the anticipated case, he died suddenly of a heart attack.

It has been estimated that the fees Marcello paid Wasserman for his work on the deportation case amounted to over $2 million dollars by 1979.

In summarizing Marcello's story, common sense and logic indicates that the powerful Marcello's entire life and fortunes were at great risk due to the actions of Attorney General Robert Kennedy and his brother Jack. Marcello and Trafficante (and associates) were violent men, in a violent Mafia society, where gruesome actions against enemies and friends were quite routine events. Marcello had the means, the motive and the opportunity to kill President Kennedy to avenge what he perceived as persecution and to prevent the government to deport him and/or incarcerate him.

A cadre of cohorts was assembled, allegedly including several rabid anti-Castro Cuban terrorists, as well as an assortment of organized crime figures under Marcello's direct control, including David Ferrie. There is much doubt that Oswald fired the fatal shots that killed Kennedy and wounded Governor Connally. However, my experience during thirty (now fifty) years as a military person and a law enforcement veteran force me to doubt very much that one shooter, with that old rifle, could accurately fire three rounds in seven seconds, from that angle, position and distance, at a person in a vehicle moving away from him at 11 MPH, fifteen minutes after sitting in the TSBD lunchroom reading yesterday's newspaper. I also am convinced that very possibly another round was most likely have been fired from the knoll at Dealey Square. Acoustics and ballistic experts have laid out that theory quite convincingly, as related in earlier chapters.

The author worked the streets of Miami for many years and had contact with Santos Trafficante, Jr. and his associates. It was also not unusual to come in contact with several Mafia figures during a shift, such as vacationing Angelo Bruno, Tony Zerilli, and a host of other national hoods while working the northeast section of Miami. These were vicious hoodlums who would just as soon kill someone, friend or foe, if it interfered with their organized crime business. I knew Frank Sturgis and others of Watergate fame, some of whom had a role in this case. Also, having had contact with the CIA during the tumultuous years of the 1960's and 1970's, there is little doubt that that criminal forces were positioned and directed by a combo of government and Mafia forces to effect the killing.

The author was a Task Force (tactical) uniform supervisor in 1969 and was shortly thereafter promoted to Lieutenant. A new Miami police chief, Bernard Garmire, assigned me to command the Strategic Information Unit (Intelligence). One of his first instructions to me concerned Santos Trafficante, Jr. The chief, new in town, had moved into a home in the northeast Miami neighborhood and soon discovered that Trafficante was living on Northeast 71st Street, several blocks away, a fact that embarrassed the boss. He wanted to know what we could do to jail him or induce Trafficante to move out of the City of Miami's jurisdiction. I informed the Task Force members of the Chief's concerns and the officers responded with unorthodox tactics. It seems that each time Trafficante traveled to his card club at West Flagler Street and 27th Avenue or to a liaison with a social friend, his wife Mary Jo would receive a telephone call at home with the details of Santos's destination. This, along with some strict traffic enforcement and other tactics, prompted Trafficante to purchase a home next to his attorney, Frank Ragano, in the City of North Miami Beach. The Chief was delighted with Trafficante's move and asked me for details. I advised him it was best that he not know his department's involvement.

Much of this chapter was prepared sometime in 1997 or 1998, while I was conducting a background investigation of the Detroit Mafia for a private customer while operating a Private Investigation agency in Miami. Since that time I have become aware of the 1995 Bahamas meeting that was attended by numerous professional Kennedy Assassination researchers and experts as well as the head of Cuban Security, Fabian Escalante, where he named Eladio DelValle, Tony Cuesta, and Trafficante's bodyguard, Herminio Diaz Garcia, as participants in the Dealy Plaza killing of November 22,1963.

I have listened to (on several occasions) the informer Willie Somersett tapes recorded by Sgt. Everett Kaye (Miami PD) between the informer and militant Joseph Milteer, where it was said that President Kennedy would be killed on his November 1963 southern trip by a high powered weapon fired from a tall building. Sgt Kaye (a great friend) worked for me in Intelligence and was a top investigator. I last spoke with him about this case the day before he passed away in an Ocala, Florida hospital, several years ago.

In 2012, I again questioned retired Sergeant Andy Giordano (one of my Sergeants in a Robbery tactical squad in the early 70's) in reference to the Eladio Del Valle murder case, which Giordano handled while assigned to the Miami homicide squad. Giordano told me that he received no federal government help in locating vital witness in the Dominican Republic (he came back empty handed) but had made some progress on the investigation. Giordano advised he took a week off after the first month of the murder investigation. Upon his return to work in the homicide office, Sergeant Giordano found his case file empty, except for the original report made the day Del Valle's body had been found. Giordano's co-workers advised that the CIA, the FBI and Metro-Dade sheriff's detectives had all reviewed his file, separately, while Andy was out of town. It was unknown which agency had removed the contents.

Andy Giordano passed on a several months ago.

PART XII

THE FIELD ASSASSINS

PERSONS OF INTEREST

Some of the persons of interest that have surfaced in JFK literature during the past fifty years are listed below.

Some of the allegations some authors have made are downright bizarre. Others have obvious merit. This author has examined numerous files and articles on these subjects but the following narrative is meant only to be a thumb-nail sketch of the persons mentioned over the past 50 years by investigating committees, journalists and independent researchers, The term, Persons of Interest", has no legal meaning as far as I know, but is often used in the media.

The biographical information and public record information on the 'persons of interest' in this chapter was obtained from many sources, including Wikipedia, the Mary Ferrell website, www.archives.gov/jfk, JFKLancer publications and JFKLibrary.org as well as public records.

Jack Lawrence- He was arrested the day of the assassination in Dallas. He was a used car salesman at a Dallas Lincoln-Mercury dealership and had been on the job for one month prior to the assassination. On that day, he came to work all sweaty, 30 minutes after the Kennedy hit. He had left the dealer's car he had borrowed in a parking lot behind the wooden fence on top of the grassy knoll. He was arrested that night after co-workers said he might be involved but no charges resulted. Lawrence actions were very suspicious but no additional information has surfaced connecting him directly to the assassination conspiracy.

Eugene Hale Bradling @ Jim Braden. He was in the Dal-Tex Building next to TSBD at the time of the assassination. The elevator operator notified the police and Braden was arrested by Deputy C.L. "Lummie" Lewis and taken to the Sheriff's office. Braden was staying at the Cabana Motel in Dallas that day. Braden said he went to use a phone in Dal-Tex building. He was released after three hours but the police did not know his correct name. Under the name Bradling, he had a record since of 35 arrests since 1934 and was on parole.

On November 21st, Brading visited H. L. Hunt, Lamar Hunt's son. He was staying at the Cabana Motel with Morgan Brown, an ex-con who was connected to David Ferrie. Bradling was a Mafia courier (for Meyer Lansky), operating from room 1701, Pere Marquette building, in New Orleans. This was an adjacent office that was being used by David Ferrie who was doing pre-trial work for Carlos Marcello. Lawrence Meyers was also at the Cabana Motel with Jean West. Jack Ruby called Meyers at the Cabana the night of 11/21. Brading was photographed at Dealey Square after the hit.

Brading says he was walking on Elm Street looking for a cab after the assassination. He went to the Dal-Tex Building asking use of phone. He says he went to the 3rd floor via freight elevator but the phone out of order. The elevator operator turned him in to Dallas police as being suspicious. Taken to Sheriff's office and interrogated but was released later that day.

Braden was almost assuredly in contact in Dallas with Jack Ruby prior to the JFK assassination. He was briefly detained in Dealey Plaza minutes after the president's murder, but those JFK assassination researchers who have mentioned Braden prefer to cast him as a "Mafia" figure rather than as Lansky's man on the scene in Dallas.

James Files -A convict serving many years in jail confessed to being involved in the Kenned assassination. The confession was made to Robert G. Vernon (22nd March, 1994) claiming he was one of the JFK shooters.

Author Bob Vernon later claimed that Files' story was completely false. Others also have found Files' story a total lie. Guess he was just trying to get out of jail. The Files story will not be repeated here.

Charles V. Harrelson, (Woody's father) was a Dixie Mafia hit man. He was arrested September 1, 1980, for killing Federal Judge John Wood of San Antonio. Wood was hit by a high-powered rifle shot. Harrelson, 25 in 1963, later claimed he was involved in the JFK hit. When arrested in 1980, he had a business card of R.D. Matthews, Dallas hood. Indicted with Harrelson on the John Wood murder was Carlos Marcello's brother, A man named Jimmy Charga hired Harrelson to kill Judge Wood. Joe Charga said Harrelson got the contract to kill Wood based on the claim that Harrelson had participated in the JFK hit.

Federal Judge John Wood, called "Maximum John", was murdered 5/29/1979 by Charles Harrelson. A federal judge since 1970, Wood was killed while presiding over a trial of Janiel (Jimmy) Chagra for drug trafficking.

Prior to the Wood case, Harrelson was tried for killing Sam Degelia, Jr, a grain dealer, in McAllen, Texas. His first trial was a mistrial. The 2nd trial in 1973, he was found guilty and sentenced to 15 years. He was paroled in 1976.

Joe Charga and Harrelson were tried in the Judge Wood case. Harrelson got two life terms, Charga got 10 years. Janiel Charga was acquitted when his brother would not testify against him. Joe testified that Harrelson claimed to have shot Kennedy. Joe Charga died in prison in 1977. Jimmy Charga died in 2008, at age 63. Judge Wood was killed by one shot in the parking lot of his condo. Harrelson was alleged to have been paid $250,000 for the hit.

Rich Lauchli, a Minuteman member from Collingville, IL, a suburb of St Louis, was Involved with the Ammo Depot at Belle Chase Naval Station in Louisiana and/or US Naval Blimp Base, 45 miles south of New Orleans at Houma, La. The Sclumberger Well Service raid was on July 31, 1963. Lauchli purchased explosives from McLaney group, working from Minuteman headquarters in Norbormo, MO. He was a member of the Counter Insurgency Council. Associates include John Martino and Orlando Bosch.

Guy Bannister -According to Jerry Brooks, the Anti-Communist League of Caribbean was headed by Guy Bannister. He was also a member of Minutemen and associated with Frank Sturgis. (See Edwin B. Kaiser, Jr.) Associates include Rich Lauchli, John Martino, and David Ferrie.

Santos Trafficante, Jr.- Trafficante opened the San Souci in Havana and also the Black Magic Lounge. Lewis McWillie was the pit boss at the Tropicana in Havana for Trafficante. In 1946, Trafficante's father sent him to Cuba to look after Trafficante's interests. Santos's father died in 1954 and Santos Jr. took over, effectively being the leader of the Mafia in Florida and in Cuba.

The Director of the FBI, J.Edgar Hoover, had denied for years the existence of a national Mafia, until November 14, 1957, when Sergeant Edgar Croswell of the New York State Police got suspicious up in the Endicott, N.Y. area. Croswell observed numerous high-end autos at the secluded home of Joseph (Joe the Barber) Barbara, a suspected organized crime figure. Croswell called in reinforcements and rounded up over sixty of the top Mafia figures from around the United States who were having a national crime summit at Barbara's home. Santos Trafficante from Florida and Joseph Marcello, Carlos's brother from Louisiana, was among the big time hoodlums gathered that day. Approximately forty other hoods escaped through the woods. Twelve days later, Hoover inaugurated a Big Time Criminal program.

Although best known as the head of the Mafia in Tampa, Trafficante actually functioned as Meyer Lansky's chief lieutenant in the crime syndicate and as Lansky's liaison with the CIA in the Castro assassination plots.

After Sam Giancana's murder, Santos Trafficante Jr. was overheard on a FBI tape the following:

"Now only two people are alive who know who killed Kennedy, and they aren't talking".

Carlos Marcello - - The 1979 Assassination Committee announced: "extensive investigation led to conclude the most likely family bosses of organized crime to had participated in such a complicated assassination plan were Carlos Marcello and Santos Trafficante" "The Committee found -as we have noted - that both Mafia leaders had "motive, means, and opportunity".

A lead from the spring of 1963 is a statement made to the FBI by Eugene DeLaparra, who worked in 1963 at a restaurant owned by Bernard Tregle, who heard Tregle and two men talking - as they looked at an ad for a cheap rifle - "There is a price on JFK's head and other members of the Kennedy family... Somebody will kill Kennedy when he comes down south.

Another lead came from Gene Summers of Darien, Georgia, in March or April of 1963, at the Town & Country Restaurant in New Orleans, who saw the restaurant boss give a wad of money to a young man. Joe Poretto, a top level Marcello man, was the manager of the restaurant.

The head of the Mafia in New Orleans, Carlos Marcello owed his status to Meyer Lansky who was his chief sponsor in the crime syndicate. Marcello could not have orchestrated the Kennedy assassination-as some suggest- without Lansky's explicit approval.

Carlos Marcello finally went to jail in 1983.

Bernardo De Torres, a Cuban born, Miami Private Investigator and the 2506 Brigade Intelligence commander,

Was captured at the Bay of Pigs and was an associate of Frank Sturgis. De Torres was also a member of the Interpen group. He was alleged to have been one of three who visited Silvia Odio, and was called "Lepoldo, "according to Ms. Odio. He volunteered to work with Jim Garrison but was suspected of funneling information back to the CIA. Later, De Torres worked for Mitch WerBell, the arms merchant.

Rolando Otero (a Miami bomber) said De Torres was involved with the Kennedy hit. The House committee (HSCA) believed that he was involved with the Kennedy murder, and gave him limited immunity. It has been said that De Torres has a picture of Dealey Square on November 22, 1963, in a safety deposit box.

Lawrence Howard, a now deceased member of Interpen group was a bilingual ex-soldier who trained anti-Castro Cubans. He was associated with Loran Hall and William Seymour as well as David Ferrie.

Orlando Bosch, 37 years old in 1963, is a Cuban exile and a CIA backed operator, who was head of Coordination of United Organizations (CORU) and a member of Operation 40. He was a trained pediatrician but has devoted his life to violent Anti-Castro activities. One of his most violent acts was the principal planner of the downing of the Cubana Air Lines with 73 people aboard in Barbados, along with Luis Posada and Michael Townley. He was also suspected of being a planner of the assassination of Orlando Letlier, a Chilean government leader who was killed in Washington D.C. Bosch was given safe haven in the United States by Pres. George H.W. Bush in 1976, when Bush was head of the CIA.

Bosch did his pediatric internship in Toledo, Ohio and came to Miami in 1960. He tried to organize an anti-Castro rebellion in Cuba in July of 1960. He was in contact with the CIA in 1962 and 1963, as admitted later by the CIA. His activities are documented in the National Security Archives. At that time he was the general coordinator of MIRR and an active member of Operation 40.

In 1968 he was arrested for an attack on a Polish freighter in Miami and sentenced to ten years in prison, and served four years when he was paroled. He then moved to Venezuela and was involved in bombings against Cuban targets in Caracas. In June of 1974, he told the Miami News that he was head of Accion Cubana and did the bombings of Cuban consulates in Latin American countries. He moved to Chili in December of 1974, living in a military house. He sent bombs via mail to Cuban Embassies. He attempted to kill the Cuban Ambassador to Argentina and the 1976 bombings of the Mexican Embassy in Guatemala. He was deported to the Dominican Republic in 1976 and founded CORU. He returned to Venezuela in September of 1976. He was overheard saying he was involved in Letlier bombing and the bombing of the Cubana Airliner which killed 73 persons, on October 6, 1976. He was arrested in Caracas and held four years awaiting trial. At his trial, he, Luis Posada and Michael Townley were acquitted. In 1977, he was involved in the bombing of the Mackey Airlines office in Miami Beach.

The Cuban newspaper, Granma International published an article suggesting that Bosch could have been in Dallas in 1963 during the hit on Kennedy. Some researchers say he looks like the "dark complected man" in front of the Depository building. He was acquitted in 2011 in El Paso, for perjury in connection with an immigration charge. The Justice

Department said that Bosch had been involved in thirty acts of sabotage between 1961 and 1968.

Bosch was also arrested during this time for towing a torpedo through Miami streets. The Feds also charged him with smuggling eighteen bombs out of the country. The Miami Mayor, Maurice Ferre, visited him in jail. The City of Miami actually celebrated an "Orlando Bosch Day" on March 25, 1983.

Marita Lorenz stated that Bosch, Frank Sturgis, the Novo brothers and Pedro Lantz traveled to Dallas in November of 1963, with long firearms. She got cold feet and had Strugis fly her back to Miami on November 21, 1963.

Marita Lorenz, former lover of Fidel Castro and a CIA agent, said that Orlando Bosch was involved in the JFK killing with the Novo brothers. Miami Mayor Maurice Ferre helped Bosch and also appointed Cesar Odio, to the position of Miami City Manager. He was the brother of Sylvia Odio

(Cesar Odio was later convicted for corruption)

Orlando Bosch died in Miami at age 84.

Ignacio Novo - Ignacio and his brother Guillermo were two of the most active terrorists associated with Orlando Bosch. The Novo's were identified by CIA source, Marita Lorenz as two of the men who traveled to Dallas from Miami in the days prior to Kennedy's murder and were members of Operation Forty. Another of Operation Forty members, Frank Sturgis, claimed that "this assassination group would, upon orders, naturally assassinate either members of the military or the political parties of the foreign country that you were going to infiltrate, and if necessary, some of your own members who were suspected of being foreign agents …. We were concentrating in Cuba at that particular time".

The brothers, were both veterans of the CIA-backed Cuban exile wars against Fidel Castro. According to Marita Lorenz, the Novo brothers were part of the armed caravan that arrived in Dallas one day before the assassination.

In 1964, Guillermo Novo used a re-built bazooka to fire at New York's United Nations General Assembly building, where Che Guevera was scheduled to make an address. The shell landed 200 yards short of the UN Secretariat, landing in the East River.

Guillermo and Ignacio Novo were arrested for the slaying of the former Chilean Foreign Minister in 1976. The murder of Orlando Letelier occurred in the heart of Washington D.C. Novo was found guilty but the verdict was later overturned on a technicality.

The FBI reported that the Novo's played a role in the Miami murder of terrorist Rolando Masferrer in 1975. In 1976, the Novo brothers were working for dictator Augusto Pinochet of Chili and were suspected of involvement in the downing of a civilian Cuban airliner that resulted in the deaths of seventy three persons when a bomb exploded on board. Freddy Lugo and Herman Ricardo were arrested for the violent crime and admitted that the Novo brothers, Orlando Bosch and Luis Posada were involved in the conspiracy.

In 2000, Novo brothers, Luis Posada, Gasper Jimenez and Pepe Remon were identified as members of a team that attempted to assassinate Cuban President, Fidel Castro, in Panama. In 2004, President Moscoso of Panama pardoned the group.

Guillermo Novo, an associate of Orland Bosch and Luis Posada, was also a member of the Operation "40" group. Novo also worked with General Pinochet in Chili and was alleged to be involved with downing of Cuban plane that killed 73 people, along with Luis Posada, Orlando Bosch, Herman Ricardo and Freddy Lugo.

Novo was involved in the Orlando Letelier murder in Washington, D.C. on 9/21/1976, with Alvin Ross and Ignacio Novo, his brother. They were acquitted on a technicality. In 2000, at the University of Panama, the Novos were involved in the attempt to kill Castro, along with Luis Posada, Gasper Jimenez and Pedro Remon. In 2004, Pres Musogso of Panama pardoned them for that crime.

"Monkey" Morales (himself a terrorist bomber) was the informer who pointed out Bosch as the one who shot a bazooka at the Polish ship in Miami. Freddy Lugo and Herman Ricardo of Venezuela were arrested for the Cubana Airliner bombing. Ricardo worked for Luis Posada's security company in Venezuela. The admitted the crime and said it was planned and arranged by Orlando Bosch and Luis Posada.

In 1974, it was alleged that Bosch was involved in the murder of Jose Torriente in Miami, and then skipped the country. In July of 1976, Bosch was questioned by the Secret Service in connection with a plot to assassinate Henry Kissinger. Peter Kornbluh, head of the independent "National Security Archives" Cuba project said: "the verdict of history, rendered by formerly secret CIA and FBI intelligence reports, and court records, is that he (Bosch) was a mass murderer masquerading as a freedom fighter".

According to Marita Lorenz, the Novo brothers were part of the armed caravan that arrived in Dallas one day before the assassination of President Kennedy. Many years after Dallas, the Novo brothers were later convicted of participating in the murder of a Chilean dissident in collaboration with international adventurer Michael Townley, who himself had ties to high-level figures implicated in the JFK conspiracy. Both were associated with Orlando Bosch, Luis Posada and Frank Sturgisall members of the Operation 40 group.

Manuel Rodriguez Orcarberro, Alpha 66 Member. Buyer of guns from John Thomas Massen, a Dallas gun dealer (who some said is an Oswald look-a-like) Luis Posada, born in 1928, was a former CIA agent.

He was a suspect in the Cubana Air Lines bombing conspiracy. He took refuge in Honduras but later served four years in prison. A Bay of Pigs veteran, Posada attempted to assassinate Castro in Panama in 2000. He came to the US in 1961 and was trained by the CIA at Fort Benning, Ga. He was a member of Operation 40 and was involved in the attempt to kill the Guatemalan President in 1965. Posada began associating with Bosch in 1965. The CIA said Posada was involved in a plot to kill Henry Kissinger.

Posada was the operations chief for DISIP in Venezuela until 1976 and w. was a private investigator in Venezuela. Associates include the Novo brothers and Gaspar Jimenez in CORU. Posada was involved in tourist bombings in 2007. In the year 2000, he was caught in Panama with 200 lbs of explosives. Posada was ordered deported from the US in 2005, but a judge stopped the order.

Hermino Diaz. Diaz, an expert rifleman, with a long history of anti-Castro activities, traveled to Cuba with Tony Cuesta and others on May 29, 1966, to assassinate Fidel Castro. They were intercepted by Cuban authorities and Diaz was killed in a shoot-out. According to Cuesta, Diaz had told him while en route to this attempted hit, that he had been involved in the

Kennedy assassination. Cuesta told this story to Reinaldo Martinez, who worked in a Cuban infirmary as an inmate.

Upon returning to Miami upon his release, Martinez was also told this story by Remigo Arce, who had previously introduced Diaz to him in pre-Castro days. The source of this information was presented in Anthony Summers' book, "Not in Your Lifetime", based on his 2002 interview with Martinez. Another source was Cuban Security Chief, General Fabian Escalante, who said Diaz was one of the people we (Cuban State Security) feel was most definitely involved in the plot against Kennedy. Escalante also declared that Eladio Del Valle was also involved, but less evidence was present. The source of Escalante's views was presented by author Claudia Furiati in "ZRRIFLE" (Ocean Press, 1994).

Diaz had been the bodyguard of Santos Trafficante, Jr. in Cuba and was later the Security Chief at the Havana Riviera Hotel. We may learn more about Diaz when the U.S. files on Tony Cuesta are released in 2017. Much of this information was also posted by Armando Fernandez, former professor at the University of Havana and an instructor at the University of Miami.

Frank Sturgis -American Frank Sturgis was a true soldier-of-fortune during his entire life. The Virginia born Sturgis became a US Marine at 17, later serving as a US Army intelligence officer in Germany. Sturgis moved to Miami in 1957 and became involved in Cuban politics. He joined forces with Fidel Castro, training his anti-Batista troops and gunrunning for Castro. When Castro took over Cuba in 1959 he installed Sturgis as gambling czar as well as appointing him to a high ranking Air Force position. When Castro revealed his communist beliefs, Sturgis became a fierce foe, joining up with anti-Castro forces, and eventually becoming a member of the super-secret Operation 40.

Sturgis began a relationship with Fidel Castro's lover, Marital Lorenz, as well as Pedro Lanz, Orlando Bosch and other rabid anti-Castro fighters. Sturgis was a paid operator, but not an agent, of the CIA according to government documents. In mid-November of 1963, Sturgis and Lorenz traveled by auto to Dallas with other Operation 40 operatives for a "big job"

Sturgis, Lorenz, the Novo brothers, Pedro Lanz, Oswald, Patrick Henning, all stayed in a Dallas motel on the days preceding JFK's murder. Lorenz claims the group met - and received money from -CIA agent Howard

Hunt. Lorenz also claimed that Jack Ruby came to the hotel and conversed with Sturgis. The two-car caravan also contained many firearms, including long rifles.

Into the 1970'a, Sturgis remained active in his spying and involvement in terrorist acts. Sturgis was one of the Miami operatives who were arrested for the Watergate burglary, along with Bernard Barker, Virgillo Gonzalez, Eugenio Martinez and James McCord. This burglary, which eventually ended President Nixon's presidency, resulted in Sturgis being sent to Danbury federal prison.

In the 1970's, investigator Bernard Fensterwald claimed in his book, "Assassination of JFK (1977), that Sturgis was heavily involved with the Mafia, particularly Florida mob boss Santos Trafficante, Jr. and Meyer Lansky.

During the "Liberty Lobby" civil case, author Victor Marchetti was sued by Howard Hunt. In the second trial, the jury decided that Marchetti had not been guilty of libel when he suggested that JFK had been assassinated by people working for the Central Intelligence Agency(CIA).

The author's last contact with Sturgis was in the mid-1080's during a retirement celebration for one of the author's best friends who was leaving the Miami P.D. to become the Chief of Police in another Florida city. The author spotted Sturgis among the guests and questioned the honoree why such a nefarious character was present alongside many of the top Miami law enforcement officers. The author's friend replied," Frank is a close personal friend". The author's reaction? "I was speechless and astonished".

It would not be too difficult to pen a full length book on the life of Sturgis. He was truly a "soldier-of-fortune". and one of the most prolific and resourceful of the most active anti-Castro group, Operation Forty. His claim, in later years, on not being present in Dallas on November, 22, 1963, is certainly rebutted by the CIA and DEA agent Lorenz. The author has several nephews, any one of which would gladly offer an alibi for their uncle.

Investigator Gaeton Fonzi wrote in his book," The Last Investigation", "A character like Frank Sturgis illustrates some of the dilemmas in investigating the JFK assassination. He can't be ignored. He is, by his own admission, a prime suspect. He had the ability and the motivation and was associated with individuals and groups - and even employed - assassination as a method to achieve these goals". (106) Fonzi was an investigator for the US House (HSCA) investigation of the JFK murder.

Frank Sturgis died in 1993.

<u>Joe Campisie</u>, second in Dallas Mafia structure.

No convictions - owns Egyptian Lounge in Dallas. He knew Ruby since 1947 and visited him in jail after Ruby shot Oswald. His associates include R.D. Matthews, Ralph Paul, Jack Todd, Benny Binon and the Marcello brothers.

Campisie was apparently well known to the Dallas police department. He was noted by many reports as the number two man in Dallas' organized crime organization, under Joe Civello.

One evening in the mid-1970's, the author was on a visit to the Arlington, Texas office of E-Systems Inc. who were manufacturing mobile digital systems (vehicle computers) for the Miami P.D. The Dallas Assistant Chief, Jim Everett, a personal friend of the author, was taking me and two colleagues from Stanford Research to dinner at a popular BBQ restaurant. The Chief, two of his detectives and I, were lined up waiting for a table behind 100-150 other customers. Along came a man with two companions who greeted the Chief by name and asked why we were waiting in line, stating, "You are the Chief, you should not have to wait". The man had us accompany him to a side door to be greeted by three employees. The employees re-located three tables of patrons who were in the middle of dining, to the back area and set up a table for the nine of us in their place.

After a fine meal, (no waiting) the man grabbed the check and paid the full amount.

Upon departing the restaurant, I inquired of Everett who this generous man was. To my astonishment, Jim advised that the man was Joe Campisie, a high ranking Dallas organized member. I said, "Oh my God, I hope the FBI didn't take photos". Jim laughed and said that it was highly unlikely.

Everett also told me that Chief Curry's estimate of the number (Thirty) of Dallas police officers who made frequent visits to Jack Ruby's club was off by about two or three hundred. (LOL)

Everett, a smart honest law enforcement professional, advised that Dallas was a small 'big city' where many criminals and police officers knew each other from elementary and high school despite going separate ways after adulthood. I observed the same situation in Miami, although as an outsider (a Yankee). Many of my Miami officers grew up with the area 'bad guys', some of whom were life-time neighbors.

All in all, the Dallas P.D. did many things right despite a few grievous errors by the Chief and the Homicide Captain. Dallas has taken their share of blame while the FBI, CIA and Secret Service have escaped their share.

Charles Nicoletti was a leading figure in the Mafia in Chicago. He worked under Tony Accardo and Sam Giancana and got the reputation as an effective contract killer. He was also was involved in the CIA plots to overthrow Castro... On 29th March, 1977, Charles Nicoletti was murdered in Chicago. He had been shot three times in the back of the head. George De Mohrenschildt died the same day. Both men were due to appear before the Select House Committee on Assassinations where they were to be asked about their involvement in the assassination of JFK.

Chauncey Holt was interviewed by John Craig, Phillip Rogers and Gary Shaw for *Newsweek* magazine (19th October, 1991). Holt related that the other two men (Nicoletti and Moceri) were long time associates of Peter Licavoli. Both of who had been involved in Cuban politics and had been involved with Jimmy Hoffa. They were long-time associates of not only Licavoli, Moceri had known Licavoli longer than he had. Nicoletti was also a hit man of some not and a an enforcer. Holt said he didn't know if he was on the payroll of the CIA or not, or whether he was working independently. The same with Moceri. Holt had no idea who paid them.

Homer Echavarria = A Secret Service Report on Homer Echevarria (Warren Commission Document 87)

relates that on November 21, 1963, a government informant Thomas Mosley, was negotiating the sale of machine guns to a Cuban exile named Echevarria. In the course of the transaction, Echevarria said that "we now have plenty of money - our new backers are Jews" and would close the arms deal "as soon as we [or they] take care of Kennedy." The next day, Kennedy was assassinated in Dallas.

Mosley, an ATF informant, reported his conversation to the Secret Service, and that agency quickly began investigating what it termed "a group in the Chicago area who may have a connection with the JFK assassination." Echevarria was a member of the 30th November group, associated with the DRE with whom Oswald had dealings the previous summer. Mosley said the arms deal was being financed through Paulino Sierra Martinez and his J.G.C.E. Sierra interestingly, was connected to Bobby Kennedy's effort to unite various exile groups, through Harry Ruiz Williams.

This Secret Service investigation was soon taken over by the FBI. The FBI quickly dropped the case, leaving this explosive statement unresolved. The Warren Commission received the Secret Service reports but did not direct the FBI to take any action in the matter. It is worth noting is that in 1995, the Secret Service destroyed presidential protection survey reports for some of Kennedy's trips during the fall of 1963, including the cancelled Chicago trip planned for the beginning of November.

Dave Yaras, a Chicago guy, was long time friend of Jack Ruby and later reported to work as a hit man for Sam Giancana. Also associated with Jimmy Hoffa. Helped establish Local 320, Teamsters, in Miami. Worked for Mafia in Cuba after Batistia thrown out. Was Chicago mob liaison with Cuban refugees? His 14 arrests, includes murder. He was arrested for the murder of James Regan, who ran a press agency in conflict with Carlos Marcello's race Wire Company. Yaras made an 11/21/63 telephone call to Barney Baker in Chicago. Ruby, a few days earlier, had a 17 minute call with Baker. Ruby's sister said that Yaras and Patrick were Jack's best friends from Chicago.

The 3 minute call Yaras received on 11/21 in Miami from Baker, puts him far from Dallas, hours before JFK hit.

William "Rip" Robertson was an CIA operative. A former Texas Marine joined the CIA in 1947 and served as a Paramilitary Operations Officer in their famed Special Activities Division. He was assigned to the Executive Action operation that was designed to remove unsatisfactory foreign leaders from poser. He was involved in the overthrow of Guatemala President Arbenz in 1954. Later Robertson was discovered to be responsible for ordering a British ship bombed; he had misidentified it as a Russian ship. Afterwards he was deemed an outcast by the CIA. He then worked as an advisor to Nicaraguan President Somoza. Prior to the Bay of Pigs he resumed work for the CIA. During the battle at the Bay of Pigs,

Robertson commanded the ship Barbara J, while CIA agent Grayson Lynch commanded the ship Blager. Robertson also led a unit of Cuban exiles in the Congo crisis. Robertson died in 1973 in Laos due to the effects of malaria. Some JFK reseachers point out that he appears in Dealey Square on the day Kennedy was killed.

David Ferrie - an enigmatic adventurer and CIA contract operative, Ferrie was closely involved with Lee Harvey Oswald during Oswald's stay in New Orleans in the summer of 1963, working alongside Oswald out of Guy Banister's headquarters. The investigation of Ferrie by New Orleans District Attorney Jim Garrison ultimately led to Garrison's discovery of Permindex board member Clay Shaw's ties to both Ferrie and Oswald.

Marita Lorenz - A former CIA contract operative, she testified under oath that one day prior to the assassination of President Kennedy she arrived in Dallas in an armed caravan of CIA-backed Cuban exiles who were met by not only Jack Ruby, who later killed Lee Harvey Oswald, but also CIA official E. Howard Hunt.

In 1977 Ms. Lorenz told the New York Daily News that in the fall of 1963 she met Lee Oswald in an Operation 40 safe house in Miami. She said she met him again at the home of Orlando Bosch along with Frank Sturgis, Pedro Lanz, and two other Cubans (later describing them as the Novo brothers). The group studied street maps of Dallas and she suspected (then) they were planning on raiding an arsenal. She also testified under immunity to the US House Committee (HSCA) that was investigation President Kennedy's assassination.

Ms. Lorenz gave a long interview to New York Daily News reporter, Paul Meskil and he wrote long articles in the newspaper entitled, "Ex Spy Says She Drove to Dallas with Oswald and the Kennedy assassination team".

Meyer Lansky - Chief executive officer and de facto "treasurer" of the international crime syndicate; active in gun-running on behalf of the Israeli underground; collaborated closely with American intelligence on a number of fronts; later settled in Israel. Researchers who have claimed that "the Mafia Killed JFK" have pointedly refused to acknowledge Lansky's pre-eminent positioning in the underworld.

Seymour Weiss- Meyer Lansky's chief bagman and liaison with the political establishment in Louisiana, he later served as a director of the

CIA-linked Standard Fruit Company and may actually have been a high-ranking CIA contract operative in New Orleans at the time of the JFK assassination.

Sam Giancana - a Mafia boss from Chicago, Giancana was a player in the CIA-Mafia plots against Castro; later murdered, probably at the behest of Santo Trafficante, Jr. His family says that Giancana admitted having been involved in the planning of the JFK hit.

Johnny Rosselli - A roving "ambassador" for the Mafia, Rosselli was the primary conduit between the CIA and the mob in the plots against Fidel Castro; may have arranged the murder of Sam Giancana for Trafficante, and was later murdered himself.

Mickey Cohen - Meyer Lansky's West Coast henchman; Jack Ruby's role model and a gun-runner for the Israeli underground, Cohen collaborated closely with Israeli diplomat Menachem Begin prior to the JFK assassination; Cohen arranged for John F. Kennedy to meet actress Marilyn Monroe who was assigned the task of finding out JFK's private views and intentions toward Israel.

Al Gruber -- a henchman of Meyer Lansky's West Coast operative, Mickey Cohen, Gruber and Ruby spoke by telephone just shortly before Ruby killed Lee Harvey Oswald. It is believed that Gruber gave Ruby the contract on Oswald on behalf of his superiors.

Michael Mertz - A former French SDECE officer and the Paris connection for the Lansky-Trafficante heroin syndicate; alleged to have been one of the actual gunmen in Dallas on November 22, 1963. Said by some to be the legendary CIA contract killer, QJ/WIN.

Jean Soutre - a liaison for the French OAS with the CIA's E. Howard Hunt, Soutre maintained contact with Guy Banister's CIA- and mob-linked gun-running headquarters in New Orleans. Soutre may have been in Dallas at the time of the JFK assassination. There is evidence linking Soutre to James Jesus Angleton's intrigue inside the CIA that affected French intelligence in a dramatic way.

Thomas Eli Davis III - A world-travelling mercenary with apparent links to Jack Ruby and Lee Harvey Oswald. Davis was taken into custody by the Algerian government for his subversive activities alongside Israeli agents in supplying weapons to the French OAS just prior to the JFK assassination. It is said that CIA operative QJJWIN, one of the reputed assassins of President Kennedy, helped secure Davis's release from prison.

Gordon Novel -Born in New Orleans in 1938. According to Alan J. Weberman in his book, "Coup D'Dtat in America", "In his youth, Gordon Novel belonged to a neo-Nazi group and was arrested and charged with bombing a Metairie, Louisiana, theatre that admitted blacks". In the early 1960s Novel ran an electronics firm which specialized in selling equipment used for bugging.

It was claimed by Jim Garrison that Novel was formerly a member of the Central Intelligence Agency and was an associate of Sergio Arcacha Smith, David Ferrie and Guy Banister. It was also reported that Novel worked with the Cuban Revolutionary Front during the Bay of Pigs operation via the CIA proprietary, the Evergreen Advertising Agency. Author, Paris Flammonde (*The Kennedy Conspiracy*), claims that Novel was questioned on five separate occasions following the assassination of John F. Kennedy.

Jim Garrison discovered that Sergio Arcacha Smith, David Ferrie and Guy Banister had been involved in a CIA operation to pick up "war material" for the Bay of Pigs attack at from the Schlumberger Well Company. Garrison subpoenaed Novel but he fled to Ohio. However, James Rhodes, the Governor of Ohio, refused to extradite him unless Garrison agreed not to question him on the assassination.

A few weeks after Novel fled from New Orleans a woman cleaning his old apartment found a pencilled draft of a letter wedged under a plastic cover alongside the kitchen. The letter was addressed to a Mr. Weiss. This letter was passed to Jim Garrison who concluded that it was a letter to Novel's CIA contact. "I took the liberty of writing you direct and apprising you of current situation, expecting you to forward this through appropriate channels. Our connection and activity of that period involves individuals presently about to be indicted as conspirators in Garrison's investigation."

Novel also said in the letter: "We have temporarily avoided one subpoena not to reveal Double Chek activities or associate them with this mess. We want out of this thing before Thursday 3/67. Our attorneys have been told to

Expect another subpoena to appear and testify on this matter. The fifth amendment and/or immunity (and) legal tactics will not suffice." Alan J. Weberman has pointed out that E. Howard Hunt worked for Double Chek in Miami.

In an article in *Ramparts Magazine*, William Turner claims that Novel admitted that the pick up at the Schlumberger Well Company was one of "the most patriotic burglaries in history." Novel is also said to have confessed that on the day the munitions were picked up, he "was called by his CIA contact and told to join a group which was ordered to transport munitions from the bunker to New Orleans."

In 1974 Jack Anderson reported that as a result of Watergate break-in, Charles Colson asked Novel to build a "degaussing gun" to erase tapes stored at the CIA and the White House that would incriminate Richard Nixon.

In an interview in 2006 Novel rejected the claims that he was a CIA agent: "I'm not a CIA agent. I'm affiliated, I work with, and we have a mutual admiration society based upon my relationship with the individuals I work with.... The CIA has multiple sides but it's been my experience over the years that they're basically the only good guys in the entire United States government. They're really patriots. Most of 'em are patriots and I've never known... I personally have never known them to do anything criminal, ever. And they didn't kill John Kennedy and they didn't kill a lot of people that they've been accused of causing the death of but I don't know that to be true. So I can tell you that my experience with 'em has been like dealing with Eagle Scouts". Gordon Novel died on 4th October, 2012.

William Seymour, Born in Fort Benton, Montana. Seymour spent three and a half years in the United States Navy in the Asiatic Pacific region. Seymour was a member of "Interpen", (Intercontinental Penetration Force) that was established in 1961 by Gerry P. Hemming. Other members included Loran Hall, Roy Hargraves, Lawrence Howard, Steve Wilson, Howard K. Davis, Edwin Collins, Dick Whatley, James Arthur Lewis, Dennis Harber, Ramigo Arce, Ronald Augustinovich, Joe Garman, Edmund Kolby, Ralph Schlafter, Bill Dempsey, Manuel Aguilar and Oscar Del Pinto.

This group of experienced soldiers were involved in training members of the anti-Castro groups funded by the Central Intelligence Agency in

Florida in the early 1960s. When the government began to crack down on raids from Florida in 1962, Interpen set up a new training camp in New Orleans. The group carried out a series of raids on Cuba in an attempt to undermine the government of Fidel Castro. This involved a plan to create a war by simulating an attack on Guantanamo Naval Base. During this period Seymour travelled around America with Loran Hall and Lawrence Howard. Michael Rohde, a lawyer who met them during this period, described Hall and Seymour as "two extremely dangerous, committed individuals.

On 25th September, 1963, a Cuban exile, Silvia Odio had a visit from three men who claimed they were from New Orleans. Two of the men, Leopoldo and Angelo, said they were members of the Junta Revolucionaria. The third man, Leon, was introduced as an American sympathizer who was willing to take part in the assassination of Fidel Castro. After she told them that she was unwilling to get involved in any criminal activity, the three men left.

After the assassination of John F. Kennedy Ms. Odio claimed that Leon was Lee Harvey Oswald. Odio gave evidence to the Warren Commission and one of its lawyers commented: "Silvia Odio was checked out thoroughly... The evidence is unanimously favorable... Odio is the most significant witness linking Oswald to the anti-Castro Cubans." (107)

On 16th September, 1964, FBI agent Leon Brown interviewed Loran Hall on behalf of the Warren Commission. Brown claims that Hall admitted that he, Lawrence Howard and William Seymour made a visit to a woman who could have been Silvia Odio. However, when Hall was re-interviewed on 20th September and was shown a photograph of Odio, he claimed she was not the woman he met in New Orleans.

Several investigators, including the Cuban Secret Police, claim that the other two men with Oswald were the infamous Novo brothers.

The FBI interviewed Silvia Odio again on 1st October, 1964. They showed her photographs of William Seymour, Loran Hall, Lawrence Howard and Celio Castro Alga. She claimed that "none of these individuals were identical with the three persons... who had come to her apartment in Dallas in the last week of September, 1963." Her sister, Annie Odio, who was also in the apartment at the time, also stated that "none of the photographs appeared similar to the three individuals in her recollection."

Seymour was also interviewed by the FBI and they established that he had been working for Beach Welding and Supplies Company, Miami Beach, Florida at the time when it was suggested that he visited Silvia Odio.

The author, Anthony Summers, suggests that the visit had "been a deliberate ploy to link Junta Revolucionaria, a left-wing exile group, with the assassination". However, G. Robert Blakey interviewed Seymour, Loran Hall and Lawrence Howard and claims that they did not visit Silvia Odio.

PART XIII

SPLIT VERDICTS

YOU ARE THE JURY

In our country we still honor the Constitution by declaring that everyone charged with a crime is presumed innocent. That being true (so far), we can all speculate based on evidence that has surfaced over the past half-century. The author has related much evidence in the Kennedy and Tippit cases, although reams of other documents exist and yet others have not yet been released. However, based on the knowledge you have learned to date, how would you vote on a jury concerning the main players in these cases.

(Take the quiz before your read the author's opinion)

This last section is an opinion chapter for both the author and the potential readers of this book. Other than Jack Ruby and Lee Oswald, no other arrests were made in these three murders discussed in this book. Too much time has passed for any possible prosecution but it is desired by millions of citizens that the real truth be revealed. This is an effort to assist in this goal being accomplished.

Being a ' person of interest' in not a legal term for an actual law breaker. It is a method for the media to call attention to suspects in a case even though no charges have been filed. In this case, it can be said that no charges will ever be filed. If any legal charges were filed, the person charged would retain the presumption of innocence until proved otherwise.

Your choices are Guilty, Not Guilty or Hung Jury.

(Author's opinion will follow your vote)

1-Lee Harvey Oswald

Charge: Murder of John F. Kennedy

Guilty _____ Not Guilty _____ Hung Jury _____

◆◆◆

2-Lee Harvey Oswald

Charge: <u>Conspiracy</u> to murder John F. Kennedy

Guilty _____ Not Guilty _____ Hung Jury _____

◆◆◆

3- Lee Harvey Oswald

Charge: Accessory Before the Fact of them Murder of John F. Kennedy

Guilty _____ Not Guilty _____ Hung Jury _____

◆◆◆

4- Lee Harvey Oswald

Charge: Murder of Dallas Police Officer J. D. Tippit

Guilty _____ Not Guilty _____ Hung Jury _____

♦♦♦

5-Lee Harvey Oswald

Charge: Attempted murder of General Edwin Walker

Guilty _____ Not Guilty _____ Hung Jury _____

♦♦♦

6- David Ferrie and Guy Bannister

Charge: Accessory Before the Fact/ Conspiracy to Murder Pres. Kennedy

Guilty _____ Not Guilty _____ Hung Jury _____

♦♦♦

7 - CIA Officers, William Harvey, Howard Hunt, David Morales, and David Phillips

Charge: Conspiracy to Murder Pres. Kennedy

Guilty _____ Not Guily _____ Hung Jury _____

♦♦♦

8- Carlos Marcello

Charge: Conspiracy to murder John F. Kennedy

Guilty _____ Not Guilty _____ Hung Jury _____

◆◆◆

9-Santos Trafficante, Jr.

Charge: Accessory Before the Fact & Conspiracy to murder John F. Kennedy

Guilty _____ Not Guilty _____ Hung Jury _____

◆◆◆

10-Secret Service Officer Roy Kellerman & Admiral Burkley

Charge; Obstruction of Justice (Removal of a homicide victim's body prior to a legal Texas autopsy)

Guilty _____ Not Guilty _____ Hung Jury _____

◆◆◆

11-Orlando Bosch

Charge: Conspiracy to murder John F. Kennedy

Guilty _____ Not Guilty _____ Hung Jury _____

◆◆◆

12 -Guiillermo Novo & Ignacio Novo

Charge: Conspiracy to Murder John F. Kennedy

Guilty _____ Not Guilty _____ Hung Jury _____

◆◆◆

13- Frank Sturgis

Charge: Conspiracy to Murder John F. Kennedy

Guilty _____ Not Guilty _____ Hung Jury _____

◆◆◆

14 - Eladio Del Valle & Herminio Diaz

Charge: Conspiracy to Murder John F. Kennedy

Guilty _____ Not Guilty _____ Hung Jury _____

◆◆◆

HOW SAY YOU? LET US KNOW

WEBSITE ADDRESS FOR "3 Killers at Dallas"

For Posting Comments and Book Ordering Information

www.JFKCASE-SplitVerdicts.com

THE AUTHOR'S VIEW

The first murder, the JFK assassination, has probably been the most-investigated crime in American history. Yet, five decades later, there remain questions regarding the number of gunmen, the true motive, and the masterminds (if any) of the killing of John F. Kennedy.

The case was 'wrapped' up in hours by the F.B.I. with the arrest of Lee Oswald by the Dallas Police Department and the case ruled by the Warren Commission to be the sole act of one man, Oswald. My law enforcement and military experience convinces me that a complex case such as this killing would not lead to completion and declaration of a 'sole assassin and non-conspiracy' in such as short period of time, and has offered some facts to rebut that theory.

We look again at Oswald. Let's face it; Oswald was a willing tool of the U.S. Government from the time of his military service until the day he died. He was not a "lone nut", but one of the tools in the CIA's box of tricks and mysteries, regardless of the agency's declared declaration of their actions as being 'right and necessary'. Oswald may have supplied one of the murder weapons that killed JFK, (some say he did not) but the fact remains that he did not fire the fatal shots at Kennedy. He would have to have been "Houdini" that day, being in two places at the same time. Oswald was indeed the best possible "Patsy" his handlers could find.

A figure no less than the head of the Dallas police department made two remarkable statements six years after the crime.

In an interview with the Dallas Morning News on November 6, 1969, Dallas Chief of Police Curry states:

"We don't have any proof that Oswald fired the rifle, and never did. Nobody's yet been able to put him in that building with a gun in his hand" (108)

In an article in the New York Times on January 17, 1970, Chief Curry stated:

"The physical evidence and eyewitnesses account do not clearly indicate what took place on the 6th floor of the Texas School Book Depository building at the time President Kennedy was assassinated". (109)

There can be no doubt that Oswald was involved in the conspiracy himself. He was also the cold blooded person who gunned down Dallas Officer

J.D. Tippit. Oswald also attempted to assassinate General Walker months earlier.

It is the author's opinion that a jury would convict Oswald of Murder (of Officer Tippit), Attempted Murder of General Walker, and Conspiracy to Murder John Kennedy. There is insufficient evidence that he was the one who fired the fatal shots at JFK and would be found not-guilty on that charge.

Charge #1 - Not Guilty of the Murder of Pres. Kennedy

Charge #2 - Guilty of Conspiracy to Murder JFK

Charge #3 - Guilty of Accessory Before the Fact of Murder of JFK

Charge #4 - Guilty of the Murder of Officer Tippit

Charge #5 - Guilty of the Attempted Murder of General Walker

The TOTALITY of the facts that have dripped out over the last fifty years has convinced the author, and many others, of the above facts.

◆◆◆

Charge #6 -Guy Bannister and David Ferrie -

The role of Guy Bannister and David Ferrie was critical in carrying out the conspiracy of Mafia head Carlos Marcello to affect the violent death of President Kennedy. Bannister, the former Chicago FBI head, with prior Naval Intelligence service, was the New Orleans private detective who was the obvious contact between the CIA, the anti-Castro Cubans and the Marcello's operation. Ferrie, who died suspiciously as the Garrison investigation was focusing on him, was acting as Marcello's legal aide during the felony trial that coincided with the run-up to Kennedy's death. Ferrie had long been associated with the violent anti-Castro group that was members of the infamous "Operation Forty". Ferrie was also Oswald's commander in the Louisiana air cadet program that a young Oswald was involved with. Both Ferrie and Oswald operated out of Bannister's New Orleans detective office in the months preceding the assassination. Ferrie's actions after the JFK hit was quite suspicious in itself as many have said he was positioned to ferry (he was an accomplished pilot) away participants in the murder conspiracy.

It is the author's opinion that sufficient circumstantial evidence existed to find Ferrie and Bannister guilty of being an Accessory Before the Fact, of the JFK homicide.

Charge #6 - Guilty

◆◆◆

Charge #7 -THE CIA

The Clandestine division of the CIA produced numerous characters in their ranks that had an obvious role in the JFK killing or in the post-event cover up. David Phillips, Howard Hunt, David Morales, William Harvey, etc, performed acts that rivaled James Bond in the quest to do away with America's enemies. The "Northwoods" project and the testimony regarding the CIA's involvement in terror acts against the government of Chili are two of the most egregious examples of how our government went wacko to achieve a result.

Through all the fog of disinformation, phony stories and dumb theories on the assassination of President John Kennedy, we must apply some common sense and logic. Who or what organization can plot every detail and plan every stage to attempt the assassination of an elected leader in diverse cities such as Chicago, Tampa, Miami and Dallas, all in a three-week period, in November of 1963? Only CIA officers coordinating with Mafia members could assemble and execute such a complicated crime - and be successful at it.

In Chicago, Latin suspects were involved according to the Chicago police and Secret Service agents. In Tampa, the alleged source of hit men were associated with Santos Trafficante, Jr. In Miami, the planned plot was reveled by a police recording of a militant Minuteman, Joseph Milteer.

In Dallas, a valuable and efficient informer for the CIA, DEA, and New York city police, Marita Lorenz, advised under oath, that the rabid anti-Castro gang headed by Orlando Bosch, traveled to Dallas for a 'big job' just prior to the assassination, and the purpose of the trip was certainly not to attend the Pepsi convention.

Pre-knowledge of the assassination by Santos Trafficante, Jr and Joseph Milteer, among others, was not just speculation.

The placement of an Oswald 'look-a-like' at several locations were not fantasies. The immediate blame placed on President Castro of Cuba by CIA- influenced media did not happen without advance pre-planning. The drip - drip - drip of post assassination accounts, many from credible sources, buttress the fact that the intricate pre-coordination and post-cover up was the work of experts, not the product of a 'lone nut'.

The example of the Northwoods project and the Chilean revelations showed clearly that our government was totally committed to eliminate Castro regardless of the methods used. The assassination of Chili's General Sepulveda, as well as the numerous assassinations and terror bombings, provide ample proof that Uncle Sam would stoop to anything to accomplish their goals.

Other than Howard Hunt, in the author's opinion, prosecution of any of the CIA operatives would have no chance of success as there would be an avalanche of conflicting evidence, submersed in the 'secrecy' aura. Jurors would be totally confused. However, strong central government control is necessary to prevent these excesses in the future.

◆◆◆

Charge # 8 - Howard Hunt, Guilty of Conspiracy to Murder JFK

Any criminal involvement of William Harvey, David Morales, David Phillips or other CIA officer would most likely result in a Hung Jury or a Not Guilty verdict.

◆◆◆

Charge #9 -Carlos Marcello & #10 Santos Trafficante, Jr. (THE MAFIA)

The Mafia, in persons of Carlos Marcello and Santos Trafficante, Jr., had very strong motivations to eliminate Kennedy and recoup Cuba's casinos. The CIA angst over JFK pulling air cover from the Bay of Pigs venture and the fear that Kennedy would make some accommodation with Castro was their prime motivation for coordinating their actions (as they had done previously) to execute this operation.

Much of the proof has already filtered out despite the efforts of the FBI's head, J. Edgar Hoover, President Johnson and the CIA. The bungling by the Secret Service and their destroying of the files are significant. We won't even go into the shenanigans that our military intelligence agencies had pulled as they successfully covered their butt by destroying any meaningful records. We are reminded of the statement of the head of the US House's 1979 probe into the assassination, Professor Blakey, years after he headed the investigation, that he was fooled by the CIA. Blakey admitted he was given wrong or incomplete testimony by the CIA during his tenure as chief of the HSCA (US House) committee. Blakey was finally convinced of the baloney he was fed. He now says that he would never again believe anything the CIA told him unless he (Blakey) was able to verify the facts independently.

Marcello himself had vowed to kill either Jack or Bobby Kennedy (the Attorney General), as documented by several witnesses. Mafia heads do not make promises such as this without carrying them out, as top law officials and Mafia members themselves can vouch for. Marcello's hatred was intense and as he himself pointed out, a patsy could be found to blame. Oswald himself, as indicated earlier, was a courier in his uncle's numbers racket in New Orleans, an operation sanctioned by Marcello.

Marcello and Ferrie were both attending the Mafia leader's trial in New Orleans and Bannister was observed in his own office on the day of the assassination, but ample circumstantial evidence exists to implicate them in the conspiracy. Marcello's counterpart in Miami, Santos Trafficante, Jr., related to witnesses that JFK would be hit prior to the next election. Trafficante, head of the Florida mob, had numerous associations over the years with the cast of characters that allegedly committed years of violent acts to bring down Castro. Trafficante had been bounced out of Cuba (and his casinos) by Castro which promoted him to be involved with John Rosselli and the violent anti-Castro group that made numerous attempts on Fidel's life. His motivation for helping Marcello conspire to murder JFK was based on the theory that if Kennedy could be murdered and the blame placed on Castro, the U.S. would take drastic action to stomp down on the Cuban communist island. One hoped-for result would be the resumption of the lucrative casino operations that would come about, ruled by Trafficante.

One of Trafficante's bodyguards, Eladio Del Valle, was identified as one of the Cuban Government Security Agencies prime suspects in the slaying of our president. Del Valle himself was found murdered in the trunk of a car in a Miami shopping center parking lot the same day as David Ferrie turned up dead as he was being questioned by Jim Garrison's investigators. The Del Valle murder file in Miami police headquarters was stripped of its contents after being reviewed by the CIA, the FBI and Dade Co. (FL) Sheriff's investigators, although the idendity of the agency that did pilfer the files has not been determined.

It is the author's opinion that Carlos Marcello was materially involved in setting up the Kennedy killing and would vote for conviction on Conspiracy to Murder

The author also believes that Santos Trafficante, Jr. provided logistics, financing and personnel to participate in the killing and would vote to find him guilty of Conspiracy to Murder.

There appears to be ample circumstantial evidence that Carlos Marcello, with assistance from Santos Trafficante, Jr., was the principal planners of the assassination. They had the means, the motive and the opportunity to carry out this crime. The author, as a juror, would have to vote for a conviction on these charges.

Obtaining a conviction on these persons would have been very difficult as Santos Trafficante remarked to his attorney, Frank Ragano, upon the revelation of the murders of John Rosselli and other persons of interest in this case, "Now only two know who killed the President, and neither of us is talking". (The other was Carlos Marcello)

Charge #9 Carlos Marcello - Guilty of Conspiracy to Murder Pres. Kennedy

Charge #10 Santos Trafficante, Jr., Guilty of Being an Accessory Before the Fact of the Murder of Pres. Kennedy

◆◆◆

Charge #11 thru #14 the Anti-Castro Cubans

I sadly conclude, that by examining the totality of evidence available that has seeped out over fifty years, that it is my (the author's) opinion that the United States Central Intelligence and the Mafia plotted in concert to kill JFK and the long time violent gang headed by Orlando Bosch and Frank Sturgis appear to be the most logical persons-of- interest that had the ability to lead and carry out the murderous street operation in Dallas on November 22, 1963.

Who had the interest, capability, the motivation, and had such a long history of violence? Orlando Bosch, Frank Sturgis and the Novo brothers, among others, working with rouge CIA personnel such as Howard Hunt, David Phillips, and other members of the huge CIA station (JMWAVE) in Miami during the early 19650's., were very well equipped, financed, and experienced to handle the "big job" (116).

Charge #11-14 Due to the credible testimony of Marita Lorenz and others evidence, I would be in favor of voting for conviction against Orland Bosch, Frank Sturgis, and the Novo brothers for Conspiracy to Murder.

The gang of violent anti-Castro terrorists under the leadership of Orlando Borsch will go down in history as being a group that killed more people than Ted Bundy and overturned (or attempted to overturn) more governments than Napoleon. Many of the heinous acts were either under the obvious control and or direction of the U.S. Central Intelligence Agency. These violent acts and others were apparently motivated by the intense hatred against Fidel Castro and his communist regime in Cuba. One would be hard pressed to identify a country in North, South, or Central America (and some in Europe and Africa) that did not experience the targeting for terror actions by Orlando Bosch and his gang, some in concert with the CIA.

Since 1959, over one million Cubans have successfully made the transition from communist Cuba to the U.S.A. These energetic and intelligent people have transformed South Florida into an international city bustling with new businesses and beautiful skyscrapers. They are truly an amazing people who have made our country greater. This band of terrorist anti-Castro thugs, who have plagued many nations with their violent acts, have disgraced the multitude of these fine Cuban-American citizens, many of whom also hate Castro and communism, but despise the horrific acts this small group have carried out.

Despite some evidence, a jury would have to find Eladio Del Valle and Herminio Diaz not guilty of Conspiracy to Murder JFK, due to insufficient evidence.

Insufficient evidence would block similar charges from even being filed against their associates, Patrick Hemming and Pedro Lanz.

◆◆◆

After considerable thought and study, it is the author's opinion that the 3 Killers at Dallas were in fact the Mafia, the CIA and the Anti-Castro Cubans.

Maybe, just maybe, the planned release of additional federal assassination documents in 2017 will uncover the real truth. But, I doubt it.

◆◆◆

I leave you with a few quotes from author G. Paul Chambers that were contained in his 2012 book, "Head Shot". (110)

"the complexity of the science of this case has allowed the fantasy of a single assassin to fester for fifty years".

"There is a fundamental disconnect between the American citizenry and the government and news media that exist to protect it".

"A government that unabashedly has to lie to its citizens and a news media that backs it up is a frightening combination".

"Eyewitness testimony is the least reliable evidence you can have. Eyewitness testimony only has value in science - only has meaning - when it is supported by physical evidence."

WEBSITE ADDRESS FOR "3 Killers at Dallas"

For Posting Comments and Book Ordering Information

www.JFKCASE-SplitVerdicts.com

INDEX

BIBLIOGRAPHY

Adams, Don, FBI Agent - "From an Office Building w/High Power Rifle", Trine Day Publishing, 2012

Armstrong, John, magizine article, "Probe:, Jan-Feb 1988

Black, Edward, article in Chicago Independent, November 1975

Bolden, Abraham, "The Echo from Dealey Plaza...", Crown Publishing, 2009

Breslin, Jimmy, "A Death in Emergency Room One", article in the Miami News, November 24,1963

Chambers, G. Paul, "Head Shot", Prometheus Books, 2012

Conway, Debra, "The Secret Service Agents on the Mall", JFK Lancer, 2001

Crenshaw, Dr. Charles, "JFK, Conspiracy of Silence", Signet, 1992

Dankbaar, William, "JFK Murder Solved", Dankbarr's website, 2005

Davis, John H., "Mafia Kingfish" : Carlos Marcello and the Assassination of John F. Kennedy, McGraw-Hill, 1988

Doherty, Philip, "Miami Police Worksheet", X-Librus self- published, 2012

Dudman, Richard, article in New Republic, Dec. 21, 1963

Duffy, James P., and Vincent Ricci, "The Assassination of John F. Kennedy: A Complete Book of Facts", Thunder Mouth Press, 1992

Epstein, Edward Jay, "Inquest", Bantam, EJE Publications, 2011

Epstein, Edward Jay, "The Secret World of Lee Harvey Oswald", McGraw- Hill, 1978

Feldman, Harold, "Fifty One Witnesses: The Grassy Knoll", Idlewild Publishers, 1965

Finck, Dr. Piere, "Autopsy", and US House Interview, 1977

Flynn, Vince, "High Treason", Simon and Schuster, 2007

Fonzi, Gaeton, "The Last Investigation", Thunder Mouth Press, 1993

Garrison, Jim, "On The Trail of the Assassins" Sheridan Square Press, 1988

Gibson, Donald, "The Kennedy Assassination Cover Up", Krosbka Books. 1999

Groden, Robert, "The Killing of a President" Bloomsbury Publishing, 1993

Groden, Robert, and Harrison Livingston, "High Treason", 1999

Hurt, Henry, "Reasonable Doubt". Rinehart and Winston, 1985

Hancock, Larry, "Someone Would Have Talked", JFK Lancer Publications, 2010

Kurtz, Michael, "Crime of the Century", University of Tennessee Press, 1993

Lane, Mark, Plausible Denial, Thunder's Mouth Press, 1991

Lane, Mark, "Rush to Judgment", Holt, Rinehart & Winston, 1966

Lifton, David, "Best Evidence", Macmillon, 1981

Marrs, Jim, "Crossfire", Carroll & Graf Publishers, 1989

Meagher, Sylvia, "Accessories After The Fact", Bobbs- Merrill, 1967

Menninger, Bonar, "Mortal Error", St. Martin's Press, 1992

Miller, David, "The JFK Conspiracy", Writer's Club Press, 2002

Philbrick, Herb, "I led Three Lives: Communist Counterspy", McGraw Hill Publications. 1952

Russo, Guy, "Live by the Sword", Bancroft Press,1998

Scott, Peter Dale, "Oswald, Mexico, and Deep Poliotics,

Bancroft Pres, 1994

Shenon, Philip, "A Cruel and Shocking Act: The History of the JFK Assassination, Macmillan, 2013

Shipman, Tim, article in London Sunday Telegraph, Feb 2, 2007

Sneed, Larry, "No More Silence", Google Oral History, 1998

Sullivan, William, "My Thirty Years with the FBI", Norton Publishers, 1979

Summers, Anthony, "Conspiracy", Paragon House, update, 1991

Talbot, David, "Brothers", Free Press, 2007

Trafton, Conner, "The JFK Investigation", article "The Three Shot Theory", 2012

Turner, Nigel, "The Men Who Killed Kennedy, The Smoking Gun:, Episode 7, 2003

Scheim, David, "Contract on America", Argyle Press, 1983

Waldron, Lamar, "Ultimate Sacrifice", 2005

Waldron, Lamar, "Legacy of Secrecy"

Waldron, Lamar, "The Hidden History of the JFK Assassination", 2013

Wecht, Dr. Cyril, "Cause of Death", 1993

Weisberg, Harold, "Whitewash" self-published, 1966

Weisburg, Harold, "Whitewash II", Mary Ferrell Press, 2007,

Wilkes, Donald, Jr., ":Intriguing Mystery: the Secret Service and the JFK Assassination", Popular Media, 2012

NOTES AND CITATIONS

The statements, affidavits, and interviews with law enforcement or federal commission attorneys, that were given by the eye-witnesses to the Kennedy murder at Dealey Square, were sources utilized by the author. The information was obtained from the Warren Commission and other government documents are on the Internet. The specific source of other statements or interviews by private researchers and/or media representatives will be noted in the text or by citation.

1   Author's run for Congress. A note in the first chapter about the US House seat that JFK first held is of personal interest to the author. In 1984, the author had the honor of running for a seat in the U.S. House of Representatives in Mass. 7th District, which then (1984), encompassed many of the same towns and cities that JFK represented. The result, however, was not too favorable as the author ended up a distant 3rd of 7 candidates.

I probably would have been shut out completely if it weren't for the numerous voters named Doherty in that district as well as my mother's vote (I hope). Guess Mass. was not ready for a person with conservative views (still not).

2   HSCA (US House) 1979 report findings, see 1-B

3   Edward Jay Epstein, "Inquest"

4   US House (HSCA) 1979 Final Report

5   Oswald's note to wife, Warren Report, p-183-189

6   Warren Commission, Appendix X, p-596)

7   Warren Report on Frazier's examination, p-183-187

8   Warren Commission document 6H-298

9   Warren Commission document CE2003

10 W.C. (Warren Commission) "Shaneyfelt", Exhibit No. 26

11 W.C. document 7H-544-558

12 Harold Weisberg, "Whitewash II", 2007, Mary Ferrell Press, p-37-38

13 Harold Feldman's survey of 121 witnesses from his book, "Fifty One Witnesses, The Grassy Knoll", published in "The Minority of One". March 1965. The statements are registered in the 26 volumes of the Warren Report. "Fifty One held the shots sounded as if they came from west of the depository

14 Dictabelt study by the House Select Committee on Assassination, (HSCA),1979. The HSCA issued a report in which they concluded that there was a high probability that two gunmen were involved in the assassination and that President Kennedy was "probably assassinated as a result of a conspiracy". The findings were based on an acustic analysis study of the Dictabelt performed by Dr. James Barker, et al, of Bolt, Beranek and Newman.

15 The National Academy of Science's (NSA) Committee on Ballistic Acoustics concluded "reliable acoustic data do not support a conclusion that there was a second gunman"

16 The HSCA (US House of Representatives) retort was that the NSA panel study was seriously flawed, backed up by a study by D.B. Thomas, a government researcher, who said it was 96% certain that there was a shot from the Grassy Knoll. Mr. Thomas' study was published in "Science and Justice", a quarterly publication of Britain's Forensic Science Society, in March 2002

17 Arthur Summers, "Conspiracy", (1991) update

18 Warren Commission testimony of Secret Service Agent Roy Kellerman, Vol. 2, pp-66-112

19 Warren Commission testimony of Secret Service Agent William Greer, Vol 2, p-112

20 III-25 Warren Commission testimony of Governor Connally, Vol 4, p-129

21 III-26 The HSCA (US House) Summary Report. 1979, on the assassination of President Kennedy

22 III-27 Same as #26 (Statement contained in the Summary Report)

23 Warren Commission testimony of Secret Service Agent Sorrells when questioned by Counsel Mr., Stern, on 5/7/1964, Vol. 4, pp-548

24 III-29 Written statement by Secret Service Agent Paul Landis to the Secret Service office, dated 11/27/1963

25 III-30 Testimony of Dallas County Sheriff Decker to the Warren Commission, 4/16/1964, Vol 7 - when questioned by Counsel Leon Hubert

26 III-31 From deposition by Dallas police officer J.W. Foster to HSCA counsel Joe Ball, at Dallas US Attorney's office, 4/9/1964

27 Warren Commission testimony, March 9, 1964

28 Jim Marrs, "Crossfire", p-35

29 Warren Commission testimony of Charles Givens, March 8, 1964

30 Conner Trafton, "The JFK Investigation", an article for the American University website, Article was entitled "The Three Shot Theory", 2013

31 Tim Shipman article, London Sunday Telegraph, February 2, 2007

32 Warren Commission, Hearings, vol 3, p-446

33 Warren Commission, Exhibit #239, Oswald's Firearm Proficiency

34 Warren Commission, Vol 11, p-302), Oswald's Firearm Testing, December, 1956

35 Sighting of Oswald or an Imposter at firing range, Warren Commission, vol 22, p-763

36 Sgt. Ellis "There was a bulltet hole in LIMO windshield", told to interviewer Gill Toff in 1971 as related in David Lifton' book, "Best Evidence".

37 St Louis Post-Dispatch reporter, Richard Dudman's, in article for the New Republic, December 21, 1963.

38 Ms. Glanges observed hole in LIMO windshield as told to attorney Doug Weldon, noted in Nigel Turner's book, "The Men Who Killed Kennedy",1999

39 George Whitaker of Ford Motor Co. related this story on the LIMO windshield to attorney Doug Weldon and it was noted in Nigel Turner's book, +The Men Who Killed Kennedy", 1999, published after Whitaker's death, with the permission of his family.

40   Secret Service Report, 11/27/1963, #180-10099-10390, Agent Charles Taylor,

41 Bill Ashby for Arlington Glass Co. related to researcher Robert Smith and reported by David Lifton in book, "Best Evidence", 1992, Signet Books

42 Doug Horne, researcher, presented this information in a article, "Hiding in Plain Sight", 2012, on website, Lou Rockwell.com

43 Syliva Meaher, "Accessories After the Fact, p-72, 1967, Skyhorse Publishing

44 Testimony of Dallas Officer M. L. Baker to the Warren Commission on March 25, 1964, relating to his confronting Oswald in the Depository building.

45 Warren Commission Reprot, Chapter 4, p-18

46 Movements of the black laborers working at the Depository building during the assassination are contained in the Warren Report, p-68)

47 Testimony of Jeraldean Reid to the Warren Commission, March 1964, Document 3H270

48 Warren Commission testimony of Charles Givens, March 8, 1964

49 Warren Commission Document H-169, Witness Arnold Rowland

50 Author Jim Marrs, "Crossfire", p-81

51 Warren Commission testimony of Victoria Adams, March 7, 1964

52 Affidavit of Billy Lovelady, Nov 27, 1963, p-36

53 Affidavit of Bill Shelly to W.C., CE2003, p-59

54 Sylvia Meagher's book, "Accessories After The Fact", p-71, reference to the confrontation Roy Truly had with Lee Oswald at the Depository building shortly after the fatal shots.

55 Anthony Summers' book, "Conspiracy", p-80

56 Sylvia Meagher's book, "Accessories After the Fact", P-71-72

57 Location of Oswald when shots were fired, Author Anthony Summers describes in detail in his book, "Conspiracy", p-74-83

58 Carolyn Walthers interview with the FBI, December 4, 1963

59 Testimony of Amos Euins to the Warren Commission, 2H-208

60 Jim Marrs' book, "Crossfire", p-329

61 Testimony of Royce Skelton to the Warren Commission, 6H-236

62 Anthony Summers update book, "Conspiracy", 1991, Paragon House

63 Warren Commission Exhibit CE399

64 Anthony Summers update book, "Conspiracy", 1991, Paragon House, p-35

65 Same as above, p-37

66 Dr Boswell's interview with the Journal of American Medical Association, 1992, as related in website, "The JFK 100, by Dave Reites

67 Dr. Piere Finck' book, "Autopsy", p-325

68 Sylvia Meagher's book, "Accessories After the Fact", page 137-139

69 Warren Commission Exhibit CE387

70 Newspaper article by Jimmy Breslin, Miami News, November 24, 1963

71 US House (HSCA Committee), Report, VI, p-179

72 Assassination Records Review Board (AARB) report, June 2, 1998, by investigator Doug Horne. (see AARB transcript, 7/16/1996, Attachment #8)

73 Doug Horne's 32 page report, on Internet at www.archives.gov/medical/jfk

74 Dr. Charles Crenshaw, "JFK, Conspiracy of Silence", 1992, Signet

75 G. Paul Chambers' book, "Head Shot", 2012, P-10

76 Lamar Waldono's book, "The Hidden History of the JFK Assassination, 2013, p-35

77 IV-9 - Warren Commission Exhibit 3H-148

78 Testimony of Witness Domingo Benavides to the Warren Commission, April 2, 1964, Vol 6

79 Anthony Summers' book, "Conspiracy", p-89

80 Warren Commission Report,, P-56

81 Statement of witness T.F. Bowley to Dallas Police, 11/22/1963

82 Testimony of witness Jim Burt to the Warren Commission, CD-205

83 Lee Oswald's' revolver, Warren Commission Exhibit # CE-143

84 Ballistic Report on Oswald's revolver, Warren Commission, Section 5, p-59

85 Discrepancies in Oswald's bullets discussed in U.S. House (HSCA) Report, Vol. VII, p-381

86 Warren Commission Report, p-314, Description broadcast on JFK suspect.

87 Henry Hurt's book, "Reasonable Doubt", p-149-150

88 Jim Marrs, "Crossfire, The Plot That Killed Kennedy", 1989, Correll & Graf, Publishers

89 Book by Peter Dale Scott, "Oswald, Mexico, and Deep Politics, 1994,

90 Sylvia Meagher's book, "Accessories After the Fact", p-243

91 Same as above - p-243

92 Anthony Summers, "Conspiracy", p–440

93 Same as above, p–442

94 Same as above, p–444

95 Edwin Black, Chicago author/investigator, article for the Chicago Independent, November 1975

96 Abraham Bolden's book, "The Echo from Dealey Plaza...", 2008, Crown Publishers. Bolden was a former Secret Service Agent based in Chicago.

97 Lamar Walden and Thom Hartann's book, "Ultimate Sacrifice", 2005, Described the Tampa plot in detail.

98 The book, "The Assassination of John F. Kennedy", by James Duffy and Vincent Ricci, document many of the facts of the assassination.

99 The book, "High Treason", 2nd ed., 1989, by Robert Groden and Harrison Livingston. Discusses the breakdown in protection for Pres. Kennedy.

100 David Wilkes, Jr. book, Intriguing Mysteries - The Secret Service and the JFK Assassination, 2012 reports that there was inadequate Secret Service protection for President Kennedy, 2012,

101 Don Adams, retired FBI agent, wrote {From an Office Building With a High-Powered Rifle", 2012. Assigned in 1963 to track militant Joseph Milteer by the FBI. His account differs from the official FBI version.

102 Memo from Assistant Attorney General Katzenbach to White House presidential aide, Bill Moyers, dated November 25, 1963. FBI 62-109060, JFK 48 file, Section 18

103 William Sullivan, the number three man under J. Edgar Hoover, wrote a book, "My Thirty Years with the FBI", claimed that Hoover would do anything to protect his own image.

104 FBI Agent Keenan told interviewers that Hoover and Sullivan sent him to Mexico City to investigate Oswald's contacts there but the CIA and the Embassy gave him no assistance whatever. Keenan said that "this was perhaps the worst investigation that the FBI was ever involved in". Keenan was ordered home after 3 days in Mexico City.

105 A confidential Private Investigation Report on the Detroit Mafia, by the author (Chief Doherty) in 1997, which branched into to the Hoffa disappearance and the Kennedy murder, described in detail organized crime's (and Carlos Marcello and Santos Trafficante, Jr., in particular) numerous threats on the life of JFK.

106 Gaeton Fonzi, an investigator for the US House (HSCA) wrote in the "The Last Investigation", 1993, New York Thundermouth, that Sturgis, by his own admission, was a prime suspect in the JFK killing.

One of the most informative sources for the possible involvement of the CIA in the JFK assassination is a book by Gaeton Fonzi, an investigator for the US House (HSCA) committee investigation of the Kennedy assassination. Fonzi wrote a book ("The Last Investigation") detailing his excellent work in the attempt to track down the truth of what really happened in Dallas. Gaeton Fonzi's masterful retelling of his work investigating the Kennedy assassination for two Congressional committees is required reading for students of the assassination and the subsequent failure of the government to solve the crime. The Last Investigation is a compelling post mortem on the House Select Committee on Assassinations, as well as a riveting account of Fonzi's pursuit of leads indicating involvement by officers of the C.I.A.

107 "Spartacus Educational" website story on Sylvia Odio.

108 Dallas Police Chief Curry's interview with the Dallas Morning News, November 6, 1969

109 Chief Curry statement to the New York Times, January 17, 1970.

110 G. Paul Chambers, "Head Shot - The Science behind the JFK Assassination", 2012, Prometheus Books,,2012, p-40-41

111 Anthony Summers book, "Conspiracy", p-94

112 The location of the disposal of Hoffa's body was provided by an confidential informant of the author, during a 1997 investigation of the Detroit Mafia.

113 Lt Charles Sapp, head of Miami P.D.'s Intelligence Unit in 1963, confirmed this motorcade cancellation in an interview with Anthony Summers in 1988.

114 The wife of Bernard Barker was an employee under the author's supervision in the late 1970's at the Miami police department's computer operations center. The author has no recollection of knowing this fact at the time and can not recall even having any conversations with her about her husband or any other subject.

115 Former Washington Post reporter, Jefferson Morley, has been attempting for years, through an FOIA request, to obtain more information on CIA agent George Joannides. Joannides, who toiled at JMWAVE in Miami, was later called out of retirement to be the liaison between the CIA and the US House (HSCA) Committee investigating the JFK killing, but hid his earlier assignment from House Chief Counsel Blakey.

116 Article, "Salon" magizine, "The Coddled Terrorists of South Florida", by Tristan Korten and Kirk Neilsen, January 14, 2008